An Insider's Guide to Cloud Computing

David Linthicum

PEARSON

An Insider's Guide to Cloud Computing

Copyright © 2023 Pearson Education, Inc.

ISBN-13: 978-0-13-793569-7
ISBN-10: 0-13-793569-2

Library of Congress Control Number: 2022923586

4 2023

Trademarks

Warning and Disclaimer

Vice President, IT Professional
Mark Taub

Director, ITP Product Management
Brett Bartow

Executive Editor
Nancy Davis

Development Editor
Ellie Bru

Managing Editor
Sandra Schroeder

Project Editor
Mandie Frank

Copy Editor
Chuck Hutchinson

Indexer
Tim Wright

Proofreader
Barbara Mack

Technical Reviewer
Jo Peterson

Editorial Assistant
Cindy Teeters

Designer
Chuti Prasertsith

Compositor
codeMantra

Special Sales

For information about buying this title in bulk quantities, or for special sales opportunities (which may include electronic versions; custom cover designs; and content particular to your business, training goals, marketing focus, or branding interests), please contact our corporate sales department at corpsales@pearsoned.com or (800) 382-3419.

For government sales inquiries, please contact governmentsales@pearsoned.com.

For questions about sales outside the U.S., please contact intlcs@pearson.com.

Cover image credit: Space Wind/Shutterstock

Pearson's Commitment to Diversity, Equity, and Inclusion

Pearson is dedicated to creating bias-free content that reflects the diversity of all learners. We embrace the many dimensions of diversity, including but not limited to race, ethnicity, gender, socioeconomic status, ability, age, sexual orientation, and religious or political beliefs.

Education is a powerful force for equity and change in our world. It has the potential to deliver opportunities that improve lives and enable economic mobility. As we work with authors to create content for every product and service, we acknowledge our responsibility to demonstrate inclusivity and incorporate diverse scholarship so that everyone can achieve their potential through learning. As the world's leading learning company, we have a duty to help drive change and live up to our purpose to help more people create a better life for themselves and to create a better world.

Our ambition is to purposefully contribute to a world where:

- Everyone has an equitable and lifelong opportunity to succeed through learning.

- Our educational products and services are inclusive and represent the rich diversity of learners.

- Our educational content accurately reflects the histories and experiences of the learners we serve.

- Our educational content prompts deeper discussions with learners and motivates them to expand their own learning (and worldview).

While we work hard to present unbiased content, we want to hear from you about any concerns or needs with this Pearson product so that we can investigate and address them.

- Please contact us with concerns about any potential bias at https://www.pearson.com/report-bias.html.

Contents at a Glance

1   How "Real" Is the Value of Cloud Computing?. 2

2   The Realities and Opportunities of Cloud-Based Storage
Services That Your Cloud Provider Will Not Tell You About 22

3   The Realities and Opportunities of Cloud-Based Compute
Services That Your Cloud Provider Will Not Tell You About 44

4   Innovative Services and Public Clouds: What Do You
Really Pay For? 64

5   Containers, Container Orchestration, and Cloud
Native Realities. 88

6   The Truths Behind Multicloud That Few Understand 110

7   Cloud Security Meets the Real World. 132

8   Cloud Computing and Sustainability: Fact Versus Fiction 152

9   The Evolution of the Computing Market 172

10   Here's the Future of Cloud Computing from an Insider's
Perspective... Be Prepared. 198

11   Wrapping Things Up: Miscellaneous Insider Insights 224

Index. 244

Table of Contents

Chapter 1: How "Real" Is the Value of Cloud Computing?   2

What We Thought We Knew. 2

       The Return to the Utility Model. 3

       The Elusive "Cost Savings" 4

       It's Not CapEx Versus OpEx, and It Never Was. 5

       This Is About Business Value, and It Always Was 6

What Could Go Wrong? 12

       Too Much Focus on Operational Cost Savings That Seldom
           Became a Reality. 12

       Too Little Attention Paid to the Cost of Skills 13

       Cloud Providers Thrive on Profit. 14

What Went Right? 14

       Agility, Innovation, and Speed Become King. 14

       Best-of-Breed Put the Business Back in Control 16

       Security Is Better in the Cloud. 17

       Development Is Better in the Cloud. 18

Call to Action 19

**Chapter 2: The Realities and Opportunities of Cloud-Based Storage
Services That Your Cloud Provider Will Not Tell You About**   22

Cloud Storage Evolves 22

Junk Data on Premises Moved to the Cloud Is Still Junk Data. 23

       Lift-Fix-and-Shift. 25

       Cloud Storage Abstraction: Shortcut or Innovation? 27

       The Fallacy of Structured Versus Unstructured Data Storage. 30

Secrets to Finding the Best Cloud Storage Value 33

       What If the Best Cloud Storage Is Not in the Cloud?. 33

       Leveraging Storage Growth. 38

       Add-ons Needed 39

How Will the Business Leverage Cloud Storage? 40

Automation Is King 41

Weaponizing AI 42

The Future of Cloud Storage 43

Call to Action 43

Chapter 3: The Realities and Opportunities of Cloud-Based Compute Services That Your Cloud Provider Will Not Tell You About   **44**

The Trade-offs of Multitenancy................................... 45

The Realities of Resource Sharing...46

Costs Versus Consistency 48

Cross-Partition and Cross-Tenant Hacks 49

CPU Performance, Meet the Internet 51

The Slowest Components Determine Performance 52

How to Speed Things Up Through Design 53

Picking the Most Optimized Compute Configuration 54

Paying Too Much for Cloud Compute? Here's Why....................... 57

Picking the Right Operating Systems 58

Picking the Right Memory Configurations........................ 59

The Concept of Reserved Instances 59

Going Off-brand.. 61

Leveraging Second-Tier Cloud Providers..62

Leveraging MSPs...62

Multicloud by Necessity..63

Call to Action 63

Chapter 4: Innovative Services and Public Clouds: What Do You Really Pay For?   **64**

AI/ML 66

Overused? 67

Overpriced? 68

Finding the Right Use Cases 69

Business Optimization of AI..70

Serverless. 71

You Really Are Using Servers 72

Cost Versus Value..73

Finding the Right Use Cases 74

Finding Business Optimization 75

DevOps/DevSecOps 75

No Cloud DevOps...77

All Cloud DevOps...77

Some-Cloud DevOps..77

Finding Business Optimization 78

Analytics. 78

Connecting the Data Is Key 79

Analytics Over and Under..81

AI Convergence 81

Finding Business Optimization 82

Edge and IoT 83

Edge and the Cloud Realities 84

Cloud Controls the Edge 84

Edge Computing and IoT Realities..85

Finding Business Optimization 86

Emerging Technologies. 87

Call to Action 87

Chapter 5: Containers, Container Orchestration, and Cloud Native Realities   88

Containers 89

What Works...90

Containers: What Doesn't Work 91

Container: Cost Considerations 92

Containers: Make the Tough Choices..93

Container Orchestration and Clustering 93

    Container Orchestration: What Works 96

    What Doesn't Work 98

    Container Orchestration: Cost Considerations 99

    Container Orchestration: Make Tough Choices 100

Cloud Native 101

    What's the Right Definition of Cloud Native? 102

    Portability Argument 104

    Optimization Argument 105

    Cost Argument 106

Technology Meets Reality 108

Call to Action 108

Chapter 6: The Truths Behind Multicloud That Few Understand   **110**

Hybrid Cloud Realities 110

The Move to Plural Public Clouds 113

    Best-of-Breed? 114

    Price 116

    Business Realities 116

Multicloud Upside Realities 118

    Lock-in Realities 118

    Power of Choice 119

    The Need to Own Your Destiny 122

    Risk Reduction 122

    Security Issues 123

    Governance Issues 123

    Ops Issues 123

Multicloud Downside Realities 124

    Cost of Complexity 124

    Cost of Heterogeneity 125

Lock-in 126

Security Issues 126

Governance Issues 127

Ops Issues 127

Key Concepts for Multicloud Success 127

Call to Action 130

Chapter 7: Cloud Security Meets the Real World   **132**

An Insider's Guide to Cloud Security Fundamentals 133

Step 1: Protect 134

Step 2: Detect 135

Step 3: Respond 136

Step 4: Track 136

What Cloud Security Worked 137

Data Encryption 137

Identity-Based Security 138

Security Automation 138

AI/ML Integration 139

What Cloud Security Didn't Work 139

Remove Focus from Non-Cloud Systems 139

Failure to Manage Complexity 141

Little Focus on BC/DR 142

Lack of Security Talent 142

The Rise of Non-Native Cloud Security 144

The Movement to Cross-Cloud Security 144

Security Peer-to-Peer Authentication 145

Security Abstraction and Automation 146

Security Intelligence (AI) 146

Security Observability 146

The Rise of Proactive Security 147

The Importance of Observability...147

Pattern Searching 149

AI 149

The Rise of Security Automation 149

Call to Action 151

Chapter 8: Cloud Computing and Sustainability: Fact Versus Fiction   152

Initial Thinking: Cloud Data Centers, Bad 155

More Data Centers, Bad...155

More Shared Data Centers, Good 157

The Politics of Sustainability. 158

Finally, Sharing Is Possible 159

The Greenness of Multitenancy..160

Not All Clouds Are Equal 161

Resource Optimization and Sustainability.......................................165

Green Application Development? 166

Multicloud as a Sustainability Weapon? 167

What Is Your Real Impact? 169

Call to Action 170

Chapter 9: The Evolution of the Computing Market   172

Forced March to the Cloud?. 173

The Shift in R&D Spending 174

Leaving Systems Behind 175

More Consumption, but Prices Stay Static. 177

The Power of a Few Players 178

This Is About Market Capture...180

Why They Don't Work and Play Well Together.....................................180

Will Public Cloud Providers Become Like Video
Streaming Services?..181

The Emergence of Commoditization 183

    Rise of the Supercloud or Metacloud 184

    Likely Cost Shifts over Time 185

The Emergence of System Repatriation 186

    Why Organizations Move to a Hybrid Model 187

    Why You Need to Justify the Move to Cloud as a
    Business Value 187

The Rise of Federated Cloud Applications and Data 188

Traditional Systems Remain…Why? 192

Battle for Human Talent 193

    What to Exploit Right Now 194

    The Secrets of Keeping Cloud Talent 195

Call to Action 197

**Chapter 10: Here's the Future of Cloud Computing from an
Insider's Perspective… Be Prepared** **198**

Continued Rise of Complex Cloud Deployments 199

Refocus on Cross-Cloud Systems 202

    Cross-Platform Security 202

    Cross-Platform Operations 204

    Cross-Platform Observability 205

    Cross-Platform Governance 210

    Cross-Platform Financial Operations (FinOps) 211

    Cross-Platform Data Federation 213

Changing Skills Demands 214

    Cloud Generalists vs. Cloud Specialist 215

    Less Code, More Design 216

    Architectural Optimization Is the Focus 217

Cloud Security Shifts Focus 217

Cloud Computing Becomes Local 219

Industry Clouds Become Important. 220

Where Is Edge Computing? 221

Call to Action 223

Chapter 11: Wrapping Things Up: Miscellaneous Insider Insights   **224**

Cloud Can Make Life Better 224

      Cloud Supports Remote Work. 225

      Support for Remote and Virtual Enterprises. 227

      Support for World Changes and Evolutions 228

      Support for Sustainability 229

      Democratization of Computing. 229

      Punching Above Your Weight 231

Changes in the Skills Mix 233

The Objectives Change. 236

The Market Absorbs the Weak, and the Weak Emerge Again. 237

Cloud Technology Continues to Be a Value Multiplier 240

Call to Action 241

Index   **244**

About the Author

David Linthicum is on most top-10 lists of technology innovators and influencers, including cloud computing, edge computing, AI, and security technology. David is a best-selling author of more than 15 books and more than 7,000 published articles. He is also the originator of many business-related technology concepts, including enterprise application integration (EAI). He's an innovator within service-oriented architecture (SOA), and now cloud computing and the use of cloud computing for digital transformations.

With his remarkable ability to design, explain, and implement technology solutions to solve existing business problems and create new opportunities, David rose rapidly through the corporate ranks from programmer to CEO, with stops in between that helped inform his holistic view of enterprises. Based in Washington, DC, David currently serves Global 2,000 clients as Deloitte's Chief Cloud Strategy Officer, where he drives new innovations and market offerings, and leads people and projects, as well as thought leadership outreach. This includes on the "Deloitte On Cloud Podcast," as well as several *Forbes* and *WSJ* articles.

David's 60+ courses on LinkedIn Learning consistently appear on the "Popular Courses" list and provide course content on cloud computing, cloud architecture, cloud security, cloud governance, cloud operations, AI, DevOps, and many other concepts related to cloud computing and enterprise technology in general. He's also an adjunct professor for Louisiana State University (LSU), where he's created courses on DevOps, Cloud Computing, Cloud Architecture, and other courses that are in demand by the LSU student body. David has done over 1,000 conference presentations in the U.S. and abroad, often as a keynote speaker at conferences related to enterprise technology. He has hosted over 2,000 Webinars on the correct use of enterprise technology, including cloud computing, edge computing, AI, DevOps, and data science.

To my father,
Ronald Gerald Linthicum,
April 7, 1939 - March 27, 2014.
None of my accomplishments have been made without your
encouragement and guidance. We miss you, Dad.

Acknowledgments

There are a bunch of people to thank for this book, including Nancy Davis and Ellie C. Bru at Pearson. Also, many people behind the scenes who do the copy editing, layouts, graphics, and even the physical printing. Also, the audio engineers who assisted with the audio version of this book.

I also want to thank Thomas Erl, a major tech author and friend, who was instrumental in getting me back in touch with Pearson, after 13 years since my last book, and myself swearing off book authoring in favor of blogs and podcasts. I'm back as a book author. Let's see how this goes.

Of course, the book would not be as readable were it not for Linda Crippes, my editor and writing advisor, who has taken many paragraphs to something that's enjoyable to read. We've worked together for so long that, at this point, I'm not sure when we started. Just glad to have somebody to assist in that department since my brain works better in speaking mode than when I write.

I also want to thank the reviewers, including Jo Peterson, who provided some great feedback on this "very different type of book." She provided many of the better ideas as we break new ground here. It's always good to have a team of smart people who make sure your ideas are not too crazy.

Keep in mind that my opinions here, which is most of the book, are mine and mine alone and not necessarily that of my current, past, or future employer. That said, this book was carefully written as not to create conflicts of interest, or cause concerns with any independence issues.

Finally, I want to thank my wonderful clients, who provided me with the experiences required to write a book like this. I'm in business to make them successful, and I feel privileged to say their successes reflect my own.

We Want to Hear from You!

As the reader of this book, *you* are our most important critic and commentator. We value your opinion and want to know what we're doing right, what we could do better, what areas you'd like to see us publish in, and any other words of wisdom you're willing to pass our way.

We welcome your comments. You can email or write to let us know what you did or didn't like about this book—as well as what we can do to make our books better.

Please note that we cannot help you with technical problems related to the topic of this book.

When you write, please be sure to include this book's title and author as well as your name and email address. We will carefully review your comments and share them with the author and editors who worked on the book.

Email: feedback@community@informit.com

Reader Services

Register your copy of *An Insider's Guide to Cloud Computing* at www.pearsonitcertification.com for convenient access to downloads, updates, and corrections as they become available. To start the registration process, go to www.pearsonitcertification.com/register and log in or create an account.* Enter the product ISBN 9780137935697 and click Submit. When the process is complete, you will find any available bonus content under Registered Products.

*Be sure to check the box indicating that you would like to hear from us to receive exclusive discounts on future editions of this product.

Preface

This book blows open the cloud computing industry's secret doors and finally says the quiet parts out loud.

Many of us know about or have experienced cloud computing outcomes that did not live up to expectations. Some outcomes were outright cloud failures that made no sense. Learning through trial and error is an expensive way to solve the problems.

There are thousands of secrets in the cloud computing industry. If revealed, these secrets could help more enterprises succeed with cloud projects their first time and avoid expensive do-overs or the ongoing expenses of a cloud system that "more or less" works, but not really and not ideally.

Cloud technology providers spend billions in marketing dollars to keep you unaware of certain secrets. Wouldn't it be nice to know cost-optimized ways to leverage cloud computing services that can cut your cloud bill in half? Or, how to leverage cloud service providers using multicloud and hybrid cloud configurations that allow you to shop in a larger pool of technology and get the best price for best-of-breed technology?

Don't feel singled out or alone. The current cloud skills shortage almost guarantees you will have a blind spot or experience gap in some or many sections of your cloud project. Providers realize there is a certain lack of knowledge within most enterprises. They also recognize that there are two general types of organizations that leverage or are about to leverage cloud.

The first type spends millions more than required on cloud computing solutions, largely due to a lack of staff familiarity with the minutiae of the cloud computing industry; thus, the enterprise remains oblivious to the pitfalls. It's not in a provider's best interest to educate away their profits.

The second type comprises a smaller minority: those enterprises that are in-the-know and understand what others don't. This includes knowledge of long-held cloud secrets that were once whispered about in conference rooms or spilled over drinks at cloud conference happy hours. They might even know more than their providers about certain aspects of cloud computing.

This book reveals many of those secrets, as well as the secrets that swirl around the hidden values of emerging technologies such as artificial intelligence, containers, no-code, and serverless computing. There is information about what works, what doesn't, and how to pick your best resources for migration or net-new cloud-based application development.

Finally, and most important, this book reveals why some workloads and data sets don't belong in the cloud…for now. We also review the true value of cloud computing in general.

Other secrets will spill, such as the actual value of cloud computing when it's applied to your carbon footprint, and the folly of some cloud technologies that were hyped just a few years ago that are now worthless and should be avoided. Also included is a discussion of "game changer" technologies that have small marketing budgets and should be examined more closely.

Regardless of how much you think you know, it's always best to start (or continue) a project with the most relevant information. Some of the secrets revealed in this book will change your odds of success with cloud computing by a little or by a lot...often by a lot.

Why I Wrote This Book

For this book to have any value, it must provide information in a candid way and not hold back on issues that many editors and book publishers would find a bit risky. For example, discussing the real value of cloud computing regardless of how the larger cloud providers now define it. Or, looking at the claims of sustainability in the cloud computing and technology markets, and letting you know the current expectations and core benefits with comparisons to what we're seeing in real-world projects.

This book's primary purpose is to provide the positive realities of what cloud technology can bring to today's enterprises and to reveal some often-unexpected downsides. The surprises tend to happen when organizations approach cloud computing incorrectly, or when the public cloud providers themselves don't have a good handle on how their clients should leverage their technology.

The misuse of and misinformation about cloud computing technology are the two most common problems. Yes, the technology does have value, but what you use and how it's used determine its value. Every day we learn more about what works, what doesn't, and how to make sure cloud computing works best for an enterprise. Cloud providers, technology providers, and those charged with selecting and configuring this technology must work together. It's also good to know if and where your providers themselves might still have some blind spots.

What struck me about the cloud computing market in general is that the billions of dollars spent on cloud marketing seems to spin cloud technology as something that can't fail. Marketing has a big impact on how organizations leverage the technology. It can also obscure some important information if potential clients don't know the right questions to ask prior to selecting cloud providers or cloud technology. And yet, how can you get the answers if you don't know the questions to ask?

This lack of knowledge leads to a few probable outcomes:

First, and the most helpful thing that could occur, would be failure. Although nobody likes to fail, at least we understand that what we did was wrong, and we back up to try a different approach with another cloud technology selection and configuration. Although this effort costs time and money, if you apply the lessons learned, the movement to the correct, near-optimized solution will be a win.

Second, and the most negative of these outcomes, is to select a cloud technology solution that's under-optimized. It costs way more than it should and does not bring the ultimate business value back to the enterprise. The issue here is that the solution works, which is the only metric that many cloud architects and developers use to measure their success. It doesn't seem to matter that it costs the enterprise up to a half a billion dollars in lost revenue. Who has the knowledge to consider the cost savings of a near-optimized configuration and the business value that ultimately gets left on the table with an under-optimized system? I would strongly question the opinions of the cloud architects and developers who installed and still believe that their underoptimized system "works."

More often, underoptimized situations go undetected. The bad solution continues to hurt the business ongoing. Chances are that you have an underoptimized example in your own career. If you don't, reading this book will help keep you in that rare air.

The outcome of trial and error is success. A success on the first try requires selection of the right technology with a configuration that gets as close as possible to full optimization, in terms of cost efficiency and value that's returned to the business. Luck doesn't get you there. It's a matter of being open-minded from the very beginning of a cloud project. What is most likely to work best for a particular project, given the requirements and current state of the technology? Look beyond the hype and noise to see what the technology can do as well as what it can't do.

Cloud migration and/or development projects are not considered fully successful unless they approach optimized efficiency and return optimal value to the business. That criterion makes fully successful projects rare. Not because they are hard to do, but because of existing biases, and a lack of related experiences and skills. In other words, few cloud architects and developers can see beyond the hype, misinformation, and what's popular to make potentially unpopular decisions, even if they're the right ones.

How to Read This Book

If the chapter topics seem to jump around a bit, that's on purpose. So many secrets exist around the use of cloud technology that they can't be organized into neat categories. This book organizes what I think is important to understand about the cloud computing industry into chapters that obviously go together. These chapters include knowledge and information that we see lead to successful cloud projects.

Other chapters are decoupled from the theme of the previous chapter or the ones that follow, but they build on information introduced in previous chapters and present new information on an obscured or "secret" topic. These chapters include secrets of cloud computing that most people in the industry are not willing to share.

Thus, although we talk about cloud storage and cloud computing services in the first few chapters, which are both considered foundational infrastructure services, we move quickly to more advanced cloud services such as artificial intelligence and machine learning that seem to dominate today's technology press. Then, we talk about other trends such as multicloud, and how enterprises are failing and succeeding with those technology configurations. We include what's being hyped and what works, which are two very different things.

Next, we get into a few cloud topics that seem to be making technology press headlines: cloud's ability to support sustainability and to reduce our carbon footprint and more. Finally, we discuss the likely future of cloud computing. Here we focus on what's most likely to occur versus what is predicted.

We end with a discussion of skills: how to find them and how to build your own. To build net-new cloud-based systems, it's critical that project leaders know how and where to build new skill sets into the enterprise, as well as how to find, attract, and keep the right skills. We also look at how to manage your own skills to become someone with talents that enterprises will pay top dollar to attract and/or retain.

What Benefits Can You Expect?

The core benefit to reading this book is that you'll be "in the know" about things that most of the cloud providers, technology vendors, consultants, and other players would rather you not know. Armed with this information, you'll be able to ask specific questions around the use and cost of the technology under consideration and many other factors to question that you'll learn about here.

To use a very simple example, let's say a new business will soon launch and you're in charge of finding a system to manage inventory. You want to determine the specific type of cloud storage that will best support a new inventory system for the enterprise's possibly unique type of inventory. You need to consider different types of storage, such as object, block, and file storage, and understand the implications of how each operate as well as the different price points of each. Moreover, you need to understand how particulars such as deals for goods can be obtained when the enterprise buys ahead of need, and when this will likely work to the enterprise's benefit and when it will not.

There will also be opportunities and challenges with cloud heterogeneity. Multicloud provides you with the ability to select best-of-breed technology and services. However, the price of this choice is complexity. The number of different system types and brands that you must operate over the years to come will require different skill sets and interfaces.

The complexity of it all becomes the challenge. Always keep an eye on the number of moving parts and configurations required to become successful. Determining the best balance of choice and complexity for each project, as well as for the enterprise, will result in a near-optimized system that brings the most value to the business.

Information presented in this book will not tell you exactly what to do step by step, one-size-fits-all. It *will* arm you with the right knowledge to make your ventures into the world of cloud computing more likely to succeed.

Chapter | **1**

How "Real" Is the Value of Cloud Computing?

Try not to become a man of success but rather try to become a man of value.

— *Albert Einstein*

We defined the value of cloud computing 20 years ago…and have kept redefining it ever since. It's become a source of confusion among those who must explain the value of cloud computing in the form of a business case.

In this chapter, we look at how we initially defined the value of cloud computing, how and why it changed throughout the years, and the current reality of "cloud alue." We also talk about what's just pure junk science.

What We Thought We Knew

The value of cloud computing is perhaps one of today's most debated topics in the world of business technology. We made many assumptions when cloud computing first became a hyped technology concept. Much of our initial thinking about the value of cloud computing got hit in the face with reality when most businesses did not realize those anticipated values, at least, not in ways the values were originally defined and promised.

This failure to recognize values led to serious reevaluations around how to define the true value of cloud computing. We based these new assumptions and metrics on the values businesses see in terms of increased revenue, higher stock prices, and, in some cases, the movement companies could make to dominate their marketplaces in a true disruptor fashion, much like Uber, Amazon.com, Netflix, and others that leveraged cloud computing as a true force multiplier.

Back to our first thoughts about cloud computing, we saw value in the ability to get out of the business of owning and operating hardware, software, and data centers. Most stakeholders understood the value that computers could bring to a business in terms of automation and data management, but the costs of owning the hardware and software were prohibitive at the time. They also took notice when the business needed a new system to automate a process or store data, and the result was many millions of dollars spent on new servers, storage systems, power supplies, and data center space, as well as the group of people needed to maintain everything.

This cycle prompted the computing industry to take another look at the time-share model, which was how businesses initially consumed computing in the early days of automation. Back then, many companies offered time-sharing services that could leverage powerful (at the time) computing and storage systems, and clients would pay only for the time that they remotely leveraged the computers. As a result, the cost of owning a physical system experienced a significant drop.

New innovations such as minicomputers and then the personal computer, along with local area networking (LAN) and wide area networking (WAN), opened new possibilities. It became more advantageous to the business to own your systems. After the initial investment, you had unlimited access to compute and storage systems that you owned and depreciated.

The Return to the Utility Model

In basic terms, today's move to cloud computing is simply a return to the old utility model of time sharing. The ideas are the same: You leverage a system that's offered and maintained by somebody else, and you pay only for the resources you use.

This approach is much like we leverage other utilities, such as electric power for our homes and city water services. Yes, we could leverage power from our own eclectic generators, or we could dig a well. When you weigh the initial investment required, it's usually more cost effective in cities and suburbs to purchase these services from centralized providers and tap into their existing infrastructure.

Of course, cloud computing is much more sophisticated than traditional time sharing, considering that we now leverage remote systems via broadband networks. We can do so as if we own the systems rather than leverage yesterday's tightly controlled and managed services. However, the consumption models of yesterday and today are very much alike. Both are metered services where you pay only for the resource you leverage and the amount of time you leverage it.

How did cloud computing drive our return to the utility model? Here are the influencing factors:

- **Today we better understand the value that businesses put on capital.** We once considered millions of dollars' worth of computing equipment and data centers just part of the cost of doing business. These days, businesses eye those investments as capital boat anchors that do not allow them to fund areas of the business with a higher ROI potential. For example, the purchase of another company could provide better channel access to the market, or businesses might spend additional money on innovation that could result in unique differentiators that enable the business to become a market disruptor.

- **When another company provides core operational services, that frees up the costs of hiring and maintaining those skills.** When businesses went into the systems operations business, the number of people needed to operate those systems exploded. Staffing costs leapfrogged to include hard-to-find and costly skill sets.

- **The value of moving to a more innovative state through the use of technology.** Today, most innovation happens in the cloud. If you want to leverage best-of-breed, then you're on a forced march to the cloud: It's where you'll find the most effective and efficient best-of-breed technology. Databases, security, development, and operations are all state-of-the-art within public clouds such as AWS, Google, or Microsoft. This is where vendors made and will continue to make most of their research and development (R&D) investments.

The Elusive "Cost Savings"

"Cost savings" was the initial battle cry of cloud computing for good reasons. Until then, most Global 2000 companies built their own data centers and filled them up with expensive and quickly depreciating hardware and software. This led to IT departments that grew much faster than the revenue to justify the growth. Soon everyone wanted to get IT costs under control and align IT spending more closely to the minimum values that stakeholders required from their IT investments.

Around the end of the 1990s, enterprises saw an opportunity to get out of the IT cost spiral. We could no longer spend $2 and project $1 in returned value. Something needed to change. The time was ripe for a fundamental shift in the way that we built, deployed, and leveraged applications and data. Along came the time-share model in its new incarnation.

Most in IT understood the legacy time-share model, although we had a more intermediate step in the '90s known as application service providers, or ASPs. These differed a bit from modern Software as a Service (SaaS) providers. Basically, they were off-the-shelf software programs that ran over the newly emerging open Internet, and just became a host for applications you would normally run in-house. Since these applications were not purpose-built for use by multiple users over the Internet, scalability and performance were problems often reported by those who leveraged ASPs. Also, the ASPs did not utilize modern mechanisms that you find in today's clouds, such as virtualization in support of multitenancy.

However, ASPs had the same value proposition as modern cloud computing. ASP value included cost savings, easy upgrades, and payments only for the time that you leveraged the applications and data. In other words, these were the first early tries at cloud computing. At the time, they fell short in what could be delivered. The desire to find a new consumption model for technology remained, with the same cost-reduction battle cry.

SaaS, such as Salesforce.com and others, showed up shortly after the ASP market tanked. There were several differentiating and attractive factors that favored the early SaaS providers. The applications were purpose-built to be multitenant products that could support the ability to service thousands of simultaneous users. They could scale to the processing loads that the customers required. They maintained a good uptime record, and even offered better security than was currently available with traditional on-premises applications.

Thus, SaaS (initially called "on-demand applications") paved the way to Infrastructure as a Service (IaaS) and Platform as a Service (PaaS). The National Institute of Standards and Technology (NIST) defined and standardized both terms around 2008, which led to today's "official" cloud computing definitions that include private clouds, public clouds, community clouds, and hybrid clouds.

It's Not CapEx Versus OpEx, and It Never Was

The goal here is to provide a brief history of cloud computing. It's important to understand where we started and how our thinking evolved around cloud cost savings (value). It's also helpful to understand why our initial definitions of the business value of cloud computing completely changed over time.

Back to CapEx versus OpEx (see Figure 1-1). The shift to OpEx from CapEx initially appeared on the scene as a hyped technology change. Most businesses viewed OpEx as the means to realistically define cloud computing's business value. OpEx changed the way we consumed computing and IT in general, which in turn provided the ability to get IT costs under control. These approaches seemed logical at the time, and OpEx became a prominent presentation point by those who promoted the use of cloud computing at the time.

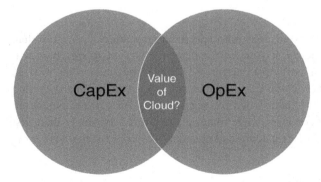

FIGURE 1-1 In the early days of cloud computing, the idea was to adopt operational expenses (OpEx) and thus reduce Capital Expenses (CapEx). This proved to be a wrong assumption.

The argument was sound. Reduce the amount of money spent on traditional computing systems and data centers and free up that capital to put back in the business. The trade-off would be a shift to operating expenses that aligned to usage. The more IT resources we used, such as storage and compute, the more we paid. This was known as "being elastic" in terms of scaling up and scaling down and increasing and reducing costs to fit current needs.

Sadly, most real-life cloud computing experiences challenged the CapEx versus OpEx way of thinking about cloud computing value.

Any quick web search will reveal that cost overruns around cloud migrations and cloud operations became the norm. The reasons vary when you ask what went wrong. The answers come down to two core issues: first, unrealistic expectations about where to find the value of cloud computing; and second, incorrectly defined metrics.

This Is About Business Value, and It Always Was

Here's a hard reality: Most of the benefits we see from the use of cloud computing are not in operational cost savings or from saving capital for more strategic uses of the funds. It's about cloud computing's transformative business value. Transformative business value is much more viable than any CapEx versus OpEx set of metrics would have you believe. It's also more difficult to understand. Basically, we can call this "hard" versus "soft" business value.

Hard value is easy to determine. Let's say the use of cloud computing saves us 10 percent in operational savings, such as using storage and compute from AWS, Microsoft, or Google, versus from our own hardware in our own data center. What we often fail to factor in are new skill sets, including the additional costs of those skills. Additionally, many of us don't fully understand or correctly plan for the costs of data ingress and egress to and from cloud providers. Moving enterprise data to and from on-premises data storage to cloud-based data storage typically involves a fee each time you do it. Usually, by volume.

Other issues arise around hard costs when the staff does not understand why things cost more than expected, which includes the costs of inefficiency. If you don't understand why it happens, how will you prevent it from happening? These are the costs that enterprise IT shops encounter when they do not have a good handle on management of new cloud costs, such as storage, compute, databases, and artificial intelligence. Indeed, prepare for sticker shock when you see what happens when resources are allocated and then not deallocated, or, more common, when things are just more expensive than first estimated. For instance, if the costs involved of expanding and changing the use of technology were not originally understood.

Soft value is where we should define the real value of cloud computing from the beginning. However, the term *soft* comes from the fact that we're defining value as something that's hard to determine—for example, the value of business agility, speed to market, and the real value of market differentiating innovation (see Figure 1-2).

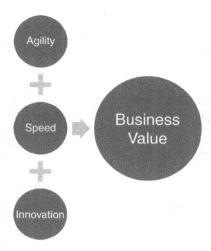

FIGURE 1-2   The true business value turned out to be more difficult to measure, such as the value of agility, speed to market, and innovation.

While most will agree that these soft values are more advantageous to the business than any operational savings that cloud computing can bring, we also agree that these values are difficult to determine. If I tell you that cloud computing will provide more business agility, your natural responding questions would be

- What's business agility?

- What's the value of increased business agility by product line?

- How do we measure the success of having more business agility?

- How do we know if the value of business agility cost justifies cloud computing in the first place?

Same goes for speed to market and innovation. Most will struggle to define these spongy concepts for a specific business. Let's try to create a set of approaches to define the worth of these soft values.

Figure 1-3 shows a typical value curve that most businesses see when they implement cloud computing. Notice that the curve is not a straight line; instead, it inflects around the midpoint when the enterprises get about 30–40 percent of the applications and data sets migrated to the cloud. Of course, at some point the value diminishes as the technology moves into more of a maintenance mode.

> **Note**
>
> There is an investment being made with new value returned during the initial migrations to the cloud. Then there is an increase in value as expansion begins and the enterprise realizes the soft values we define here, values that include business agility, speed to market, and innovation. All these values will increase by using cloud computing. Eventually, there is a move to the maintenance stage when the move to cloud slows down and the enterprise focuses on continuously improving the cloud services in support of the soft values.

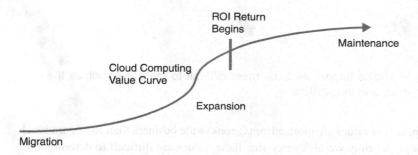

FIGURE 1-3 The cloud computing value curve shows where the return is equal to or greater than the amount invested, which is typically farther down the path than most businesses understand at the outset of a cloud project. Indeed, for most businesses, cloud computing has yet to return the values that were advertised in the early days of cloud computing.

Agility

Business agility, or just "agility," is the business's ability to change around business requirements. Examples of agility include moving into new markets via an aggressive acquisition strategy, where key business processes and data need to be quickly integrated. Or, adding a new "game-changing" product such as a traditional core manufacturer adding a line of electric vehicles. Agility includes anything that has a value multiplier if these improvements can quickly be placed into production and thus drive more revenue, and even improve stock prices.

The trouble with agility is that you don't know what the value will be until you see the effects of the system's ability to drive more agility. Therefore, we must rely on estimates around what we think the value of more business agility will bring. This means doing complex modeling that considers many different factors that make up the value of business agility estimations. Of course, some of these assumptions, such as market acceptance as a factor, may not turn out to be correct.

To predict the unpredictable, you need to determine a best- and worst-case scenario. What is the value of agility if all assumptions are correct, meaning they meet or exceed estimates? Or what is the value if the assumptions fall short? For instance, we assumed that an emerging market could be found in a specific area, such as robotic lawnmowers. However, the market was slow to grow due to an economic downturn where luxury items such as lawnmower upgrades saw diminished demand (worst case). Or, just as likely, the cost of gas skyrocketed to a point where electric lawnmowers are seeing demand that outpaces initial estimates (best case). Most of the time, the reality will fall somewhere in between.

Keep this in mind: Increased agility returns huge values for most enterprises. However, the degree of value will greatly vary from one enterprise to the next, and with how they can or want to weaponize business agility to find more markets and thus revenue.

It will take some creative thinking to figure out the soft value of agility in your enterprise and how cloud computing can enhance its business agility. How you understand your business and create these estimates will also come into play. Each business will have a different value for business agility and a different way that you determine what you think that value will be.

Basically, the more value you place on business agility, the more valuable cloud computing will be to your business. Indeed, the value of business agility will be many times that of any investment in cloud computing. Operational savings should not be the main consideration, or sometimes no consideration at all when your enterprise looks at the true value of cloud computing. This is a value indicator that we missed back when cloud computing began.

Speed

Speed is a bit different than agility, but kind of the same. Speed focuses on your ability to move fast in a single business direction, whereas agility focuses on your ability to change your business fast.

Like agility, speed (such as speed-to-market) will have various degrees of value that depend on your business and the markets you serve. For example, a box factory in the Midwest might place a very low value on speed. The market demand for boxes usually doesn't change with enough velocity to put a premium on moving fast.

However, another company will place a very high value on its ability to expand production of a product based on current or projected explosive demand. A simple example would be a trending children's toy at the onset of the holiday season. Cloud computing allows the enterprise to scale up production processing to much higher levels, which will increase the speed of production to meet changing demand. Thus, the enterprise obtains more revenue. Therein lies the soft value of speed-to-market, which usually exists within the value of agility.

Innovation

Innovation is perhaps the most underrated value of cloud computing. It often gets overlooked for the same reasons that speed and agility get overlooked. Determining its value is also just as difficult. Putting a dollar figure on innovation will take much deeper analysis to predict, specifically what value innovation will bring to any individual enterprise.

With that said, the value of innovation is relatively easy to understand. For example, Uber used innovation to figure out how to create one of the world's largest transportation and delivery services, and it did so without owning a single vehicle. Cell phone manufacturers took the innovation leap to make small and powerful computer systems that now fit in our pockets. Innovative leaps by these companies now define most if not all their value in the marketplace, and they had to effectively leverage technology to get there.

Cloud computing supports innovation by giving enterprises cheap and almost instantaneous access to technology. In the relatively recent past, it would have cost several million dollars to access AI to drive innovation in your company. Today, cloud-based AI systems are much more advanced than the AI technology of just 10 years ago, and AI might cost only a few dollars a month to run. Even better, you can leverage today's AI by just clicking a box on a public cloud provider's dashboard.

The same can be said for very large analytical databases, advanced processing systems such as high-performance computing (HPC), the Internet of Things (IoT) development, edge computing development, containers, and anything else the innovator wants to create that could launch the company to a different competitive level.

Indeed, almost all of today's innovations occur in the cloud, and have since about 2015. Those who build and deploy this technology understand that the market they need to build for is "the cloud." It's unsurprising that enterprises spend almost 90 percent of their R&D dollars on cloud-based technology rather than on traditional systems. This is the reason that security, operations, governance, databases, and AI systems are now better in the cloud than on premises. This will remain the case for the next few decades.

We know that most businesses place a high value on innovation, but how high is it for your business? This typically depends on the following business attributes:

- **The market that your company falls within.** For instance, an enterprise in the finance vertical will typically gain much more for key innovations than an enterprise would gain in the agriculture vertical. Take our box company example mentioned previously. It's a sound business, but it's doubtful the company would gain a great deal from innovative capabilities around improvements to boxes. It's a different story for tech company disruptors. (Not to pick on the box industry as noninnovative; it's just an example.)

- **Your current position in the market.** Innovation is more valuable to larger companies with an existing market and customer base. The bigger you are, the more you must gain from innovation. Conversely, big companies are known for driving less innovation than their smaller counterparts.

- **What are the most likely innovations?** In some instances, companies redefine themselves through net-new innovations. For instance, a boat company invents a new way for boats to float above the water using an innovation around magnetic levitation (MagLev). This is an innovation that falls outside of traditional offerings with net-new technology that could disrupt the existing boat market and create a net-new market that does not yet exist. Others may create innovations that are not as game-changing. An automotive parts manufacturer might create brakes for cars that last two times as long as traditional brakes. Innovative, yes. But not revolutionary.

Figure 1-4 shows how innovation value may appear in the cloud value curve we introduced previously. In this model, innovation driven by cloud adoption significantly increases, well behind the rate of cloud adoption. Depending on the business attributes listed previously, your curve may not be as steep, or it might only slightly slope up. The key here is to understand the true value of innovation. Not just in general terms, but how the true value of innovation relates specifically to your business.

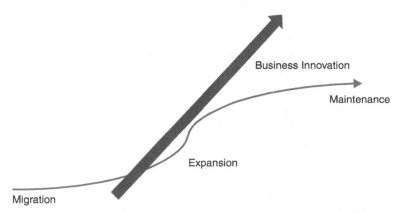

FIGURE 1-4 A core value that cloud computing brings is the ability to drive business innovation. This means that companies can become disruptors rather than be disrupted.

How do you define the soft values of cloud computing for your enterprise? Here are a few recent schools of thought:

- What are the differences in values between the business having the soft values of agility, speed, and innovation in place and not in place? What are the values minus the costs of migrating to the cloud, including all migration, development, and operational costs? For example, if the business does not have cloud computing in place to support these soft benefits, what is the sell-price value of the business? Now, what is the value of the business if these soft benefits are enabled using cloud computing? We can call this the "value differentiator calculation" to determine true value.

- Define and project the increase in revenue by putting these soft values in place using cloud computing. Let's say a business experienced revenue at 6 times all costs in 2010. When the business migrated 50 percent of the applications and data to the cloud by 2015, they experienced revenue at 14 times all costs that included migration and operational costs of the new cloud-based systems. Now you can assume that the use of cloud-based systems, including the accompanying soft values, will produce 8 times more revenue.

- Here we say "assume" because other market factors could drive sales up or down by increasing or decreasing the company's ability to sell more goods and services. Some simple market factor examples are the pandemic and current gas prices that were unforeseen a year before they happened. Both events drove businesses both to and away from certain markets. In this context, think about the production of face masks versus office furniture, and the production of electric cars versus RVs. This quickly becomes a complex calculation that should factor in as many variables as possible. Thus, this example might not be a good determination of value, considering that we're only looking at revenue differences rather than considering the true value of the business, or what you could sell the business for at any given time.

The way you define the value differences will always be unique to your business, either estimated prior to moving to the cloud when creating a business case or when evaluating the post-value benefits after cloud systems are in place. I could present any number of formulas and metrics here, but none will apply to your specific business.

Yes, you could make incorrect assumptions if you force fit someone else's idea of a value calculation to your business. While you can certainly use the value calculation concepts in this book as a starting point, your best bet is to form your own ideas and models based on the needs of your actual business and your understanding of their values.

What Could Go Wrong?

Taking another step back in time, if our first ideas around defining the value of cloud computing were mostly wrong, what exactly went wrong and what exactly went right? I always think it's a good idea to figure out what did not work and why. Don't just ignore a failure and hope nobody notices. The reality is that we're wrong a lot about the true value of technology, and we need to focus on how to make better technology value assumptions moving forward.

This is not about pointing blame at the many who promoted cloud benefits as just an OpEx versus CapEx, including promises of lower operational costs. Today, we need to find the true value of cloud computing and admit where these value concepts can be improved. Generally speaking, let's look at what went wrong.

Too Much Focus on Operational Cost Savings That Seldom Became a Reality

For many businesses, cloud computing can provide operational cost savings. However, clearly the industry overpromoted the concept of operational cost savings at the onset of cloud computing.

A variety of unconsidered things happened. An example would be not accounting for the higher costs of public cloud services that ended up being the services leveraged versus the basic cloud services that defined the initial value.

We often priced the use of cloud services using simple storage and compute service prices to support migrated applications with analog platforms (e.g., Linux on premises versus Linux in the public cloud).

Tempting new services and enabling technology in the cloud soon arrived, adding costs, but were too tempting to ignore. These included AI and machine learning, advanced databases, serverless computing, edge computing, IoT, containers, and any number of technologies the tech press promoted over the last 10 years.

While the use of these technologies by migrated and net-new applications significantly raised the cost of public cloud computing for most of those use cases, it was the right call to make. By focusing on the soft values I described earlier in this chapter, the value and use of these emerging technologies easily offset the higher operational costs. For many companies, the use of these technologies and the pragmatic innovation they provided "made" the company. This is certainly the case with better known disruptors such as Uber, Airbnb, Netflix, and other companies that quickly learned how to weaponize cloud computing. Often, the amount of time taken to migrate a service to the cloud ends up being double or triple the time that is first estimated. This increase is due to a lot of reasons, but the majority of the time it's simple poor migration planning. Moreover, the client is paying for the legacy system and the new cloud environment at the same time.

Even though the cost of cloud computing turned out to be much more than we initially thought, those who made the decision to pivot to the types of cloud technology where they found more exponential value often found more soft values. They made the right decisions. It all depends on the specific business. It's more impactful for some businesses to place more weight on the soft values that cloud computing brings than it is to stick to a static cloud computing budget. Sometimes it's not.

Too Little Attention Paid to the Cost of Skills

The cost of good people with good cloud skills turned out to be a whole lot more expensive than we once thought. In 2010, a cloud computing specialist or an experienced consultant cost about $35–$45 USD per hour, or about $80,000 per year if salaried. That person had general cloud computing skills, such as understanding cloud storage, cloud compute, and the configuration of cloud platforms. There was very little specialization when cloud computing first appeared, and most "cloud people" were generalists.

Today, it's a seller's market that does not seem to be affected by the existing unemployment rate. If you're a cloud computing generalist in 2023, you'll likely make at least $75 USD per hour, or about $140,000 per year in salary. However, if you're a specialist and focus on specific technologies such as data analytics in the cloud, AI, or machine learning, or if you are a cloud computing architect, then the salaries and hourly rates carry huge premiums. It's not unusual for a cloud technology specialist with specialized certifications (such as those provided by the larger cloud providers—AWS, Microsoft, or Google) to command $200 per hour, with salaries well over $275,000 on the top end.

Remember, you make and pay the market rate for talent. It turns out today's costs for certain skills are at a much higher premium than many anticipated in the budget phase. Indeed, the current cost of talent is often the highest cost of moving to the cloud or building systems in the cloud, with the actual cloud costs being a much smaller portion of the budget.

The higher salaries and rates just confirm that cloud computing skills are in demand since cloud computing is in demand. This demand is largely due to businesses finally figuring out the soft values I described here. Even these higher salaries are a drop in the bucket compared to the overall value that most businesses can find when they use cloud computing services.

Cloud Providers Thrive on Profit

Many focus on greed as a primary reason that cloud costs are too high, whether that greed involves the cost of skills that I just described or the cost of cloud computing services themselves. What's clear is that cloud computing providers are in business to make money, just as your company is in business to make money. As such, providers will drive as much profit as they can, and that will reflect in higher fees and fee structures as cloud computing matures.

These prices do not surprise anyone who has been in technology longer than a few years. Nor did it surprise us when many of the large enterprise technology players jacked up the license fees for their older technology. These databases, platforms, legacy hardware, and other systems that enterprises once depended on are now legacy technologies that vendors won't further improve. Today, technology providers focus almost exclusively on cloud products.

The days of watching public cloud prices drop are at an end. Don't be surprised that the cloud providers now want to maximize the returns on their technology investments. The cloud providers will charge clients the value that they believe they bring to the business. These costs will in turn drive more profit for the cloud computing providers.

Today's new technology offerings come with new and higher prices. Volatile prices add a new dimension of difficulty to planning for hard and soft costs. However, if higher cloud costs also increase business value, the costs become more of an observation than an obstacle.

What Went Right?

On a more positive note, let's turn our attention to what went right. It's important to understand what assumptions came true to find the true value of cloud computing. Here "in the right," we can determine the true value of cloud computing. We can also identify the true value drivers and pivot to support new patterns of thinking about value. It's all about focusing on the soft values we covered previously.

Cloud computing is still an evolving technology, which means we will redefine cloud value for years to come. However, much of what we cover in this chapter will evolve as well, albeit I suspect the same soft values will remain consistent for at least the next 20 years.

Agility, Innovation, and Speed Become King

As we covered earlier in this chapter, today's end state understanding of the value of cloud computing seems to focus on the value of agility, innovation, and speed. Because we already covered these soft values in detail, we do not cover them again in this section. Instead, let's review how we concluded that these were the right soft values to focus on.

Many businesses have different motivations to leverage cloud. For some, such as startups with little funding, cloud computing was their only option. They could purchase powerful computing resources at reasonable prices and forgo yesterday's requirements to spend millions of dollars on data center space, hardware, software, and people to run everything. These companies had "no choice" but to move to the cloud. Even companies that were built in the cloud served as nice use cases for those still trying to figure out the business value and how to migrate to the cloud.

The unique factor about startups "born in the cloud" is that their motivations to utilize cloud computing back then echo the reasons that enterprises should leverage cloud now. What often differs is that these startups also enjoyed OpEx savings. They had no existing data centers. Cloud was cheaper, and they paid only for what they used, which directly aligned to the revenue that the cloud-based systems brought back to the business.

While this direct alignment to usage and revenue was certainly true for most smaller or startup companies, enterprises did not share the same experiences since such a small portion of their IT systems were cloud-based systems, and thus it was difficult to determine the amount of revenue a cloud system generated at different levels of use.

For example, let's say a .com startup keeps all web and revenue-generating systems on a public cloud provider, say AWS. If the startup gets a cloud bill of $1,000 for a single month and sees $100,000 in revenue to show for that bill, and the next month's bill is $2,000 and there is $190,000 of revenue that month, it's easy to draw a direct correlation from the usage of cloud-based systems to revenue.

A larger company might see the same cloud bills from one month to the next. However, because it has only 10 percent of its systems migrated to public clouds, it's difficult to figure out which systems, cloud or not, directly related to an increase or decrease in revenue. Worse, most larger enterprises don't track revenue generation per system, cloud or not, so they don't have the mechanisms in place to figure out how much revenue relates to any specific system, cloud or not.

You might think that smaller cloud users, including startups and other small businesses, would prove the initial thinking around CapEx versus OpEx values. However, a few things emerged around some of the startups that left the traditional business case assumptions in the dust and change the focus of larger businesses to the soft values we covered in this chapter.

Why? Well, many of the businesses that first leveraged cloud through economic necessity became industry disruptors and found that cloud computing was a better weapon than just a utility service. Netflix, Uber, eBay, PayPal, and Airbnb, all early adopters of cloud computing in their startup phases, learned quickly that cloud was much more than a money saver.

Keep in mind while these are the brands that most people trot out when talking about the cloud computing benefits of agility, speed, and innovation, thousands of other lesser-known businesses have found the same value. Many of those businesses are also industry disruptors with explosive growth. Or, they are about to disrupt an industry, such as prescription drugs, logistics and supply chains, insurance, home automation, and other industries where the current leaders proved less than innovative and agile.

In the end, customers will vote with their dollars just as they did with Netflix over Blockbuster Video, or Uber over any city taxi service. If you think these disruptions are at an end, think again. Over the next 10–20 years, we'll see an entirely new crop of disruptor brands emerge. All will have the same two things in common: They will recognize the value of cloud computing technology, and they will weaponize it to dominate an industry.

Weaponization of cloud computing differs from disruptor to disruptor, but the primary values these disruptors found and will find in the cloud include

- The ability to quickly adapt. For example, pivoting to new and more lucrative markets during the initial growth phase of the company.

- The ability to out-innovate larger businesses. For example, the ability to leverage AI systems to provide a better customer experience.

- The ability to scale without slowing down the business. Startups that leverage cloud computing could go from 100 customers to 1,000,000 customers with basically the same infrastructure. While their cloud costs rose, so did revenue to cover those costs.

- The ability to keep up with market demand. As demand rises, startup disruptors that use cloud don't worry about keeping up with changes in demand. They can both pivot and increase velocity as needed to support the business. Most of the time with the click of a mouse.

Best-of-Breed Put the Business Back in Control

Initially, cloud-based platforms were not best-of-breed in any way, shape, or form. They were just simple storage and compute solutions. As cloud evolved and became the focus of most R&D budgets, public clouds became the location where innovation occurred, and thus where the best technology could be found. This includes databases, application development, AI and machine learning, analytics, serverless, and containers, as well as upcoming approaches such as IoT and edge computing.

Those in the cloud had access to more innovative best-of-breed technologies to build and deploy their systems. Many of these systems became game-changing technologies that defined their business. Again, the successful disruptors learned how to effectively leverage this technology to support their business and to create a new space such as ride-sharing and house-sharing applications that are now industries worth multiple billions.

The unique part about this wave of change is that it put the control back into the hands of the business. In the past, most businesses depended on a handful of technology providers or whoever owned the platforms they leveraged to support their existing systems. Diverting from those primary providers meant higher costs and risk, which was typically not an option for most Global 2000 companies. Thus, best-of-breed from their providers was rarely best-of-breed in the marketplace because they were limited to a small pool of technology providers.

The rise of cloud computing opened the technology market for those committed to cloud computing. Because most technologies have a cloud-based version that exists within public clouds, those are now options as well. The key advantages here include easy and open access to the newest and most innovative best-of-breed technologies.

Because we're no longer dependent on a specific technology that supports our existing traditional platform, we can focus on all technologies that we need or want to deploy. Any platform configurations can be done on public cloud providers; thus, there are no limitations that hinder what technologies you can leverage. That puts control back within the business that leverages cloud computing.

Technology providers spend about 90 percent of their R&D budgets to build technology specifically for clouds. Therefore, the newest and most innovative technologies are found in the cloud. Given the access advantages we just covered, this means there are no limitations as to what technologies we can leverage, and these technologies will be the latest and greatest.

The key theme here is control. No longer is a business stuck with whatever technologies worked with past platform decisions. Instead, businesses control all aspects of what technologies they leverage, how they leverage them, and can be certain that the best-of-breed technologies they need to meet business requirements can be found in the cloud. This is far more liberating than most people understand right now, but they will.

Security Is Better in the Cloud

Security was the most common argument against cloud computing, certainly public cloud computing, and it's a criticism that you'll still hear today. I once called this "hug your server" paranoia. Public cloud providers use data centers that you'll never see or enter. How can your data and systems be safer if you can't physically see or touch ("hug") the hardware it runs on?

Around 2014, those in the know noticed a shift in security offerings. Again, most of the technology providers' R&D budgets are now spent in the cloud. This spending includes development of new and innovative security solutions. Cloud providers spent and will continue to spend an enormous amount of money to shore up their native security offerings. Many cloud experts, including myself, have declared that cloud computing systems are now more secure than most traditional systems.

As you can see with Figure 1-5, the reason the security situation happened so quickly is easy to understand. Most R&D spending in the enterprise software space occurred and occurs in conjunction with a cloud platform, with private, hybrid, and public clouds as the target for that solution.

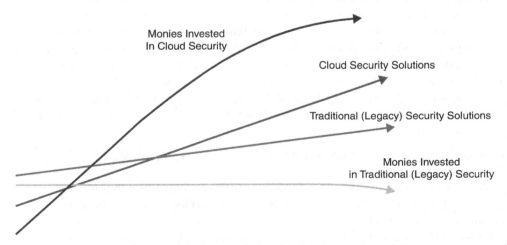

FIGURE 1-5 As vendors invested more dollars in cloud security solutions versus security solutions for traditional (legacy) systems, cloud security became much better on cloud-based systems and platforms than on traditional on-premises systems.

As you can see in the "Monies Invested in Cloud Security" line in Figure 1-5, most of the larger cloud players spent billions to develop services for this emerging market. The larger enterprise software players also spent significant amounts on cloud-targeted products and services. Most of these companies don't break out their R&D expenditures, but it's currently estimated that they spend 85–95 percent of their R&D budgets on cloud product/service innovations, on average.

As you can see on the "Monies Invested in Traditional (Legacy) Security" line, cloud innovations and development came at the expense of traditional security systems. Traditional systems with small or nonexistent innovation and development budgets are less desirable. Many enterprise software companies now treat legacy solutions as "sunset" products. They are unlikely to invest in these solutions in the longer term. The downside of this is that enterprises still pay high license fees for these products and do not receive the same number of updates and innovative improvements as products in the cloud.

This shift is occurring across the board, but specifically within security solutions. Today's security in the cloud is often better than on-premises or legacy systems. This trend also extends to most major enterprise software systems, such as databases, development platforms, governance, operations, and any on-premises system that enterprises likely consider important to their operations.

In other words, the market shift is to the cloud. If you're not willing to pay more for less, you'd be well advised to shift as well. This is an undesirable situation for many enterprises, with the market forcing their hand to move to cloud-based platforms. I call this "The Forced March to the Cloud," which we'll discuss in more detail in Chapter 9, "The Evolution of the Computing Market."

Development Is Better in the Cloud

Current development trends are much the same as security. New cloud products provide the ability to quickly build systems to meet business requirements using innovative methods and services. Traditional development tools offer little innovation and many limitations. However, many of the traditional development approaches and mechanisms found new life in the cloud. In the last several years, public cloud providers upped their game, in terms of offering design, development, and deployment systems and services that are too compelling not to leverage. In the cloud these days, developers will have native access to advanced AI systems, big data analytics, auto scaling, and other cloud-based innovations. It's an easy decision to choose cloud-based development platforms in terms of agility, speed, and innovation, and thus value.

The trend here is to focus on development systems in the cloud that do or provide the following:

- **Automated scaling.** Developers and application architects no longer need to consider the problem of getting the software system to support higher workloads. This can be done for you automatically on most cloud-based applications. Because it's usage-based pricing, you pay only for the additional resources you use. For many businesses, the cloud resources they leverage, and thus the cost, will align somewhat with revenue. That makes it self-funding as well.

- **Continuous testing, integration, deployment, and so on.** Clouds can support emerging DevOps (development and operations) and DevSecOps (development, security, and operations) approaches and tool chains that exist entirely within the cloud. Clouds support development, but also the automation of the entire software development life cycle using an interactive and continuous improvement model.

  This is a value discussion for later, so here I don't get into a deeper discussion of DevOps/DevSecOps. However, simply put, the idea is that we can go from the design of an application to deployment using automated processes that deal with interactive testing such as performance testing, smoke testing, black box, or white box. Also, cloud DevOps provides the ability to automate the testing of application security, such as the ability to live up to predefined internal and external policies. Moreover, it can integrate and test the applications, including databases. Finally, cloud DevOps provides the ability to move to deployment, ensuring that the target platform is correctly leveraged and that we keep track of the configurations and application iterations that are released into production.

- **The ability to embed advanced services into applications that are native to the cloud, and thus to the development environment.** Advanced services provide a huge amount of value to cloud-based applications with access to advanced AI systems, large database analytics, and specialized system development such as building and deploying IoT or edge computing systems.

- **Disaster recovery (DR) is easier on public cloud platforms, and typically cheaper as well.** This is due to the fact that we can leverage other cloud platforms to do DR, and they have all of the benefits. This includes cost advantages and enterprises no longer having to maintain their own hardware just for DR operations.

Call to Action

This chapter is about how we got the initial value of cloud computing wrong and then figured it out along the way. The value drivers for cloud computing are different but more compelling than we originally thought. However, they are difficult to determine for most businesses, and thus many are still confused about how to determine the specific value of cloud computing for their business.

The call to action is to figure out what the value of cloud computing means for your business, your department, and even you personally. There are many ways to look at cloud values. It's clear that there is no single way to build a value model that will work the same for all businesses. However, it's helpful to conceptually understand the hard and soft values, and then use those concepts to come up with models that mirror the values that are most important to the business. That will result in a better understanding of the value that cloud computing can likely bring.

It's important to mention that "no cloud" is always an option. However, as I mentioned in this chapter, we're basically being forced to the cloud for many applications and data sets that might contraindicate a move to the cloud. You can't always create a sound business case to move every existing workload. If adequate vendor support remains and there is not enough value involved in moving a workload or data set to the cloud, then it should not be moved.

The concept of value is perhaps the most challenging aspect of figuring out the most optimized path to any new technology. It's easy to get overwhelmed as you make your way through the rapidly emerging maze of technology that includes cloud. Take it one bite at a time, and then make the right choices as to what should move to the cloud and what should not, with solid documentation as to why.

Chapter | **2**

The Realities and Opportunities of Cloud-Based Storage Services That Your Cloud Provider Will Not Tell You About

Nothing makes us so lonely as our secrets.

— Paul Tournier

In this chapter, we take on the pragmatic use of cloud computing resources. We focus first on storage and then move on to compute in the next chapter.

We also cover the more modern offerings such as serverless, AI, and so forth later in this book. However, we don't focus on the use and definitions of these cloud computing services; there are plenty of places you can go to figure that out. Instead, we look at how to effectively use these services to solve real business problems.

We also discuss some of the confusion around cloud services, some of it caused by the marketing messages from the larger cloud providers, some from confusion and cheerleading from the tech press, and, realistically, some of our own confusion as we think like a flock of birds and all move in the same direction. Sometimes it's the right direction, but most of the time we need to course-correct as we fly.

The purpose of this chapter, and really the entire book, is to get you flying in the right directions to effectively leverage cloud computing and other technologies.

Cloud Storage Evolves

In the beginning, Infrastructure as a Service (IaaS) providers all had one thing in common: They all provided storage systems. This includes the two dozen or so cloud providers that popped up around

2008–2010 at the beginning of the cloud hype. Storage growth exploded as raw data and binaries (for example, video and audio files) experienced such rapid growth that enterprises struggled to keep up with new and bigger on-premises storage systems. These systems included raw storage such as object, block, and file storage, as well as databases that leverage raw storage.

Storage costs soon became the focus of IT budgets, with storage often accounting for up to 60 percent of IT spending each year. It's no surprise that enterprises were eager to find more cost-effective solutions. Enter the ability to purchase storage as a utility, and thus the rapid rise of IaaS cloud computing.

What happened between then and now is that IaaS cloud providers, most of whom provided storage, were unable to keep up with better-funded hyperscalers such as AWS, Microsoft, and Google. They either exited the IaaS cloud market, got bought out, or pivoted in more unique directions. Today, practically speaking, we have only about five to seven viable IaaS clouds, with three holding most of the market.

Of course, IaaS cloud was never just about storage. Cloud compute, databases, AI, serverless, DevOps, security, governance, operational, and other specialized services (such as IoT and edge computing) provide more holistic solutions. Enterprises go to the cloud for a complete solution that will match or surpass existing capabilities onsite.

Therefore, cloud computing should be considered as an entire holistic platform, in terms of value. But it's helpful to separate and break out the larger cloud resource offerings (such as storage) to determine opportunities for better optimization of the technology itself and the cost.

Here are the primary reasons to focus on the best ways to use cloud computing storage:

- Storge is a component of most services leveraged on public clouds, including databases, AI, development, and anything that stores durable information between compute sessions. In most cases, you don't know it's working behind the scenes until you see the monthly bill.

- For most enterprises, storage is the largest portion of their ongoing cloud budget. Moreover, it increases exponentially year over year.

- Cloud-based storage systems house more and more corporate data each year. Many believe that a business's data *is* the business. As such, the importance of selecting and leveraging the best storage system in terms of security, performance, and resilience becomes a much higher priority.

Junk Data on Premises Moved to the Cloud Is Still Junk Data

Backing up a bit, let's focus on how most enterprises first leverage cloud storage. Most migrate applications and data to the cloud, and thus must pick sound analogs for their platforms (including storage and compute). Again, this initial system could leverage raw storage, such as that needed to store structured and unstructured data. However, most enterprise storage comes along with the databases they want to leverage. Examples are large relational databases such as Oracle or moving to proprietary purpose-built cloud databases such as the dozens of object-based databases that are offered only as a public cloud service (such as AWS's DynamoDB). It's helpful to first look at the process of data on premises-to-public cloud migration and then look at how and where we can find areas of improvement.

Here's the core mistake that most in IT make when they migrate data to the cloud: They move data, databases, and raw storage systems that are in a poor as-is state, including data that has no single sources of truth.

We've all seen this happen. The first outcome is a ton of redundant data that requires unneeded excess storage. The second outcome includes the larger problems of poorly designed and deployed data storage systems that lack efficiency or the ability to allow for easy change. Data in a poor as-is state on premises will be just as bad, if not worse, in the cloud (see Figure 2-1).

FIGURE 2-1 Broken and poorly designed on-premises data won't fix itself when you move the data to the cloud.

Efficiency, simply put, is the ability for the storage systems to serve people and applications in the most optimized way possible, including cost efficiency, performance efficiency, and the ability to support all business requirements such as security and governance. The challenge here is to get those in charge of moving storage to the cloud to understand that they have an existing problem to solve before they can move the data.

Most believe that the public cloud's ability to access as many resources as needed will solve many of the existing problems with performance and capacity issues. In some regards, this is true. You can certainly throw resources and money at problems, and they will become less noticeable. That is, until someone bothers to read the monthly cloud storage bill, which is likely many times what it should and needs to be. Efficiency is about doing the most with a cloud storage system to support the business goals and minimize the cost of using those resources. This level of efficiency only comes with fundamental design and deployment changes that need to occur before or during the relocation of these storage systems to a public cloud.

Support for change is the storage system's ability to support core changes in processes and thus data stored in databases or on raw storage systems. As described in Chapter 1, "How 'Real' Is the Value of Cloud Computing?" agility is a fundamental benefit (that is, soft value) of leveraging public cloud computing resources. However, having the ability to support rapid change by using cloud storage services does not mean that you have optimized agility.

For optimized agility, you must consider the core design of the database along with the current and future ways you will leverage the data. We've all had the experience of changing the meaning or structure of data to meet a new business requirement, and then we watch that change break a dozen or so applications that are tightly coupled to the data. This does and will happen if the data is not designed and deployed to support change, even if it's on a cloud storage platform that enables easy changes because resources can be instantly added and removed. Broken data is still broken data.

The bad news is that migrating data to the public cloud will usually make the situation worse for most businesses. Take some time to fix the issues before or during the migration process via major or minor design and deployment changes. Otherwise, poorly designed storage systems (including on-premises data) will be just as bad or worse in the cloud. To compound the problems, the "panic fixes" deployed in the cloud (for example, just tossing resources at problems) will result in more cost inefficiencies.

Many mistakenly think that cloud providers will also offer best practice information about moving data from on-premises storage systems to their cloud-based storage systems. Think that through for a minute. It's not their responsibility, and there is zero business incentive for them to increase your storage efficiencies and agility because poorly planned results make them more money.

This failure to provide best practices does not mean that cloud providers are working against you; they're not. The providers are in business to be experts at providing well-maintained storage services. It's their job to keep their services running and to fix any issues that arise on their end. You, not cloud providers, must be or become the expert in terms of what your business needs to solve its specific problems. It's your responsibility as a technologist to leverage the technologies in the most efficient and effective ways possible. Providers will not actively work to ensure that you'll be efficient with your own storage needs because they can't. If we fail at our end of the bargain, that's on us.

The cloud providers call this "shared responsibility." You'll encounter this term with most major cloud systems, especially security. They provide the tools, but how you use them to serve your own business needs is entirely up to you. Ultimately, your business use of their products is your responsibility.

This relationship is much like our relationship with our electric power providers. We know that a poorly designed and maintained HVAC system for our home will result in higher electric bills. With a bit of research, we can fix and/or replace the system and improve the efficiency of our electric usage. However, it's on us to act and do what's best for us or our business. Cloud storage is no different.

Lift-Fix-and-Shift

Many of us are already familiar with lift-and-shift, where we just move the applications and data from the traditional platforms to a public cloud provider with the minimum number of changes needed to make it functional in the cloud. Lift-and-shift does not look at how to optimize data storage, but at how to do the move as cheaply as possible. Lift-and-shift "kicks the can down the road" by just migrating a problem from one platform to the next. We'll eventually have to fix the problems or suffer the consequences of leveraging bad data, no matter where it exists.

Instead, we should fix issues with storage and data before or during the movement to the cloud. It's a best practice to take the existing on-premises data and improve or "fix" the data as it's moved from the on-premises storage systems to the cloud storage systems. We can call this lift-*fix*-and-shift.

Figure 2-2 depicts the basic idea. We start with the existing data, which is on traditional on-premises platforms, in most cases, but can also be on public and private clouds. The core issue is that the existing data is in a bad state, and we need to "move and improve" it. In other words, it's our intention to change the data and typically the attached applications as well, for the better.

Again, referring to Figure 2-2, we move toward a state where we eliminate data redundancy, establish a single source of truth, define a true business meaning of the data, and meet the minimum data security requirements. These are only a few of many issues we may have with the as-is state of data.

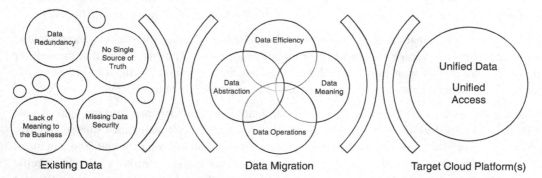

Existing Data   Data Migration   Target Cloud Platform(s)

FIGURE 2-2   We must fix data before or as it's being migrated to the target cloud or clouds. The idea is to get to a unified data storage system, with unified and meaningful access.

Moving on to the migration of the data, we have several methods to make the data easier to use by applications and humans. There are technologies such as data virtualization to hide dysfunctional physical data structures that can create an abstraction layer between the physical data and the applications and humans that need to leverage the data in more meaningful ways. The data has true meaning, such as the concept of a "customer" that may be an aggregation of 100 different data elements, from a dozen different physical databases. We move it from a confusing amount of information to place customer data in a single place where it is easy to find and to leverage, with meaningful data that we would normally associate with a customer, such as name, address, phone number, and account. This can happen only after we've fixed the data and storage issues as our data and applications move to the cloud.

The approach here is to look for a "minimum viable data layer" that can produce a single source of truth, no matter if you're looking for customer information, an invoice, sales history data, or anything else you need to know to effectively run the business. The goal is to avoid major costly and risky changes to the back-end data storage systems. This is not to say that the same data would be undiscoverable if the existing data models, structures, and storage systems were just relocated to the cloud, but the lift-fix-and-shift approach does not cost that much more than just pushing the problems down the road. Because you pay for cloud services based on the efficiency of your data and applications, you'll likely avoid a much larger bill as well as provide better data access to services that promote more efficiency, agility, and innovation, which, as we covered in Chapter 1, go right to the bottom-line value of cloud computing.

The objective illustrated in Figure 2-2 is clear. The goal with lift-fix-and-shift is to create a unified data layer, with unified data and unified access. Enterprises have long dreamed of this ideal, but most don't get there. Instead, many just layer new databases and data storage systems over old and never really figure out what the data needs to do. So, most enterprises are not there yet...even if they say they are.

A unified data layer means that we have the following advantages:

- Common views of data related to all concepts that need to be leveraged by applications, such as a single view of a customer, invoice, inventory, product, or sales record, which often number in the thousands for more complex enterprises.

- Common access to the data, typically using APIs such as services and microservices. This means we provide access to the data using a controlled mechanism. These API/services can monitor what questions are being asked of the data and how to respond with the right data in an efficient way. This capability is critical to a unified data layer because we also provide behavior that's bound directly to the data, which can be leveraged directly from an application without having to add behavior each time as to how the data gets leveraged. This access needs to be truly unified, which means the data, no matter where it exists, can be found, and then read through these unified interfaces with all the connectivity, security, and data operations taking place behind the scenes. The end game is to have access to all data, at any time, for any reason, and put the burden on the unified data access system to make this happen, and not on the end users or the developers, as was done in the past. Common access should work across all platforms, including all public clouds, private clouds, traditional on-premises systems, and so forth.

- Common security and governance define how the data is to be secured within the data. For example, allowing access only by a specific group of users and applications and then placing guardrails around this data access layer (such as allowing data access only every one second) to push off performance issues (such as those caused by a developer accidentally saturating the data with a single application). Keep in mind that common security and governance are not cloud-only, but across platforms and systems that include multicloud, private clouds, and traditional systems. The goal is to solve data security and data governance once and then use those solutions everywhere they're needed.

- Common metadata that spans applications, databases, cloud platforms, and even traditional platforms. While a discussion of master data management (MDM) is beyond the scope of this book, it's a powerful concept related to how we understand the meaning of the data within a few databases, as well as within databases operating across different cloud providers (multicloud), databases on traditional platforms such as mainframes, and any new types of platforms such as edge computing and IoT. The idea is to understand what the data means no matter where it exists and have access to it using a single unified access mechanism.

Cloud Storage Abstraction: Shortcut or Innovation?

Let's drill down a bit on single storage systems and databases, and those that operate across cloud providers or within a single provider. Here we look at how to deal with any number of the same or heterogeneous data stores that exist in a single public cloud or may exist in many public clouds. The goal is to get to a state where it really does not matter.

Building on the concepts introduced in the preceding section, again we want to deal with data complexity and find data meaning using common mechanisms that don't solve a data problem one single time, on one single cloud platform. Instead, the system should provide unified, secured, and governed access to all data using common interfaces that can span application solutions.

Unfortunately, this is a problem that enterprises rarely solve. Most enterprises still rely on several different mechanisms to access a variety of different databases. More disturbing, the data storage systems are tightly coupled to the applications. This means that any changes made to the database, such as changing the zip code attribute from five digits to nine, would end up breaking most of the applications that are coupled to that database.

It's time to do a few things better, including decoupling applications from data storage. Decoupling allows changes to be made to the physical databases without having to drive changes to all applications. More importantly, and as we learned in the preceding section, decoupling provides the ability to get to a unified data and access layer that can simplify access to the data, and do so across cloud providers, database technology providers, and other technology that may add to the complexity.

We can accomplish this goal in a few ways. First, blow up all the databases and combine the data and the data entities into a single unified data storage system that's the mother ship for all enterprise data. As you may recall, this was tried in the '80s and '90s with the acknowledgment that big honking enterprise databases from vendors such as Oracle, IBM, and others would be the destination for all enterprise data. Unified data storage would provide a single way to store and access the data.

This approach did not work for several reasons, primarily because a single database could not (and still can't) solve all our business problems. Purpose-built databases do provide more capabilities, such as providing better transactional performance or more flexibility in how data is stored. Databases that are data warehouse-focused or transactional-focused meant that we had a mix of different databases. All store data in different ways, with different meanings for the same data (for example, customer), and use different methods to access the data, everything from SQL to cryptic APIs. So, blowing up all the databases and forcing all data to move to a single database almost never works.

The second option is to change all the back-end databases to some sort of unified standard way of looking at the data. At the same time, normalize the databases so there is no redundant data being stored, and there is a single source of truth. Although you still have the same number of access approaches and mechanisms as you do data storage approaches and databases, this is the price you feel you must pay to leverage best-of-breed data storage, one that's been heavily modified to build a heterogeneous data layer that's much easier to use and understand.

Of course, there are issues with this second approach as well. Namely, you must still operate a very complex data layer and run different databases that you will need to operate and administer, including changing the physical structure of the data that must be reflected in the applications that are coupled to the data storage systems, from raw storage to sophisticated databases. While this is an improvement over the first option, you must still deal with many of the same issues you dealt with in the past, including data complexity that leads to efficiency issues. This approach is also prone to errors.

The third option involves a concept that's been around for decades, and one that I first addressed in my *Enterprise Application Integration* (EAI) book back in the '90s. Data virtualization was a game changer back then, but the technology had some evolving to do. As you can see in Figure 2-3, using the data virtualization concept, you don't have to change all the back-end databases to some sort of unified data model. Instead, you put forth an abstraction layer or a virtual database structure that exists only in software. Its structure and data representations, including metadata, map directly to back-end databases that can include objects, attributes, tables, and elements.

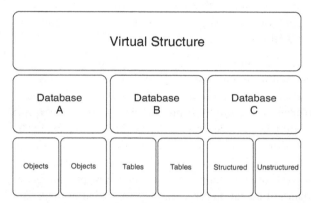

FIGURE 2-3 Data virtualization is an old technology trick that allows us to fix data issues in middleware, above the physical databases. We can map any physical structure, no matter how poorly designed, to a new abstract structure that will better represent the way that the business needs to use the data. This can be done in the cloud and/or on traditional systems.

Data virtualization technologies allow us to represent the data any way that we would like and provide unified access to the data. It's the job of these tools to translate the physical representation of the data into a virtual representation of the data. The virtual representation is more meaningful to the business because it includes a single source of truth for customer information that might be an abstraction of four different physical back-end databases, as we can also see in Figure 2-3.

Data virtualization provides several advantages. You change only the virtual structure to support a required single application-driven change rather than change the actual physical database, which could end up breaking 20 other applications that are coupled to the database. As far as the single application is concerned, the data is represented in a new way that the application requires. Any other applications connected to the database, whether they access the physical database directly or through the data virtualization layer, will see the same structure, either virtual or physical. In other words, data virtualization puts data volatility into a configurable domain.

So, why bring up data virtualization in a chapter about cloud data storage secrets? There are many benefits to using data virtualization technology as we look to modernize and cloud-enable our existing data. Today's data virtualization (a.k.a., cloud fabric) can work within a single cloud provider, and it can be made to work across multiple cloud providers. This allows us to deal with overly complex and distributed data that exists over many public clouds, private clouds, and even existing legacy systems on premises. Data virtualization deals with data in the same way, no matter where it's physically located or how it's structured.

Many view data virtualization as a work-around that just pushes off the need to fix all the back-end data stores. Data virtualization becomes a more realistic approach when it reduces the cost and the risk of changing data that's moving or has moved to the cloud. Yes, you could go to the back-end data and fix everything, and that would be a good call. However, in the real world, no one has an unlimited budget to move data to the cloud. The amount of time and talent needed to manually change all of the back-end databases is the most expensive option possible, although it will provide better business meaning and a single source of truth. Most business leaders would ask you to come up with a less expensive but still best-possible solution. Data virtualization provides a compromise.

There are downsides to all technology solutions, and data virtualization is no exception. First, you must pay for data virtualization technology through a subscription within a public cloud provider or use traditional enterprise licenses. While there are open-source solutions available, the cost of the talent and time required to customize a solution will incur an eyebrow-raising line item in most enterprise budgets. Second, there is a bit of a performance hit when you leverage a data virtualization layer. The severity of the hit depends on the complexity of your data-to-virtual data mappings, thus how much processing needs to occur behind the scenes, but it's not as good as direct native access to the database. On the positive side, the advances made in high-performance input/output systems now provide better performance. Considering that we've been at data virtualization for about 30 years, give or take, data virtualization technology is perhaps the best that it can be.

The Fallacy of Structured Versus Unstructured Data Storage

The last several years saw an explosion in the amounts of structured and unstructured data, in the cloud and not. The idea is that some data exists within a structure, such as the Oracle relational database. Unstructured data includes anything else of meaning such as documents, audio files, video files, and other information that is not a part of a formal structure. Another way to look at it is that structured data exists mostly in databases, such as object and relational databases, whereas unstructured data exists mostly in file systems, like those you would find on your laptop.

When you move all data to the cloud, structured and unstructured, it's my strong recommendation to deal with the data as a holistic concept. By this, I mean that no matter if it exists in a database or not, you can find the data, extract the data, process the data, and find meaning within the data. It shouldn't matter if you leverage deep analytics tooling, AI, or simple business processes where decisions are made to support real-time business data, such as the status of shipping a product, or an alert to production to accelerate fabrication of a specific product based on inventory levels.

Data virtualization renders structured and unstructured data the same, because we're defining a structure in middleware, which is applied on both structured data, such as a relational database, and unstructured data, such as a bunch of PDF files. You won't hear that from the average IT person who moves data to the cloud or builds net-new systems that leverage data in the cloud. The IT tendency to deal with unstructured and structured data differently remains firmly embedded in the IT psyche.

But that just leads to more data complexity and limits what developers, processes, applications, and other humans can do with the data. The end objective here is to leverage all data using a set of unified services or APIs that allow access to all data, at any time, for any reason, with the full meaning of the data available as well.

What we must deal with in the meantime is a set of data silos. Unfortunately, cloud computing just makes silos worse as we move data to data storage systems (such as databases in specific clouds). For example, let's say we start with 10 enterprise databases on premises, and a file farm of documents and binary information (such as audio files). When we move to the cloud, we end up with 7 databases on premises and 7 in the cloud. The extra 4 databases came from new requirements found in the migrated applications, plus the trend to expand database heterogeneity and complexity to meet the expanding needs of the business. So, was this the right move?

Data needs to be part of the infrastructure, much like the infrastructure requirements for networking, compute, and raw storage. No matter what type of technology stores the data, documents, or binaries, we should be able to access all this information in the most optimally useful ways for the humans, processes, or applications to access and process the data. And they need the ability to do so without dealing with semantic differences in the data that exist between databases and to be able to bind data directly to documents and binaries if there are links and meanings.

The goal is to create something like the unified data access interface represented in Figure 2-4. Here we're defining a single access point to all data, data within our data center, IaaS clouds, SaaS clouds, and so on. The data may be virtualized, meaning that we're defining virtual schemas to represent the back-end physical data, or it may be just access to the native physical schemas. What's important here is that we're accessing the data centrally, and not pushing developers and data users to work through a bunch of native database interfaces, all that are different.

Note

Whether the databases or file storage system exists in AWS, Microsoft, or Google clouds—or two or three of these options—does not matter. What matters most is that we consistently do certain things such as

- Deal with data as a single layer, where all data that's associated with a business including external data (from suppliers, for instance) exists behind a set of governed and secure database servers.

- Manage the common meaning of the data, no matter where the data exists and/or how it's defined within a specific database. We opt for more holistic understanding of repositories that exist across the databases and raw storage systems.

- Define common security mechanisms that are coupled to the data rather than decoupled within some centralized data security system. The governance policies, security policies, and authentications are a part of the data and thus easily transferable when leveraged on other platforms, such as across a multicloud.

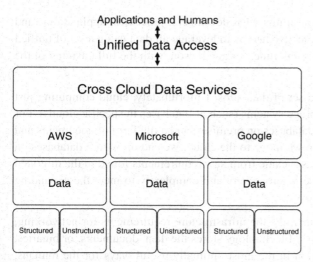

Applications and Humans

Unified Data Access

Cross Cloud Data Services

AWS	Microsoft	Google
Data	Data	Data

| Structured | Unstructured | Structured | Unstructured | Structured | Unstructured |

FIGURE 2-4   The ultimate objective of unified data access is to get to a data layer that crosses all clouds and even traditional systems. The physical back-end databases and raw storage simply function as data providers. We can leverage data from anywhere, at any time, for any reason, and (most important) use views of the data that are the most productive for the business.

Referring again to Figure 2-4, we work from the ground up to meet unified data access objectives. Don't focus on migrating the data from one database to another, but instead leverage the data where it currently exists, in whatever format it exists in. This applies to raw data such as binary files, all the way to highly structured data that may exist in a high-end enterprise database.

If you think unified data access will commoditize existing storage mechanisms, you're right. I mean, who cares what the back-end database is or the number of databases; we're looking at them the same way. If performance and functionality are good, the database can be anyone.

I'm not saying that the databases will go away, but they will have a diminished role over time. The focus on technology growth will include the tools that provide you with the ability to manage heterogeneous data, externalize that data, and provide the data as sets of services where meaning, security, and governance are bound to the data. This will exist at the "Cross Cloud Data Services" level shown at the top of Figure 2-4.

So, what specifically are "Cross Cloud Data Services?" They should consist of

- Data virtualization and/or abstraction as defined in the previous section. This is the layer that can take data in any structure or with any meaning and remap it to a common set of structures and services.

- Service management, or the ability to externalize microservices or other types of APIs that are discoverable and callable for any application, process, or a human using a data-oriented tool such as analytics.

- Security and governance, including the ability to hide some data from those who need it for processing, but allow it to be used in that process in an anonymous form. For instance, the ability to leverage a security layer that keeps the data encrypted but still allows certain information to be seen by nonhumans, such as data with governance derived from laws and regulations. HIPAA data would be an example. In a more specific example, if you analyze the rise of a viral disease to create a treatment, you will need to analyze personally identifiable information (PII) of exposed patients, but you are not allowed to view the PPI portions of the data. It will remain encrypted, become visible only to the analytics processes, and won't be seen by nonauthorized applications or any humans.

The quest for common and unified data access has been a topic of white papers and tech articles for decades. What's different here is that it doesn't matter how the data is physically stored and/or structured; we don't treat the data any differently. We must figure out how to create a single unified data layer that contains most of the services we'll need, as well as security and governance. Otherwise, multicloud and the future directions of complex and distributed cloud architectures will just lead to too much data complexity, which will prove impossible to scale. We must deal with the data access issues before we move to those architectures.

Secrets to Finding the Best Cloud Storage Value

Storage is fundamental to all cloud architectures, no matter if you create a simple cloud-based application or a complete cloud computing architecture for the enterprise. We need to persist files, information, and data as a foundation for how we do computing.

That said, it's your business needs that will determine the type of storage you'll leverage for a cloud or even a non-cloud-based solution. Business needs will depend on the industry the enterprise is in, any data regulations and laws that affect the enterprise, as well as the enterprise's ability to take full advantage of the agility and innovation benefits of cloud computing as discussed in Chapter 1. Thus, "it depends" comes up a lot when it's time to pick the right cloud storage solution...or any storage solution. It's something you constantly need to adjust and monitor to leverage the best and most cost-effective storage solutions that meet the requirements of your applications and business, today and into the future.

What If the Best Cloud Storage Is Not in the Cloud?

Here's something we often overlook when we search for a cloud storage solution: Cloud storage is not always the solution. Traditional on-premises storage could be more cost effective than cloud-based storage, even considering the potential benefits of cloud computing such as speed, agility, and the ability to better support innovation. Those soft values often make cloud computing worth the price of admission over more traditional storage solutions.

However, be sure to compare cloud-based storage to other storage solutions, such as traditional on-premises hard disk drive (HDD) storage, even when loaded with the additional costs of administration, power, and network expenses. Of course, there are other and perhaps better options, such as solid-state storage device (SSD), but let's use HDD for our comparative purposes.

Cloud computing and traditional on-premises storage are typically apples and oranges, when you think of all the add-on services you get with cloud-based storage, such as maintenance, power, networking, and a layer of experienced people who keep the cloud storage systems running. You must consider those benefits and factor them into your cost and technical decisions. However, if your enterprise produces a product that hasn't changed much over decades, where innovation or speed to market are rarely if ever factors while doing business, HDD storage could be a more cost-effective solution.

In the last few years, the price of on-premises storage, or HDD, has sharply dropped. Looking at Figure 2-5, you can see that around 2010, the prices for HDD storage leveraged for on-premises systems began to drop and continue to drop. The reasons for this are the normal ones, including better and cheaper manufacturing processes, and even the fact that cloud storage forced traditional storage vendors to become more competitive, in terms of pricing.

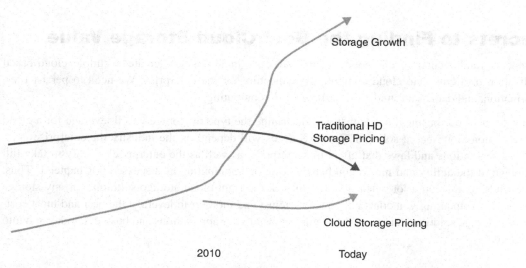

FIGURE 2-5 The prices for cloud storage remain stable and even rose over time. The prices for traditional on-premises storage systems fell in the last 10 years. While not the same, you need to consider the extra cost that comes with cloud storage. This does not mean that on-premises storage will be a better and more cost-effective solution in all business use cases, now and moving forward.

As you can also see in Figure 2-5, storage growth exploded while the prices dropped for traditional HDD storage. We now store everything. Systems that underwent digital enablement using cloud computing (or not) have nearly eliminated the use of paper. Most enterprises also eliminated duplicate information. However, we may still store the same things several times for slightly different reasons—for example, inventory data that needs to be a part of a sales transaction database but also needs to be stored in another database for compliance audit purposes.

At the same time, cloud storage pricing initially fell but mostly flattened out and then began to rise in the last few years. Of course, cloud storage comes with added capabilities from the cloud providers that make using cloud storage more useful to many businesses. However, they pay less for their core storage systems, or the physical storage that makes up their on-demand storage systems that provide the public cloud services, this due to their ability to buy a great deal of storage hardware at a time. Thus, we can assume that the profit margins improved for public cloud providers.

So, what are the general cost differences between traditional on-premises storage and cloud storage? Table 2-1 depicts a cost comparison over 10 years between traditional on-premises storage and cloud-based storage. As you can see, the core differences are that the subscription cost for cloud-based storage is $2,000 per year, whereas HDD on-premises storage costs $4,500 per unit (or units). Additional maintenance, power, and people costs for on-premises storage are combined for a total of $820 a year. This cost is wrapped into the cloud computing storage costs.

TABLE 2-1 Sample yearly cost differences of cloud versus on-premises storage. Note that we include on-premises maintenance costs that we must pay for non-cloud storage that we own and maintain in our data centers.

Cloud			On-Premises		
		Cumulative	Purchase	Maintenance	Cumulative
Year			$4,500.00		$4,500.00
1	$2,000.00	$2,000.00		$820.00	$5,320.00
2	$2,000.00	$4,000.00		$820.00	$6,140.00
3	$2,000.00	$6,000.00		$820.00	$6,960.00
4	$2,000.00	$8,000.00		$820.00	$7,780.00
5	$2,000.00	$10,000.00		$820.00	$8,600.00
6	$2,000.00	$12,000.00		$820.00	$9,420.00
7	$2,000.00	$14,000.00		$820.00	$10,240.00
8	$2,000.00	$16,000.00		$820.00	$11,060.00
9	$2,000.00	$18,000.00		$820.00	$11,880.00
10	$2,000.00	$20,000.00		$820.00	$12,700.00
Total	$20,000.00		$4,500.00	$8,200.00	

Figure 2-6 is just a graph of Table 2-1, illustrated to show a few points of interest. First, in Year 4, the cumulative cost of cloud-based storage surpasses that of on-premises-based storage, all costs assumed to be fully loaded. Thus, if we assume the business advantages are the same for both types of storage, traditional on-premises HDD storage will be more cost effective in this case. However, we must also consider many of the soft values described in Chapter 1.

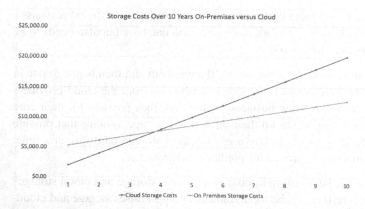

FIGURE 2-6   This graphic depicts the data in Table 2-1. At about Year 4, the on-premises storage solutions become more cost effective than the cloud. Remember to consider all costs, including operations and data center costs, when comparing the two storage solutions.

The kicker is that, for certain storage use cases, the advantages that cloud computing provides are not that helpful. "It depends" on the specific industry, business type, and/or applications to determine if a cloud computing storage solution or on-premises solution is best. And it's another indication that one-size-fits-all is not the case when it comes to picking storage solutions or other technologies for that matter.

Some questions to ask when you evaluate storage options, cloud or not cloud, include

- What is the value of agility and speed for my business and this use case?

- What is the cost sensitivity within the organization? Is saving a buck more important than making a buck?

- What is the long-term strategy for the enterprise, including the expanded or limited use of cloud computing?

- What are the security issues to consider that may make on-premises storage or cloud-based storage more advantageous?

- What is the growth of costs over time? Will it be consistent for both types of storage, as we saw in Table 2-1? Will it be highly volatile and difficult to predict?

- What are the performance requirements and issues such as sensitivity to latency? Will leveraging on-premises storage provide a performance advantage versus cloud storage leveraged over the open Internet? Is performance a make-or-break factor for the business?

- What sunk costs already exist in purchased storage equipment?

- What about existing depreciation of existing storage equipment? Will the lack of depreciation cause a tax concern?

- And so forth...

Table 2-2 is basically the same type of comparison model as Table 2-1 is to Figure 2-6, but this time the model for cloud storage costs is reduced by about $1,500 per month. In this case, perhaps the cloud storage provider (that is, an IaaS cloud provider) offered a substantial discount if the enterprise commits to a 10-year deal. Sometimes this could involve purchasing storage ahead of use, and thus the cost model for cloud will compare favorably to on-premises storage costs, because the enterprise guarantees payment up front to get the storage at a discount.

TABLE 2-2   Sample yearly cost difference of cloud versus on-premises storage, but this time modeling lower cloud costs. You can often find cloud storage bargains when you purchase capacity ahead of need or when leveraging a third-tier non-brand-name provider. Or this may become true of cloud storage as costs begin to drop again as they did when cloud computing first appeared on the market.

	Cloud		On-Premises		
		Cumulative	Purchase	Maintenance	Cumulative
Year			$4,500.00		$4,500.00
1	$500.00	$500.00		$820.00	$5,320.00
2	$500.00	$1,000.00		$820.00	$6,140.00
3	$500.00	$1,500.00		$820.00	$6,960.00
4	$500.00	$2,000.00		$820.00	$7,780.00
5	$500.00	$2,500.00		$820.00	$8,600.00
6	$500.00	$3,000.00		$820.00	$9,420.00
7	$500.00	$3,500.00		$820.00	$10,240.00
8	$500.00	$4,000.00		$820.00	$11,060.00
9	$500.00	$4,500.00		$820.00	$11,880.00
10	$500.00	$5,000.00		$820.00	$12,700.00
Total	$5,000.00		$4,500.00	$8,200.00	

Figure 2-7 depicts the data from Table 2-2 as a graph. Note that the cloud costs are lower and about even in cumulative growth with the on-premises solution's costs. The key here is that the business obtained a significant cloud discount, which made cloud-based storage the most cost-effective solution, combined with the other soft cloud benefits we previously mentioned.

So, on-premises storage solutions are not always cheaper than public cloud storage solutions, and vice versa. These are complex calculations that need to be made with everything considered. Considerations include business requirements, the cloud services you currently leverage, the cloud services you want to leverage, and (of course) the value you may or not place on the soft cost benefits of agility, speed, and innovation.

Here's where we frequently circle back to "it depends." However, these examples are accurate representations of how we can figure this out for each problem we need to solve with storage.

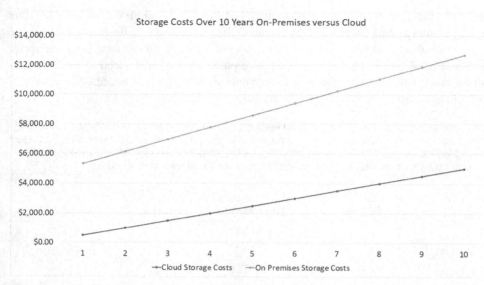

FIGURE 2-7 This graph depicts the data in Table 2-2. Note how the line items are relatively the same, in terms of cumulative growth, with the cloud storage solution providing lower overall costs for this scenario. Again, you'll have to consider your own business needs, current pricing, and other costs that may be part of your unique "it depends" situation when calculating your own storage costs.

Leveraging Storage Growth

The growth rate of your storage requirements is an asset that you can leverage in negotiations with a cloud storage provider. It may not work out as well as prices for traditional on-premises storage if you're just talking yourself into purchasing too much storage ahead of need. However, cloud-based storage can grow as needed, and you'll pay as you grow.

As you can see in Figure 2-8, a storage growth rate of, say, 1 petabyte to 10 petabytes over a five-year period should also see a reduction in pricing for that storage time. As storage growth rises, the prices of cloud-based storage should fall as a percentage of the amount of storage you leverage. The fact is that the provider will get a big chunk of cash from your business ongoing, and thus you deserve to have favorable pricing. You can promise (in writing) to grow storage at a specific rate and thus request a discount for promised future growth. Although most public cloud providers say they don't discount, most will when dealing with large enterprises' spending commitments, depending on the cloud provider. The more you use, and the higher rate of growth, the less you should pay per gigabyte and petabyte.

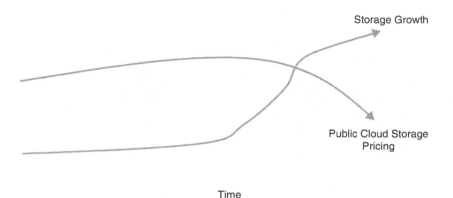

Storage Growth

Public Cloud Storage
Pricing

Time

FIGURE 2-8   As storage growth rises, the prices of cloud-based storage should fall as a percentage of the amount of storage you leverage. You can promise (in writing) to grow storage at a specific rate and thus request a discount for promised future growth. Although most public cloud providers say they don't discount, most will when dealing with large enterprises' spending commitments.

It's not uncommon when negotiating or renegotiating with a major public cloud provider to use the storage growth estimates as a bargaining chip to obtain more favorable pricing. Also keep this in mind: From a provider's perspective, they won't have much more overhead if you move from 1 petabyte to 5 petabytes. The same base costs exist for the provider to support you as a tenant, other than more physical storage space. As pointed out earlier in this chapter, the forecast is for storage space to get cheaper over time.

These discounts typically come with some strings attached. First, the provider may request that you sign a nondisclosure agreement (NDA), which means you can't reveal the price you paid for storage. Their most likely concerns are that others will use your price as leverage within their own negotiations. Second, the provider may require that you commit to a specific amount of storage use or growth over time, say a half a petabyte per year, or something as significant. This requirement introduces the risk that you won't be able to drive that promised growth (such as during a business downturn) and would still have to pay penalties when you do not meet your growth promises.

Finally, this agreement contractually locks you into a specific provider. If you find issues with that cloud provider down the road, it will be difficult to exit the contract. There is an advantage to leveraging a cloud provider as a noncontractual customer, where you can leave the cloud provider at any time, for any reason, which is why many enterprises leverage cloud computing in the first place.

Add-ons Needed

Storage does not work by itself, and many different systems need to work with storage to provide a complete solution. These systems include storage management, storage operations, storage security, storage governance, databases, database management, database security, and other cloud-based add-ons you'll need to get the most value from storage.

Of course, the add-ons you need will depend entirely on what you plan to do with your cloud storage system. I brought up this point here because those who build their cloud architecture typically remember that they need storage, of course, but many overlook the other cloud services that will keep their storage systems healthy and secure. Don't forget to factor in those necessary services and consider them in the negotiations of the storage costs with your cloud provider. Providers often toss them in for free on the front end, but they could cost thousands per month if you add them in at the last minute.

To define a solid storage solution, look holistically at the potential storage systems. Describe its current intended use, as well as its use into the future. Storage systems are often multiuse, meaning they will support thousands of applications and tools that directly access the storage system, or access the system through a database. Yes, define the use cases for the storage solution when it's accessed by a specific application, but remember its other uses as well. This includes how the storage system will be used in 1 year, 5 years, 10 years, and so on. We get deeper into this discussion in the next section.

How Will the Business Leverage Cloud Storage?

How your business will leverage cloud storage is a question that most good cloud service salespeople will ask when you shop for cloud computing storage. In most cases, you'll pick different storage systems and/or databases for specific use cases—for example, purpose-built for data analytics versus a storage system purpose-built to deal with highly transactional systems.

The three major types of storage are block, object, and file storage. Each serves different purposes. Many times, you'll leverage a database that needs a specific type of storage, and then the number of use cases that call for a specific type of database become more numerous as well. In most cases, the recommendation is to leverage different types of storage that focus specifically on what you plan to leverage with the storage system.

Figure 2-9 represents how an enterprise typically leverages storage. At the top of the stack are applications that often use automation to leverage the data, and humans who leverage the data directly, typically through a tool of some sort. At the next layer are the types of databases we may leverage, either focused on analytical data uses or standard transactional systems.

Moreover, many purpose-built databases are beginning to emerge that solve a specific problem—for example, a database that is built to store data related to medical treatments or a database designed for edge computing. The idea is the same, that we have a use case so unique that we need a specialized database to solve the problem.

Note the third layer on Figure 2-9, where standard types of storage include object and block storage that the database above it might leverage. Again, it depends on the database you leverage. Some may leverage the native raw storage system of the cloud; some could have their own way of setting up their raw storage. All use raw physical storage systems that data is persisted on a public cloud provider.

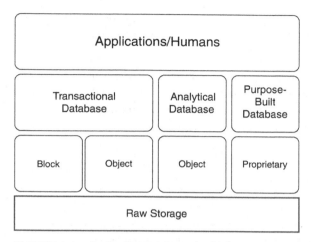

FIGURE 2-9   A storage system could have many applications and/or humans that access a specific database that is designed for a specific purpose, such as sales transactions, or for analytical purposes, such as looking at the history of sales over the last five years. In some cases, the system may leverage purpose-built databases that don't have a specific or standard type of storage, or the purpose-built database could use its own proprietary approach.

Automation Is King

In terms of cloud storage, automation means that you want to automate most of the activities around maintaining a native cloud storage system and/or database that leverages a native cloud storage system. For example, data backup and recovery, deduplication, performance tuning, auto scaling, and other functions associated with storage and database management that need to be carried out by humans or, preferably, by automation.

The objective here is to automate as much as you can. By doing so, you remove many of the reasons storage systems fail—typically some routine activity that's not carried out due to human error. This does not mean you can't make mistakes when using automation; you can. However, you do create repeatable processes that happen no matter whether someone remembers them or not, and thus remove much of the risk from storage maintenance.

Examples of storage maintenance and operations automation include

- Automated storage and/or database backup that includes migrating backups to other public cloud regions in case of localized failures. If data is lost in one region due to a hurricane, then the data that's backed up to region two remains unaffected and available for use. This data gets automatically and periodically migrated to region two through geographic redundancy to lower the risk of data loss.

- Automated security checks that include proactive scans of the storage system or database to find and fix issues with security—for example, unencrypted data that should be encrypted, and/or suspicious activity that could indicate an attempted breach.

- Automated performance maintenance such as deduplication to eliminate redundant data and increase the value of the data that's there. Also, automate the tweaking of data and/or storage tuning parameters to enhance storage and database performance. This includes items such as increasing the cache size as the database grows organically over time.

- And so forth…

Weaponizing AI

Let's not get into the functions of AI engines here; there are many other places you can go to find that information. However, it's important to mention the use of AI when looking at how to leverage data to obtain the most business value.

AI is the single most valuable thing that you can do with your cloud data. Because AI systems now live on cloud providers, the cost and risk of leveraging AI continue to decline. Many of the startup businesses that appeared over the last five years or so are built around the use of data and AI. Those businesses are now household names because AI and data *became* the business.

AI is useless unless it has data that it can use to train the AI engine. AI and machine learning are good at spotting patterns in the data, and through understanding what those patterns mean, take on a learning role that can grow well beyond any human capabilities that could try to reproduce the same analytics.

Take fraud detection. AI can look for specific transactions, say, banking transactions that tend to show patterns of fraud. We can feed training data into AI that shows known patterns of fraud and nonfraud to teach our AI or knowledge engine what a fraudulent transaction looks like. In turn, AI can look at thousands of transactions in a single minute and flag the likelihood of fraud for specific transactions. Perhaps ranking them from 0, or no likely fraud, to 10, where fraud is very likely. As the humans review what the AI engine spots, we can train the knowledge base even more when we further tag and vet transactions, and the results of the vetting get fed back into the knowledge engine.

What's important to remember is that AI only exists to provide value with a great deal of useful data, and that brings in the power of storage and databases. A common mistake is to believe that AI is like what we see in science fiction movies, where the AI engine has human characteristics. In the real world, we will leverage AI as a tool to target specific business problems that require a great deal of data and data storage to solve specific problems.

The Future of Cloud Storage

If I were to predict the future of cloud storage, the easiest thing to call out is the growth of storage. There is no end in sight, in terms of how much data we're likely to store, and it will include data of all kinds and all functions. Enterprises no longer purge data after a certain amount of time since digitized data and AI make all data valuable or potentially valuable. In a sense, enterprises have become data hoarders.

At the same time, we can't store all that data on traditional storage platforms, nor can everything be stored on the cloud. The growth of data will mean that some data storage will be on traditional on-premises systems for cost reasons in cases where the value of using public clouds is less compelling and the cost of on-premises storage is too competitive. This shift to thinking about on-premises storage will be geared toward specific types of data and specific types of companies. This does not mean that these companies are anti-cloud, only that they are pragmatic about which storage systems will provide the best value for a specific business use case.

The elephant in the room is cloud egress costs. It's kind of a ransom that you must pay when you're removing your own data from public cloud providers. I get why they charge that fee: You're leveraging a huge number of resources, including network bandwidth, and intermediate storage. In the future, with the growth of multicloud, the hope is that these fees will be reduced, as we need to move data from cloud-to-cloud and cloud-to-data center more often, and the pushback on how these egress costs will drive cloud providers to be more reasonable with egress and ingress costs.

Of course, cloud storage will continue to explode as well, and for reasons that even the cloud providers don't currently forecast. First, the instant expandability aspect of cloud storage will be too attractive for enterprises whose businesses need to quickly grow around new market opportunities. The near zero latency of cloud storage means that IT won't have to constantly think and plan around what storage resources must be added to meet the changing needs of the business. However, a few years ago, who would have thought that cloud storage would often be the more expensive option? However, it also provides the most business value, considering the type and purpose of the business. Again, we're back to "it depends."

Call to Action

Most of us look at cloud storage as table stakes for moving to the cloud. It's something that's always there, and a known asset that's easy to understand and use. As with other cloud assets, people who don't focus on the true cost and true value of cloud storage are more likely to make key mistakes: They will overpay for cloud storage, and thus remove value and add risk to the business.

The clear message is that cloud computing architects need to understand that there are no "unimportant" layers of cloud computing technology. They are all interdependent upon each other, all incur ongoing costs, you must secure and govern everything, and no layer of technology is less or more important than the other.

Chapter 3

The Realities and Opportunities of Cloud-Based Compute Services That Your Cloud Provider Will Not Tell You About

There are no secrets to success. It is the result of preparation, hard work, and learning from failure.

— *Colin Powell*

Now that we've covered storage, let's cover compute. This topic is a bit more complex. In addition to choosing public cloud computing processors, which are usually referred to as central processing units (CPUs), we must pick the platforms needed to operate those processors. The platforms themselves require choices, including operating systems, memory configurations, network connections, and even the need to define some physical storage that needs to exist.

In this chapter, we focus on what these services are, how to understand them, how to pick them, and how to obtain the best value from your cloud provider. We also look at some concepts you need to understand before you pick compute services. These concepts include how cloud hosting works, and how to understand your own requirements so you don't under- or overbuy. Additionally, we discuss how to find the best deals with known discount approaches, such as leveraging reserved instances or leveraging processors that are considered "off-brand." Finally, we review some traditional options that we often forget about in the haze of cloud computing migrations. Again, the focus is to provide you with inside information on what to leverage and how to think pragmatically about cloud-based compute.

The Trade-offs of Multitenancy

When you leverage CPUs via a cloud service, you typically share those CPUs with other cloud computing tenants. You get the services that you contract for, but you're not the only client leveraging that physical resource. You could even be multiplexed across many virtual compute servers and be serviced by several CPUs, memory configurations, and input/output management subsystems.

The problem is that you really don't know what goes on behind the scenes in terms of how a public cloud provider deals with its tenancy. Providers debated extensively about multitenancy approaches when cloud computing first started. Multitenancy choices in those days were—and still are—"share all," "share some," and "share nothing" approaches.

My first cloud consulting firm focused on creating all three types of multitenancy architectures for new and existing software companies looking to become SaaS cloud providers. They needed the ability to deliver multiuser types of services, as well as the ability to deal with resource sharing that includes CPUs, memory, storage, and so on.

It was not unusual during the early days of cloud computing to have traditional software companies approach multitenancy in rather unorthodox ways—especially when they received requests from new or existing clients that wanted to be on a SaaS or other type of cloud. Rather than leverage a true multitenant automated platform, many traditional software providers simply bolted a new server onto the rack of their so-called cloud provider services. They would assign a name and IP, and the client leveraged only that server while leveraging the provider's "cloud." This is a classic example of a traditional service disguised to look like a cloud service.

Today, most of us recognize this "bolt-on" model as silly and wasteful. At the time, most clients never understood this was happening. While it's not a true multitenant architecture, it was an approach that many used to break into cloud computing, and it formed many cloud users' understanding of a "share nothing" approach.

Although we could pick apart multitenant approaches as we did during the early years of cloud computing, they worked for the most part, and the issues that arose are long since resolved. Most public cloud providers now offer solid multitenant services that optimize performance, even though they multiplex your use of a public cloud across many different physical resources. There are still some multitenant trade-offs to consider:

- Performance can be "bursty." In many cases this is the bursty nature of most Internet connections, in that performance will speed up and slow down based on the demand on the network resources. You can see the same type of performance patterns by looking at the performance of a cloud platform. When asked to do processor-intensive tasks, certainly when there's not enough memory and CPU power allocated, you'll see performance that seems as if it's starting and stopping.

- It's difficult to predict the performance of deeper types of platform use, such as threading. A thread is a flow of execution of tasks found in processes, also called a thread of execution or thread of control. Most advanced operating systems support threading. Here you will see many of the same issues occur as previously discussed, including bursty performance. Also, launched threads may not succeed if the processor was busy for some reason, or if the application expected the thread to return faster than it did.

■ Many applications that are ported to the clouds using a lift-and-shift approach where a minimum amount of redevelopment occurs. Because the application was not developed and tested on a multitenant platform, its performance can be unpredictable.

Of course, the severity of these trade-offs depends on the cloud provider you use and how the provider specifically approaches multitenancy. These issues need to be worked out beforehand, worked around, or properly fixed after the migration. Many of these trade-offs result in more migration costs for enterprises.

The Realities of Resource Sharing

When it comes to understanding multitenancy, it's important to understand that all public cloud providers have a different approach to tenancy. What one public cloud provider says may not apply to other providers—even if they say basically the same thing. Public cloud providers consider their approach to multitenancy proprietary to their IP. Although you get some overviews around how a provider approaches tenancy, what occurs in the background or in the native public cloud system that you can't see is really what determines how the provider carries out multitenancy.

In some cases, you can insist that the public cloud provider reveal how multitenancy is carried out, typically around compliance audits that you need to support. For example, say you're a government contractor who plans to place government systems on a public cloud provider. These systems may, as part of an audit, insist that the contractor and provider reveal the mechanisms behind multitenancy for a specific cloud they will leverage. You'll find that some cloud providers are candid, having had to address this issue before. Others are not as forthcoming. If the provider won't reveal the specific details and mechanisms behind how it approaches multitenancy, and if this won't meet the needs of the audit, you need to determine that up front or face having to move off that cloud because it was later determined to be noncompliant with an audit.

The moral of this story is that you determine these details up front. Understand what the requirements are for your specific situation and if you need to have a detailed understanding of how the multitenant system manages resources. Figure that out before moving assets to that cloud.

The good news is that, for most use cases, high-level explanations will suffice. In the cases with special audit requirements, it's usually best to leave these systems in the enterprise data center and save yourself the hassle.

Putting the legal issues aside for now, it's helpful to understand the basic approaches and mechanisms that public cloud providers leverage for their public clouds, especially compute. These include

■ **Shared** is often the default and thus the approach that most cloud customers use, no matter whether they understand the concept or not. Shared means several public cloud computing accounts may share the same physical hardware. For most uses, this type of multitenancy approach is fine, and you won't even know you're sharing resources. However, performance issues such as the trade-offs we've described previously will come into play if you have special high-end requirements. As you may have guessed, a Shared model is typically the least expensive because you use fewer physical resources, all of which are shared. Figure 3-1 shows what the high-level architecture looks like, where a single physical resource is shared by many tenants. Note: The way you share resources—and how they are shared—is specific to the cloud provider's multitenant services.

- **Dedicated Instance** is when your instance (that is, running your applications) runs on single-tenant hardware. This approach typically works better for special higher-end requirements, such as applications that tend to saturate the CPUs and other resources. For all practical purposes, it's as if you host your application on your own server that nobody else uses. Of course, this approach is more costly than the Shared model because you leverage physical hardware that others cannot leverage. Also, you rarely know the physical location of hardware. The provider allocates different servers for your use, and you are typically not assigned a dedicated server.

- **Dedicated Host** is when your instance runs on a physical server with all its capacity dedicated to your use. You have complete control over this isolated server. Functionally, it's as if you purchased a server, installed it within your data center, and now have exclusive use of it. In many instances, the cloud provider may even let you know where it's physically located, although those policies differ from cloud provider to cloud provider. This is the costliest of all the sharing options listed here.

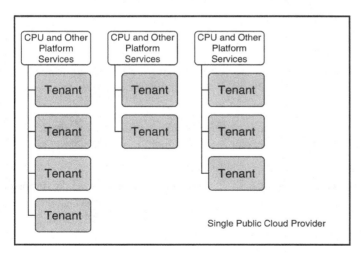

FIGURE 3-1   Resource sharing for most public clouds means that you share physical resources with many tenants or companies like yourself that need to access compute services. This is often the least expensive approach because the cloud provider can share a few resources with many tenants. As far as the tenants are concerned, they leverage a virtual resource that functions much like a dedicated server.

Costs Versus Consistency

The trade-off with compute models comes down to cost versus consistency. You either pay less to leverage physical servers that are shared with others, or you pay more for the luxury of dedicated hardware to ensure greater consistency. Figure 3-2 depicts the typical cost curve that most enterprises will encounter when purchasing compute resources from a large public cloud provider. None of this should be shocking, considering that as public cloud providers' costs go up, they will pass the cost for the additional hardware resources, such as storage and compute, on to their customers.

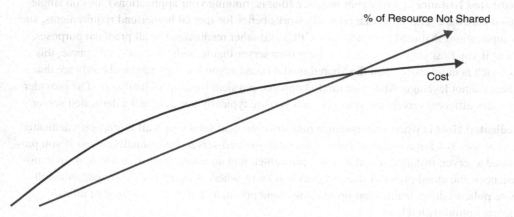

FIGURE 3-2   As a rule, costs rise as you share fewer resources in the cloud. However, at some point, the cost begins to level out but never becomes completely flat, or diminishing.

The real question then becomes, What would compel you to use nonshared resources, and how would it even justify the extra costs? In truth, many of those who insist on dedicated instances, and even those who reserve a physical server in a public cloud, typically have no need for them. The extra cost is a classic waste of money.

In many instances, customers pay much more to use a public cloud provider's dedicated resources than if they owned their own physical server, even with data center rental and maintenance factored into the equation.

In too many instances, I see this become a kind of ego play, in that someone wants to elevate the importance of their workloads to a point where they lose sight of the real goal, which is to get to the true value of cloud computing. The objective is to pay less to securely share most resources and still gain the soft values of cloud computing.

There are a few instances when it's the right move to elevate workloads and data, when the needs for consistency and control outweigh the cost factors. However, most arguments for uninterrupted performance or security concerns with shared resources prove unfounded or, more often, available within a shared model option. We're well into our 15th year of leveraging IaaS clouds and pretty much understand what shared and nonshared resources can do, and the cost trade-offs.

Despite the history and provable facts, I still see enterprises demand and deploy nonshared resources for the consistency and control reasons just mentioned. This will lead to a sizable reduction in the value that cloud computing brings to the business. In many instances, it will then lead to cloud computing having negative value that is completely avoidable. Carefully consider the business case and the technical realities before deciding that your workloads are much too important to mingle with others.

Cross-Partition and Cross-Tenant Hacks

It was not long after cloud computing became a thing that alarms began to sound around the possibility that other tenants could reach into your compute instance and grab your data or interrupt your processing. This is called a *cross-channel attack*, a *cross-partition attack,* or a *cross-tenant attack*. For our purposes, we'll use the terms interchangeably.

These "cross" concerns came from some valid realities, including the fact that you are indeed running on the same physical servers. It's logical to assume that if something were left misconfigured or a vulnerability overlooked that could be exploited, then someone or some program could purposefully reach through a logical partition and cause problems.

Experiments proved that this scenario could potentially occur, but only if there were a vulnerability on the multitenant system that was known to black hats, and thus could subsequently be exploited. The chances of that occurring, even though there was a chance, were much less than other security risks that typical applications and/or data sets encounter on a traditional platform. So, by moving to cloud, you lower your security risk. The chances that you'll be hacked tenant-to-tenant are pretty much nonexistent.

The real issue here is that multitenant just seems scary. Your application that processes sensitive, often proprietary data, runs within the same memory set and CPU as other companies' applications and data. Your cotenants could be a competitor, an illegal business, or the government.

Figure 3-3 depicts the types of attacks that tenants find of most concern, namely, a tenant being able to reach into the workspace of another tenant running on the same physical server. Or a tenant reaching across to another tenant running on another physical compute server.

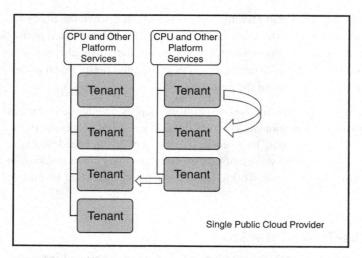

FIGURE 3-3   In the early days of cloud computing, many feared cross-channel, cross-tenant, and cross-partition hacks, or reaching to compute and storage spaces controlled by another tenant—either within the same physical CPU and platform services, or between physical CPUs and other platform services. Much of this concern has been eliminated, but it's still wise to ask your public cloud provider how this will be managed.

Cross-channel attacks are a false concern for the following reasons:

- The public cloud providers became aware of this concern years ago and built specific security measures into their systems to isolate resources used by specific tenants. Of course, providers all do this differently, but they all have their own mechanisms to detect any cross-channel intrusions.

- The data that resides within each tenant partition is encrypted at rest and in flight. If, for some reason, a tenant could reach into another partition, the data is worthless given that it's encrypted. Most public cloud providers encrypt everything to remove this security vulnerability. You maintain your private key, and even the cloud provider can't see your data without it.

- The nail in the cross-channel risk coffin is that tenants can't launch a machine instance on a specific machine, say, a specific machine where their target runs their data. Lacking the ability to choose the physical server that the tenant will run on, at least in a shared multitenant deployment, means no tenant can leverage standard approaches to access other tenant instances, such as making use of Level 3 memory cache exploitations.

Nothing I say here pushes these possibilities off as a nonthreat, only that there are many other things that should rank higher on your list of concerns in terms of cloud security. In this instance, it's okay to say, "Nothing to see here."

Keep in mind that when you play the cloud security game, it's not about creating an invulnerable security layer. Ultimately, nothing is invulnerable. It's about removing as much risk as you can, and then prioritizing and paying attention to the more likely threats.

CPU Performance, Meet the Internet

Most of those who leverage cloud computing do so using public cloud providers. Although some companies can afford dedicated connections into a cloud provider, most of us will leverage cloud services over the open Internet. That causes a few problems when it comes to CPU performance, as well as data consumption and transmission.

As you can see in Figure 3-4, applications that are network-bound cause an issue. This means that the applications leverage the Internet to transmit and receive inter-process communications (IPCs) to share data and application message traffic between applications. This does not affect applications that are designed not to carry out IPCs and data exchange over the open Internet and may be sharing data only via the much faster network that exists internal to a cloud provider. By avoiding use of the Internet and its bursty latency that often occurs, your application won't be bound to the speed of the Internet when considering overall performance.

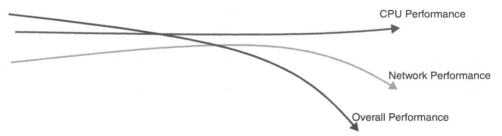

FIGURE 3-4 Although you might leverage the fastest CPUs, if you move data or inter-process communications over the open Internet, the speed of network communications will become the bottleneck. This is something that many using the public cloud attempt, but often redesign or rehost the applications and data back onsite, so that network latency is diminished.

Yes, most of us are aware of performance issues when you carry out more heavy-duty processing and data communications over the Internet. What we often overlook are changes to the criteria you should use when selecting compute platforms, including CPU speed and type, memory size, and even the operating systems you plan to leverage, such as Linux and Windows NT.

Figure 3-4 shows performance at various levels of network performance, or an increase and a decrease in bandwidth, with a significant drop-off at the end. Note that the processor speed is about the same, and even rises slightly as it moves to the right. However, as network performance decreases, it really does not matter which processor you picked because that's not what determines overall performance.

For example, let's say you have a saturated Internet router or even a denial-of-service attack. If the application or applications are bound to Internet speeds due to dependencies on IPCs or data exchanged that's needed to drive the application(s), the CPU speed and performance become irrelevant.

This is not a call to rewrite all your migrated applications to remove or reduce IPCs or data exchanged over the Internet, or communications that once existed only on your corporate network. Instead, consider the cost you'll pay for the platform, including CPU, memory, and so on.

The moral of this story: If you don't get the extra benefit of faster CPU processors, why spend the extra money?

The Slowest Components Determine Performance

Here's another way to think about buying compute. If your applications are processor bound, meaning they consistently wait for a process to complete or finish a compute cycle to continue, then you'll likely get real value out of deploying the fastest and most expensive CPUs. This includes high-performance computing (HPC) platforms that are now available, which clients often leverage in response to slow-running applications.

However, for many applications, the CPU, memory size, and speed have little to do with overall performance. It's the application design that's at fault; trying to fix the problem on the provider side just wastes money. Sometimes it costs tens of thousands of dollars extra per month to run network-bottlenecked applications on expensive CPUs and HPCs, which removes any value gained by using public clouds.

Many enterprises go wrong here when they pick cloud computing services and components, which often includes the compute platform. With an incomplete understanding of what determines overall application performance, the typical response is to upgrade and up-spend the cloud provider's CPUs. After all, it's a simple click of a mouse to do the upgrade; you don't have to visit a data center to integrate a new compute server with the other physical servers and the network. The process is so easy that you can get into real trouble with cloud spending before you realize the root causes of application performance problems.

A detailed discussion of typical application performance problems, how they are diagnosed, and how to design an application for good performance is beyond the scope of this book. However, it's an area of focus that many cloud computing and cloud application architects should better understand.

Remember: The slowest running component determines overall performance. The most frequent culprit is the network. However, storage I/O delays, omnibus latency, and yes, the CPU could also be factors.

This point brings up more complexities when you pick components to build your application(s) or system. It's not about what you spend for better-performing cloud services. It's more about the design of your application(s) or system and where the performance bottlenecks will likely exist. The kneejerk reaction to a poorly performing application is to toss money at the problem and hope that fixes it. Instead, that approach introduces a whole new set of problems. The result is that you'll spend too much for the application's infrastructure that will not solve the root cause of the performance issue.

For example, let's say a client of mine migrated an inventory control application from an existing LAMP stack (Linux, Apache, MySQL, PHP/Perl/Python) that ran in their data center to a public cloud provider. Minimum changes were made to the application, choosing instead to take a lift-and-shift approach to minimize the costs of migration.

After the migration was complete, performance issues were noted during acceptance testing. The user interface ran 40 percent slower than it ran on the traditional platform. Without truly diagnosing the problem, the application owners decided to leverage a more powerful and more costly platform, meaning a higher-end CPU cluster and more memory. The result was a 5 percent increase in performance, with the resulting performance determined to be unacceptable.

In this example, it could be any number of components or cloud services that caused the performance problem or problems. Without a sound diagnosis of what's at the root of the performance issues, you're just taking shots in the dark by renting better components and cloud services and hoping for the best.

Upon detailed diagnoses, it was determined that a combination of the database and network was the root cause of the problems. The database was fixed by changing a few tunable parameters, in this case, significantly increasing the data cache size. A failing Internet router in the department that used that application the most caused the network issue. Spending more money on CPU and memory resources did not help and only confused the matter more. By reviewing the application's overall design and usage, we identified the actual issues and fixed them for a minimal amount of money.

How to Speed Things Up Through Design

The lesson here is that the key to selecting the best compute configuration (covered next) is to first understand the design of the application that will leverage the compute instance. Many of us hate the "it depends" answer, but here it really depends on how the application was structured, and thus how it leverages compute, storage, memory, and the network.

Fortunately, you can run the application within an application profiler to understand how the application leverages infrastructure resources, such as I/O, storage, compute, memory, and network. In many instances, this is done prior to migrating the application to the cloud so that you can make a more educated determination of how to set up the target cloud's infrastructure to better support the application and data storage.

You can also understand the design of the application in other ways. A good old-fashioned review of programming code and database structure comes to mind. A review of the documentation left behind from the original design is another sound idea, as is talking to those who originally designed and built the application. During speedy migration projects, you'll find that most of those who migrate the application don't go to this level of due diligence and end up having performance problems. Reminder: Tossing more resources at the application after the fact is the costliest way to bandage over performance problems.

Enterprises consistently under- or overestimate the amount and configuration of cloud-based resources needed for a single application, or many applications. This is more than an application-level problem. It's now a holistic migration problem.

The key to understanding the resulting performance problems is to first understand the design of each application, how it leverages different resources, and thus how the target cloud compute instances should be configured, along with other services that the application may need, such as storage.

Application design needs to be considered when building net-new cloud applications or when migrating an existing application to the cloud. Almost all performance issues I encounter, in terms of applications being migrated to the cloud or built on the cloud, end up being issues that were fixed by changing the application's design.

Examples include leveraging new models for utilizing memory more efficiently, reducing calls across the network, and even performing foundational tasks such as leveraging a database caching system to reduce disk I/O and network utilization. Some of these are tweaks, such as tuning your database. Others are major surgery, such as leveraging a new and more efficient sorting approach. Potential design patterns pretty much number in the millions. It's important that you have some visibility into these patterns to make the most of your cloud deployments.

Picking the Most Optimized Compute Configuration

So, let's say we do most things right, in terms of understanding the design of our application workloads and data storage requirements. That means we pretty much know what we need for CPU, memory, and other platform requirements such as operating systems. How do we pick the most optimized compute configuration? Keep in mind that we can make mistakes here in two different directions.

As you can see in Figure 3-5, the value delivered is at its lowest points when we leverage too few resources or too many resources. If we leverage too few resources, this will save money on cloud resource usage, but application performance and resiliency will suffer, leading to a reduction in the business value the application will deliver to the business.

It's the same case for using too many resources. Although application performance and resiliency should be good, we pay too much for unnecessary resources. Thus, the extra cost reduces the value delivered to the business by overspending. We maximize the value delivered to the business when the value delivered to the business is about centered where both curves meet, and the number of resources is as fully optimized as value delivered.

Keep in mind that we may be facing a mindset issue here. Customers build in the cloud like they used to build data centers. They build like they are retailers trying to build for the Christmas rush. This is largely because it's so easy. The best analogy that I have is the current rise of food delivery services. The ease in which we can obtain our favorite foods, with pretty much no effort or pain, means that we will have the mindset to buy more, and thus get fat (or fatter). The mindset around cloud computing means that we're getting fat with cloud services that we most likely don't need.

What's interesting about this chart is that the current number of fully optimized enterprise cloud applications is pretty much zero. Most of those charged with picking cloud resources, including the CPU and memory resources, over- and underestimate the number of required resources. They end up on either end of the resource and value curves and almost never near the center. One problem is that few cloud architects don't suffer the immediate consequences of resource allocation mistakes and remain blissfully unaware of the ripple effect of their choices.

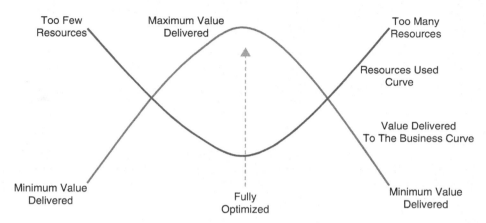

Too Few
Resources

Maximum Value
Delivered

Too Many
Resources

Resources Used
Curve

Value Delivered
To The Business Curve

Minimum Value
Delivered

Fully
Optimized

Minimum Value
Delivered

FIGURE 3-5 Here's what happens when you leverage too few or too many resources, and the corresponding effect on value delivered to the business. The objective here is a fully optimized system that delivers the most value to the business. You will find that just tossing money at problems fails to deliver the value. Also, not spending enough on the resources that you need also removes value. It's a balancing act.

Although overallocated resources result in higher cloud bills, the cloud-based application typically performs just fine, which is the metric most application owners use. Even those who underallocate resources may not know they have a value delivery problem unless they measure productivity, which may suffer due to application latency and outages. It will take time to go back and identify where a system failed to live up to expectations, but these ghosts in the machines will eventually come back to haunt you.

Again, the ability to optimize systems comes down to understanding your requirements before selecting the cloud resources you should leverage. The process should never be about guessing, nor trial and error. It should be about mathematically understanding the requirements around processor speed and memory use to get as close as you can to full optimization. This is a bit like horseshoes and darts in that you'll win this game only if you get close. Very few will obtain full optimization when it comes to business value; what's important is that you get as close as possible.

Figure 3-6 looks at your options when it comes to selecting a cloud compute platform. Selecting and configuring a compute instance sound simple; just select the CPU type (such as x86), including brand (Intel, AMD, and so on) and processor speed. However, you must also consider the number of processors configured and the size and speed of the memory. And then there are different types of processors, such as a microprocessor, microcontroller, embedded processor, and digital signal processor. Also, different processor generations, brands, and standards.

Yes, you can configure and deploy some pretty powerful compute platforms. However, it's not only about what you pick to align the platform to the requirements of the application, but what goes on behind those choices, in terms of power and cost of the compute resource.

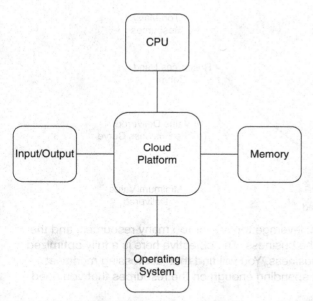

FIGURE 3-6   When picking a compute platform, you must decide the power and type of processor, number of processors, memory configuration and size, and operating system. Input/output usually needs to be configured as well.

The operating system the platform will employ focuses on the type and brand. For example, if your application runs on Linux on its traditional platform, you'll need to pick a Linux-compatible brand for cloud migration such as Red Hat, or perhaps a version created by the cloud provider such as AWS Linux. You might also pick Windows NT and other operating systems that you need to configure.

You'll find that the types, brands, and even the versions of operating systems vary a great deal from public cloud provider to public cloud provider. It would be nice to have a list here by platform. However, there could be a dozen more operating system types, brands, and configurations available by the time of publication. But I've found that most of them do the same things, and today arguing about what operating system is best has diminished returns. Don't get caught up in the silliness of becoming a believer around one specific operating system or another. Certainly, not the public clouds where changing operating systems takes a very short period of time and does not require touching physical hardware.

Normally, cloud providers give you a few choices. First, you can select one of their prebuilt configurations with the processor, memory, and operating system preconfigured for you. These "packages" are often the easy choice because these components are known to work with the provider's systems, or you can select the components a la carte from a list of prebuilt configurations provided by the public cloud provider. Or, you can select just the memory, operating system, and processor(s) that you need. So, what's the best path?

I never really liked the idea of selecting the packages that the public cloud providers put together. Not that there is anything wrong with prebuilt bundles that are known to work together, but the odds are against a prebuilt bundle meeting the exact needs of your application workload. This is especially true if you're only guessing about application requirements without having a detailed profile, and little thought is given to your exact and specific needs.

Picking the correct compute configuration is an often-overlooked art form, certainly in the world of cloud computing. Let's look again at Figure 3-6, where there are three to four components to choose. You'll also need to attach storage (perhaps a database), configure the network, and even attach special services such as machine learning and data analytics. For now, let's just keep the discussion to compute.

For most migrated applications, you'll need to profile the application workload using an automated profiling tool to determine the exact processor and memory needs. Or, you can use formulas to determine the compute needs of the application based on what it's built to do and how it should use processor and memory. Guessing is only a last resort that pretty much ensures a wrong answer.

Paying Too Much for Cloud Compute? Here's Why

A common theme in this book is that most who leverage public clouds pay too much. You'll find study upon study that proves this statement correct, but what's at the heart of the issues that break cloud budgets? If we just focus on compute issues for the moment, a few issues seem to tip the scales.

As covered previously, most of those who configure and allocate cloud computing compute resources do so without a good understanding of what the application does and how it does it. When the choices are based on uneducated guesses, most of those tasked with picking a compute configuration will select more resources than the application needs. Or, the budget-conscious could pick too few resources and then end up with an application that fails as it runs out of CPU horsepower or perhaps memory. Overbuying typically won't be identified as a problem until cloud costs finally come under audit. Eighty percent of the applications I see have typically overpurchased compute resources, spending as much as three to four times the money they should have on resources that won't be fully utilized.

Another issue? The cost tracking that cloud providers make available are not set up to let you know when or if you're overspending. To their credit, most cloud providers do offer tools to determine the size of the resources that you need. However, the tools have limited value. Typically, they're just questionnaires that those about to migrate and build net-new applications will need to fill out. In many cases, the new clients don't know what to tell the questionnaire.

Many of the mistakes being made today are by IT leaders who are just learning to understand cloud compute. How eager would you be to point out your own mistakes, ones that could be costing the business millions of dollars in unnecessary cloud resources?

The solution to this problem is obvious, but one that's rarely considered due to cost concerns. The better option is to implement a complete FinOps (Financial Operations) system that includes people, processes, and tooling that can automate the ability to determine when and if you're spending more cloud dollars than needed.

A FinOps system should also suggest changes that could reduce spending without impacting application performance and reliability. A FinOps approach and tooling will pay for itself compared to the costs involved to do a migration wrong the first time and then go back and fix it later. Implementing a FinOps system can provide a larger and ongoing return on its initial investment—this considering that ongoing processes and automation allow us to monitor costs, create policies around managing costs, and optimize the use of cloud resources with costs in mind.

Here are a few more ways to ensure that your cloud compute costs are more in line:

- **Accept outside help.** Hire people who can provide you with an objective opinion as to what you're spending on compute and where it's in line with what the workloads need. Consultants often provide this service for several businesses and thus have experience in what's optimized and what's not.

- **Deploy FinOps.** This is a subject that we cover heavily in this book. Basically, it's the ability to track cloud costs by usage, manage cloud negotiations to obtain the best prices, and do cloud cost forecasts to understand what's spent now and what will be spent in the near and far future.

- **Gain a wider understanding of cloud costs.** In many instances, the focus is on a single cloud provider. Rather than just work within their walled garden, it's a good idea to understand what the other cloud providers offer in terms of costs and compute configurations. You may find that you can pay half the cost for the same configuration on one provider versus another. We cover multicloud later as it relates to the consideration of compute configurations from other providers.

Keep in mind this all goes to the benefits of cloud cost optimization. This is both an approach as well as sets of software that allow us to optimize costs using automated systems. This means that we really don't have to think about it, it's carried out through a magical process. This is good, considering that many cloud geeks, like myself, don't seem to have an active part of our brains that deal with cost issues. This protects us…well…from us. Some of these things include better forecasting, a single pane of glass for multicloud, row-level access controls, cost tracking and forecasting, through the use of historical cost data, in-depth optimization recommendations, and automated remediation.

Picking the Right Operating Systems

For many developers, operating systems are a personal choice. I remember the operating system wars in the '90s when I was attacked by one side or the other, simply for picking one operating system over another in a review article. I learned that, in many instances, picking an OS is an emotional decision rather than an objective, technical one. If you're going to get emotional, get emotional about being true to your workload requirements and minimizing costs.

With that said, all operating systems are not created equal. The operating system you pick will affect how your applications and data leverage the processor, storage, memory, and even the network and user interface management, to cover just a few of the top attributes affected by the operating system. You'll see different performance profiles for the same basic workload on different operating systems. This includes open-source systems such as Linux, where many flavors and builds are put out by different vendors. Even the cloud providers themselves have their own versions that they sell within their cloud.

In many instances, the operating system you leverage will depend on the type, brand, and size of the processor you run. Some operating systems support only a small group of processors, typically those that support a similar architecture. This means they are not binary compatible with other processors and thus won't work with another processor. The topic of processor and operating system relationships is also beyond the scope of this book. However, it's a good idea to brush up on the subject before diving into designing specific solutions for your cloud compute configuration.

Picking the Right Memory Configurations

There are many kinds of computer memory. For our purposes, let's focus on the most important basic attributes required to select the right memory configuration for a specific workload. These attributes include size of memory, speed of memory, and type and amount of memory cache.

Memory cache provides temporary storage for frequently used instructions and data for quicker processing by the processor. The cache is an extension of a compute platform's main memory. Its use is a given in most cases. You might look for more cache to speed up processor requests that are more routine, which can be held in cache and thus are not required to be reloaded at the cost of performance. However, you can allocate too much cache that won't be used, or not enough, and that will also impact processor performance.

The speed of the memory is just that. It's the amount of time it takes memory to receive a request from the processor and then read or write data. RAM speed or frequency is measured in megahertz (MHz), and that's often how cloud providers will tell you about the speed of the memory for your compute configuration.

Finally, there's the type and size of the memory, or how much memory will be available to the application. Typically, memory size is measured in gigabytes (GBs). If, for some reason, you don't allocate enough memory, your application won't just stop processing. Instead, the operating system will begin to write to disk storage instead of writing to memory. Your application performance will suffer greatly when this occurs. Memory size is also a tunable parameter in the operating system, as to when and how the operating system leverages storage instead of actual memory.

The Concept of Reserved Instances

Did you ever get an offer to purchase something ahead of need at a good discount, something like a vacation timeshare or even a cemetery plot? Reserved instances offered by public cloud providers are the same. They are compute configurations and/or storage instances that are purchased in advance of actual need, and the provider offers a discount to pay in advance and reserve the purchases for your use.

There are a few things to discuss here, good and bad. First, let's cover the good. If you're good at planning ahead and understand exactly when and how you will need a compute or storage instance from a cloud provider, this is a good option to consider. However, based on my experiences, chances are you're overconfident about your planning abilities, most especially if this is your first cloud project. But let's assume that some of you have this superpower, and then the reserved instances may be a way to get more for less.

If you have not guessed yet, the bad around reserved instances is that most of the people planning for the use of cloud resources in the future do not have enough experience or luck to make the right choices. When they stock up on reserved instances, most overpurchase. Unlike that giant cooler the big box store took back a month after you bought it, all sales are final with cloud providers.

Figure 3-7 depicts what happens most often. Instances are purchased from the cloud provider for a predetermined cost, which is now a sunk cost. The instances typically expire after a specific amount of time, usually one to three years, and end up being largely unused. Thus, you may see a cost layout as shown in Table 3-1.

TABLE 3-1   This is an example of the business case for leveraging reserved instances: a refund.

Resources and Outcomes	Cost
10 reserved instances, x86 CPUs, 6 GB of memory, running Linux, usable for one year.	$20,000 one-time fee.
Number of instances used, 4, with the remainder returned to the cloud provider.	Considering what we paid for the reserved instances, we say that we paid $5,000 per instance.
Cost of purchasing the same instances as needed.	$3,000 per instance.
Overpaid/underpaid.	$20,000 – $12,000, or $8,000 overpaid for the same cloud resources.

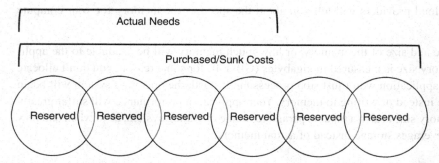

FIGURE 3-7   Although reserved instances may make sense for a small few, most overbuy and underutilize reserved instances that typically cannot be returned for a refund.

So, do reserved instances ever make sense? Sure, such as when you're relatively certain that your instance need will be X and then you use X. However, as we covered previously, most of those who do cloud resource and cost planning still don't fully understand what will be leveraged and in what amount of time.

Another scenario that would make sense is if you forecast the need for 100 compute instances over the next year. You could purchase 50 reserved instances to reduce the cost. If you fall a bit short, such as needing only 63 instances over the year, you're still ahead of the game.

In this case, you paid for 50 instances at a discount that you needed and used. With 50 instances discounted, you spent less money than if all the instances were purchased at full price as needed, even though you were off by 13 instances. Although you did not correctly predict the number of instances you planned to leverage, the strategic use of reserved instance pricing allowed you to save some money without much risk of letting the prepurchased instances go to waste. Now that more FinOps teams and tools are starting to emerge, we're seeing more enterprises take advantage of this strategy.

Enterprise Discount Program (EDP) is a cost-savings approach that most enterprises don't understand. AWS is the cloud provider known for this program, but other public cloud providers have something similar. The idea is that organizations that commit to a predetermined annual cloud spend (typically $1 million or more) can obtain automatic discounts. The discounts will vary based on spend commitment. These are functionally like reserved instances but provide more holistic cost advantages for larger enterprises that will be spending a great deal on public cloud services.

The general recommendation here is that you should avoid using reserved instances unless or until your cloud resource planning is so good and accurate that you feel it would be an advantage. For most of us, it's a gamble. Much like those subscription services you sign up for and used once or twice, they rarely deliver the value you expect.

Going Off-brand

Most people who look at cloud computing focus on the top three or four brands. After all, those are the cloud brands that most enterprises leverage, and those brands spent billions on their cloud services over the last few years to stay cutting edge and competitive. However, the big brands are not always the most optimal.

Today we can leverage reliable cloud services from any number of providers, including storage and compute services. Depending on the needs of your project, a nonmainstream brand could end up saving millions of dollars in cloud service costs over the next several years.

There also are non-cloud or less-than cloud options, such as managed services providers (MSPs). MSPs manage the services, including cloud services, for you, including major or minor brand cloud services, traditional system services, network services, or anything else that others can maintain on your behalf. Covered later, the opportunity with MSPs is to replace some cloud services with services that MSPs run while they also take care of systems that run across traditional platforms and/or any cloud platforms. Many MSPs offer built-in optimization systems, which means that they are not only managing traditional services and public cloud services on your behalf but also are able to optimize the use of these resources for you, thus reducing overall costs.

Finally, there are the opportunities and challenges around multicloud. Multicloud means you leverage heterogeneous public cloud services that allow you to deal with other services as the same. With multicloud, you can leverage many brands of storage and compute services using the best-of-breed services as well as least-cost services rather than deal with just a single cloud provider.

Leveraging Second-Tier Cloud Providers

Now that the concept of IaaS cloud computing is more than a decade old, we are beginning to see second-tier cloud providers enter the market. Of course, they only offer a fraction of the services you'll find within a major cloud provider, and they don't have as many points of presence (where the data centers are located), but a second-tier provider can offer a cost savings that makes them too compelling to ignore.

So, how much savings? Considering just compute, second-tier providers can offer the same compute configurations at prices 25–50 percent lower than those of the larger players, and you leverage the configurations in much the same manner. On one hand, they are not the premium brand, and thus you'll get some questions from those who consider the cloud brand inferior. But, if you save $10 million a year and your production workloads do not suffer, it may be worth the risk. Make sure to include testing, fully understand how you'll be billed, and do other due diligence, and the chances of success go way up.

Also, keep in mind that we now live in a cloud computing world where multicloud is now the norm. It's considered acceptable to leverage two or three major cloud brands. Add in the ability to place discount brands into your cloud services catalog to have them available for use, and this could be where the second-tier concept takes off. In this case, it's just as easy to attach a lower-cost resource such as storage and compute as it is to attach a major brand resource. Ease of implementation will push many enterprises to leverage the lower-cost resource, and perhaps send more savings to the bottom line. Also, by design, these lower-cost resources can work and play well with major brand cloud resources. Much of what is happening in the cloud world now and over the next several years will be a race to the bottom of the market.

Leveraging MSPs

MSPs differ a great deal in the services that each provides, but most will manage public cloud services for you, including provisioning, securing, and maintaining these cloud services in support of your workloads and data. They also support traditional systems, such as mainframes and traditional x85 such as LAMP-based platforms. In many instances, MSPs can be talked into managing more specialized systems such as edge computing systems and high-performance computing. MSPs often provide cloud-like services such as storage and compute that are less costly than the same services you might find within public cloud providers.

The advantage of using MSPs over traditional clouds is both cost and the ability to host several different platforms, including mainstream public clouds, and have the MSP manage those platforms. This means you have a service running in front of your cloud service that removes you from much of the work and complexity of managing all those systems on your own. For many enterprises, working with an MSP is often a lower-cost choice when compared to the costs to manage all their compute and storage services. With hundreds of MSPs in the market today, this option will continue to grow in scope.

Multicloud by Necessity

We'll address the important topic of multicloud later in the book, so we won't get too deep into it here. However, when discussing the ability to leverage different cloud brands and cloud types to save costs, remember that multicloud is a core weapon to leverage to both reduce costs and focus on the use of best-of-breed cloud resources.

Multicloud by necessity means that we consider multicloud a tool to leverage different services to provide a choice that should lead to utilizing services that are more cost effective. Multicloud provides the ability to pick the exact right services your applications and systems need, or best-of-breed, as well as pick the services that are at a lower cost point. To achieve your optimization objectives, multicloud is usually a necessity.

Call to Action

Compute is a fundamental building block of cloud-based systems. I revealed some secrets here that you won't often hear from cloud providers or other sources. It's not because they don't want you to know the truth, but that the truth around using the cloud compute resource is still misunderstood on several levels. This is certainly the case when framed within the more holistic concept of building systems in clouds.

In this chapter, we focused on what these cloud computing services are, how to understand them, how to pick them, and how to obtain the best value from your cloud provider. The idea here is to learn the tricks and get the insider path on the current cloud reality. You should now understand compute and its related services in ways and with methods that can lower your costs of leveraging cloud compute instances and increase your productivity. Cost and quantity are often at odds, but they need not be.

Chapter | 4

Innovative Services and Public Clouds: What Do You Really Pay For?

In a properly automated and educated world, then, machines may prove to be the true humanizing influence. It may be that machines will do the work that makes life possible and that human beings will do all the other things that make life pleasant and worthwhile.

— *Isaac Asimov*, Robot Visions

Now that we've covered some of the more mundane cloud services, including storage and compute, let's move on to the services that really drive cloud computing today. These more innovative and advanced services include AI, serverless, analytics, data lakes, and much more. They dominate much of what the technology press (including myself) currently writes about.

Here, we don't concentrate on the definitions of these services, which is information you can find in so many other places. Instead, we focus on how to optimize their value for the business. Most enterprises that rent advanced services from a top-tier public cloud provider only scratch the surface when it comes to their capabilities and potential benefits.

The cloud services of yesteryear were nowhere near as good as the traditional enterprise data center solutions. Those days are gone. Today's cloud-based solutions are multiples of times better than the traditional solutions, especially solutions that the top-tier public clouds can now provide. The reason is that the lion's share of all enterprise technology companies' R&D budgets goes toward cloud-based products and solutions. As a result, security is much better in the cloud, even though that seems counterintuitive to many people. There are also better databases, better development platforms, and better software packages available in public clouds.

Those who chose to stay off the cloud for any number of reasons will soon (or already) leverage inferior technology in the data center because these legacy systems receive less frequent or no updates from the provider, which means they also cost more to maintain and operate. There are reasons everyone is moving to the cloud these days. It's partly because the market evolved to give us little choice.

For our purposes, let's assume that moving to the cloud is a foregone conclusion. Your enterprise plans to leverage basic cloud infrastructure services, such as storage and compute as table stakes. The more innovative services covered in this chapter offer additional value to your enterprise, and these cloud services could even become game changers that redefine your business.

As we pointed out in Chapter 1, "How 'Real' Is the Value of Cloud Computing?" different layers define the value that cloud computing can bring to an enterprise. At the bottom layer we have basic infrastructure services (see Figure 4-1). These services support the applications and data storage systems that run the business. Basic infrastructure examples can include sales order entry, inventory management, shipping, logistics, and other systems that are common to most businesses. The target benefit of cloud computing at the bottom layer is to run these systems at a reduced cost, but these are just operational efficiencies. These are not game changer services.

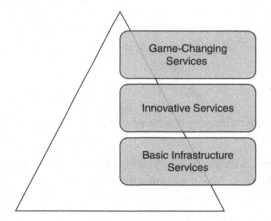

FIGURE 4-1 Cloud computing services can range from simple infrastructure services, such as those that run the business, to game-changing services, such as those that introduce innovative advantages that lead to the company becoming an industry disruptor.

Moving up a layer, we have innovative services. These services also depend on basic infrastructure services but provide true opportunities for innovation. Examples include advanced application development platforms and the ability to leverage services such as advanced data analytics, deep learning AI, massive scalability, proactive security, and anything that allows you to innovate or create unique differentiators.

Companies that leverage innovative services today include ride share companies that can leverage AI as a key differentiator to tell customers where their ride is located in near-real time, how much it will cost, and the almost exact time the ride should arrive. Ride share systems are based on simple services. By adding enhanced customer experiences using innovative cloud services, they can disrupt an existing traditional market.

For the most part, this chapter is about those innovative services. We look at what they are, what value they can bring, and how to effectively leverage them.

At the top layer, we have game-changing services. These innovative services combine to create net-new technologies and services that do not yet exist. A much earlier example of game-changing technology would be the invention of the airplane, which eventually changed how we travel long distances. These days, it could be a breakthrough in ways in which we cure diseases through genetic engineering or the ability to 3-D print construction components or entire houses. The possibilities are literally endless.

These are services and technologies that will change the way we think of things such as transportation, health care, housing, and other problems we want to solve, but we will do so in unique ways that did not exist prior to the appearance of these services and technologies.

Remember, each layer depends on the more primitive layer beneath it. Even the basic infrastructure layer where storage and compute exist needs to leverage more primitive components, such as a physical disk or a CPU, to provide the hardware services this layer needs. It's a good reference model to define different types of cloud services and solutions that exist and how they are all interdependent and work together.

AI/ML

Artificial intelligence and machine learning (AI/ML) are old concepts with new life, thanks to cloud computing.

Back in the '80s, AI was more of a high-tech experiment, with any AI advantages removed considering the high cost and lower technology capabilities at the time. You may remember computers playing chess, and IBM's Watson on game shows. It was interesting technology, but the business applications were few and far between, and it was still cost prohibitive for valid applications.

AI saw little use in the '80s, '90s, and even the early 2000s, until something came along to change all that...the cloud. Now that we can rent the infrastructure, as well as the AI engines themselves, the cost went from a minimum investment of about $1 million to a few hundred dollars per month. Today's AI technology is cheap, readily available, and with more advanced capabilities than in previous generations. It comes as no surprise that enterprises want to use AI in ways that will differentiate their business within the marketplace. Although you'll hear different definitions of AI and ML, at its essence, AI is a type of technology that leverages human-like learning capabilities. AI is the broad category of computer intelligence with implementations that can include services such as ML and deep learning (see Figure 4-2). Although there are many different definitions of ML, it's best thought of as a subcategory of AI systems that uses data to learn and find patterns. ML focuses on the pragmatic application of AI concepts that improve the value of AI for the business.

Today, most of what you see on the cloud is ML in the form of AI. ML can determine things such as a likely fraudulent transaction, in terms of patterns that may provide indicators. ML learns the patterns by learning from data specifically designed to teach the knowledge engine what certain existing patterns mean, such as data that is likely fraudulent or incorrect. It's our job, as humans, to define and set up the learning data that will "teach" the ML engine to spot specific patterns.

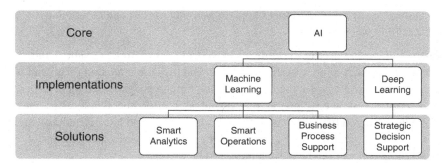

FIGURE 4-2 AI is the core concept, and machine learning and deep learning are examples of AI-related concepts or subcategories. Machine learning provides solutions related to analytics, operations, and business processing. Deep learning solutions include complex decision support and other solutions where a deeper understanding of the data is required.

Deep learning (DL) is the ability to leverage data and stimulus to find deeper meanings within data or stimulus. One can consider ML more tactically focused, meaning that we use it for more business purposes. DL can find deeper meaning within the data, sometimes finding a deeper understanding than we humans could find, such as the ability to figure out causes of some illnesses, where the problem is so complex that a single human is unable to process all of the knowledge that needs to be processed. That's why deep learning is often called "AI without limits."

It's not a good idea to get too wrapped up in the semantics of AI. You'll find that many in the world of cloud computing use AI, ML, DL, and other AI-related concepts interchangeably. While the PhD candidates may have issues with that approach, there are a lot of crossovers between the different types of technologies, which is why I just call it all "AI." Enough said about that idiom.

Overused?

Is AI overused? Perhaps initially when cloud computing providers began to offer AI as a service. The cloud made it cheap and readily available to solutions developers. As a result, AI found its way into applications that did not require AI capabilities, and the solution ended up less valuable. It's like putting high-end, high-cost racing brakes on a subcompact car. The car will stop just fine with stock brakes, while high-end brakes just waste money and resources.

These days we better understand the pragmatic use of AI: when it will prove worthwhile and when it will not. Business solutions that typically find the most value with cloud-based AI include

- **Business applications with potential patterns to find in large amounts of data.** These can be new patterns from new data, or new patterns that emerge based on what an AI engine already processes and learns from data as it processes over time. The more data that gets analyzed and the more patterns the AI system identifies, the better the AI engine gets at doing its job. We see this today in our daily lives, such as our cars learning from our driving patterns to accordingly adjust braking and acceleration. Even the smart thermostats on the wall can determine better patterns of use, including adjusting temperature based on past preferences and other related patterns, such as the current weather outside.

- **The creation of new data and/or understandings.** For example, leveraging "recommendation engines" by retailers selling online to better determine who they are interacting with and thus recommending products and services the user will likely purchase. Just based on behavior, these engines can determine your age, demographics, sexual orientation, income, location, and even the amount of education you likely had, and if you have a spouse and kids. Retailers can increase sales by using these engines, often by 20 percent or more. This "educated" means of enticing you to purchase additional products weaponizes AI.

- **An existing data set combined with AI's ability to determine new meanings.** It's why AI exists in the first place. Most enterprises realize they have valuable data, but they have not figured out ways to mine its value. Data is at the heart of all AI-enabled systems but is rarely noted as such. If you understand that there are better ways to learn from your business data, as well as gather information that is not necessarily obvious, then you can grasp the value of AI and the cloud.[1]

Overpriced?

The cost of AI dropped over 300 percent in the last 10 years, and the capabilities quadrupled (at a minimum). So why would anyone consider AI overpriced? This is more about AI's deliverable value for your specific use cases than its cost. When you leverage AI, you don't just leverage a single AI cloud service. There are many other resources that must be attached as well, including storage, compute, databases, and security, just to name the top four. To understand the real costs of AI, you need a holistic understanding of the AI service.

AI services are notoriously compute- and I/O-intensive; thus, they always incur additional costs. Also, training data is needed to analyze, and those data resources could cost you more than any AI service you leverage. Sometimes the cloud providers will "give away" the specific AI cloud service because they realize that billing will be higher for infrastructure resources the system requires when using AI.

However, some cloud providers offer bundled AI packages that include its infrastructure requirements. Some even provide AI cloud services at a fixed price per month for all the compute, storage, and AI usage you'll need. The larger players rarely offer these bundles, which means you also introduce the additional expense of leveraging AI as a multicloud deployment. We get into the risks, costs, and advantages of AI later in this book.

So, when considering the cost versus value problem of leveraging AI in the cloud, you need to consider the following questions:

- What potential value will an AI-enabled system bring, in terms of its direct ROI? What payback can you expect in hard dollars? For example, the ability to detect and stop most fraud by leveraging AI in the cloud would be based on the elimination of historical fraud losses.

---

1. https://www.infoworld.com/article/3662071/3-business-solutions-where-ai-is-a-good-choice.html

- What potential value will this AI-enabled system bring in terms of strategic ROI? For example, could you enter a new market with new innovative offerings or optimize the existing market through new processes and new understanding of the data?

- What's the all-in cost of building a system(s) using AI in the cloud? This includes costs for infrastructure, AI engine usage costs, training, and any risks that adding this technology might bring.

Answers to these questions will establish the true cost of AI, which can determine whether the cost is too high. Again, you need to consider the true all-in cost against the soft and hard values that AI can bring. For some enterprises and some use cases, this is the best bargain they will see at any cost. For others, the payback won't be as well defined. You could pay a dollar for an entire AI system, and it would still be overpriced. Always consider the clear benefits as well as the drawback costs of unnecessary distractions.

Finding the Right Use Cases

The key to finding the right AI value is to find the right use cases. What problems can AI solve to benefit the business? Conversely, where is AI overkill with costs higher than any business benefits?

There's a list of use case examples that the industry feels will benefit most from AI technology, cloud and not. However, it's better to understand the typical problem patterns that are a good fit for AI. If you make a long list of application types, such as fraud detection and health-related wearables, that may or may not be a good application of AI technology within the specific requirements of a specific use case. Instead, look at what patterns you might find within your business problem, which is much more helpful than just listing types of applications where AI has been a good fit in the past. My fear is that we will end up force-fitting AI before we have a true understanding of the problem to solve, simply because others in somewhat similar situations have profitably leveraged AI. Rocky architecture ends up adding unnecessary cost and risk.

So, if you set aside application lists created by others, how do you find the right AI application for your use case? Let's first understand why we are bothering with AI in the first place.

AI systems, especially those that leverage ML, are good at learning from large amounts of data, called training data. AI can make inferences around that data via things that humans teach the AI model (supervised learning), or they can learn on their own (unsupervised learning), or there can be some assistance from humans (semi-supervised learning), or AI can be trained through trial-and-error corrections that can be made by humans or automated processes (reinforced learning).

Reminder: I'm not going to teach you all the details behind AI and ML; there are plenty of other places to go for that knowledge. However, it helps to get an insider view of what business problems AI and ML typically solve best and how to recognize when AI technology should and should not be considered.

AI, including ML, should be leveraged only when there are things to learn, and then leverage the AI model only for business problem solutions that are a best fit for AI and ML. While the need to have a system learn from historical and ongoing data is an easy way to describe the best use case, there still needs to be a business case for leveraging this knowledge model. It's not good enough to say that you can derive additional meaning from the data, such as spotting fraudulent transactions or diagnosing a disease. Define the business case use for that trained knowledge model to be leveraged, such as marking the likely fraudulent transactions for automated investigation and resolution that will return 2 percent of net profit to the business.

Far too often, businesses build these AI systems with no solid, stated benefit to the business at the end of the day to justify the cost of leveraging AI, cloud or not. Define, memorize, and be prepared to prove the true benefit of AI, no matter whether the application seems like a good fit or not. Most AI applications work just fine, but the additional cost is unjustified.

Business Optimization of AI

Okay, AI works, but now we need to find the problems to solve that will bring the most value to the business. What do we need to consider?

Most people who look for business applications of cloud-based AI/ML do so without picking applications or solution patterns that will optimize the value that AI/ML can bring. This is close to an epidemic, as AI costs go lower and availability rises. More and more often, enterprises apply AI to solve problems that AI is unsuited to solve. As you can see in Figure 4-3, this means that about two-thirds of the applications that leverage AI/ML are underoptimized for the business and end up costing more money and time than they should. These AI projects are often hailed as initial successes, but they become a money pit that insidiously removes value from the business over time.

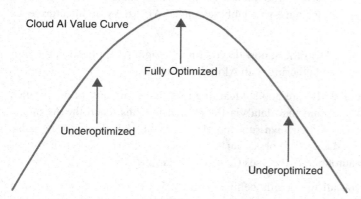

FIGURE 4-3 Cloud-based AI applications and/or solutions should leverage most capabilities of AI/ML. Applications and/or solutions that don't leverage these capabilities are considered underoptimized or inappropriate use cases. These cases cost the business time and money.

If using AI/ML has a negative effect on value, that often means we're not using AI/ML holistically. As you can see by Figure 4-4, it's usually best to set up access to AI-enhanced data by leveraging both the data and the knowledge model that's bound to the data through a holistic API. Therefore, any number of applications can leverage the "knowledge" using APIs or services, as much or as little as needed. This approach solves a few other problems as well, such as having a centralized knowledge model and data that's consistent from application to application, which should also reduce operational and development costs because you leverage the same AI/ML services throughout the portfolio of applications.

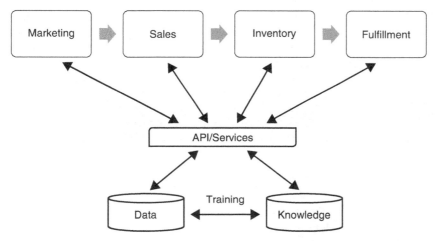

FIGURE 4-4 AI optimization means returning the maximum value back to the business to justify the use of AI technology. Most AI systems will be set up for use via multiple applications, both inside and outside of the cloud. This holistic solution can provide the best value to the business, but you must still consider your specific requirements.

Today, AI/ML is in overuse. Many believe this is a good thing, considering what the technology can do. Holistically, it often moves the business backward by leveraging applications and/or solutions that may not initially appear to be a failure, but they remove value to the business ongoing. This is the dilemma when leveraging any type of new, hyped technology, in that they are often misapplied and make things worse. The theme here is to consider the use case and its longer-term impact on the business before you jump on AI/ML.

Serverless

Serverless technology is a misnomer, in that it's about how you deal with "servers" rather than the lack of them. The technology is called serverless because you no longer need to figure out how many server and storage resources will be required to run specific applications. The number of required resources is figured out for you, on the fly, as your applications execute.

Serverless gained in popularity because it moves allocation and provisioning decisions of virtual cloud server resources from the developer to the cloud provider. The types of serverless technology available grew from simple application execution systems to containers, databases, and anything else that makes cloud resource-sizing steps easier.

You Really Are Using Servers

When we leverage serverless systems found on major public cloud providers, we often forget that we're leveraging actual servers and we'll have to pay for their use. This is not much different from when we allocated the cloud server resources ourselves (such as storage and compute) and paid for the resources we leveraged. Now that automated processes make those calls for you, the question arises: Is serverless cheaper and more efficient than more traditional approaches? The dreaded answer is: It depends.

Serverless works on the assumption that rank-and-file developers are not that great at resource planning, and often over- or underallocate the number of resources needed. Overallocation means you spend too much money, underallocation means the application could fail. Both are cost inefficient, considering the outcome.

For now, let's put aside some of the other features that serverless can bring to focus on manual versus its automatic provisioning features. When serverless is in play, the serverless system determines what the applications require, and thus allocates the precise number of resources needed for the application to execute at a particular point in time. Each provider approach to serverless is a bit different, but these functions usually operate independently, and thus the serverless system allocates resources only to execute that specific function, or a system that uses many functions. You'll get a small report when the function executes, telling how many resources it used and how much it cost to execute that function/ application. Thus, you'll have to design for your serverless system as well, considering that these applications are more function oriented.

Many people question a serverless system's ability to pick resources more cost-effectively than humans. There are two arguments to be made here. First, when we leverage automation, we usually have more cost-effective results than if it's all left to people. This is the typical case when you have more dynamic applications that are difficult to predict, in terms of resources that need to be leveraged. However, there are static applications that provide easy-to-predict resource requirements, especially if the number of resources needed is not likely to change over time. With static applications, we can also leverage special discounting (such as reserved instances) to further improve costs to allocate our own resources versus relying on serverless automation.

Determining the value of leveraging serverless anything is best answered (again) by: It depends. It depends on the size and the specific behavior of the applications, dynamic versus static, for instance. So, sometimes serverless will make sense and provide the most cost optimization, sometimes not. The trick is to understand the application patterns that will lead to the best cost optimization.

Cost Versus Value

As you can see in Figure 4-5, traditional methods of allocating resources that support application execution are not based on the application needs at the time of deployment, but what the application will need. Or you can allocate enough resources to support application execution and then manually increase those resources as the scalability and capacity needs of the application organically grow.

With traditional methods, you don't look at the number of resources that an application continuously uses, but adjust those resources up or down, based on need. Thus, your resource allocations might be perfectly aligned with the current needs of the applications only once or twice a month, at the most, because traditional resource allocation for an application workload is static. Traditional allocations are never continuously adjusting to meet the needs of the application, whereas serverless is adjusting for the exact needs of the application or function.

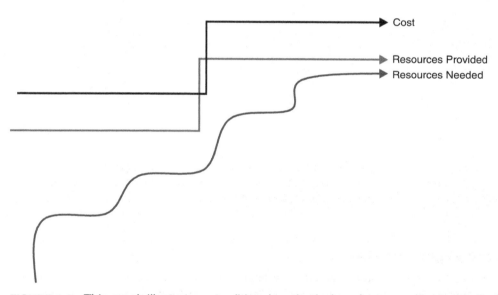

FIGURE 4-5   This graph illustrates a traditional method where humans select and allocate the number of resources needed, which means resources must be allocated ahead of need. In this example, the resources are only allocated twice—once initially and once to increase them to handle a growing application load. The capacity allocated ahead of need is largely wasted. Optimizing serverless means first understanding what you give up.

Serverless was created to work around the fact that most developers struggle to correctly size applications to the number of required resources, and they usually don't have unlimited time to do adjustments ongoing. Figure 4-6 depicts the serverless value of removing humans from this process, at least the value of automatic server provisioning. Again, as the needs go up, so do the number of cloud server resources leveraged, and so does the cost of those resources. The object is to align the resources needed with resources provided, as well as optimize cost. The question then becomes, Does leveraging a serverless model make us more (or less) cost efficient?

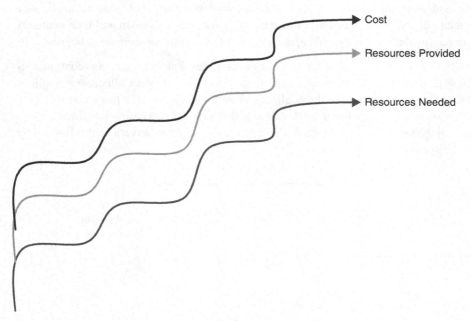

FIGURE 4-6   Serverless is a bit easier to understand. As the resources needed to run the application increase and sometimes decrease, this directly aligns with the amount of cloud resources allocated as well as what you pay for those resources.

Finding the Right Use Cases

The answer of whether or not to utilize serverless systems comes down to the use case. Applications that behave in dynamic ways also need to scale, meaning they go from using many compute and storage resources to very few, and then back to many resources again. Applications with dynamic behavior are a great fit for serverless. Serverless automation deals with the dynamic resource needs, always adjusting the number of resources up and down based on current need. Obviously, costs follow this line, as you can see in Figure 4-6, where you only pay for what the application(s) need, and you do not pay for unnecessary capacity.

Of course, not all applications are that dynamic, and they may not need to scale. In those cases, a simple equation can often define the number of required resources. In these use cases, serverless systems are usually more expensive than standard cloud resources that you manually provision and manage ongoing. Again, you could further reduce costs if you leverage discounted cloud resources, such as those purchased ahead of need. With proper planning, a nondynamic application could cost about one-third less than if you leveraged serverless resources.

Finding Business Optimization

The optimization of costs as related to need is key here. Many of those who pick serverless technology within the cloud providers do so for the wrong reasons. Often, they do not understand the requirements of their core use cases, which means they can't properly determine if they should leverage serverless or more traditional approaches.

I suspect they'll eventually figure out that serverless was not a cost-effective fit for a particular application because they did not consider the application's processing and storage needs, which were not dynamic and did not need to scale. The use of static resources that could be manually allocated and remain in place would have been a much better idea. Remember, cloud providers don't offer refunds for your poor judgment.

As we covered previously, serverless provides the best business optimization when the applications are both dynamic and consistently grow in the number of resources the applications will require going forward. For these types of applications, serverless is purpose-built to provide a more optimized solution.

DevOps/DevSecOps

Development and operations (DevOps) is also called development, security, and operations (DevSecOps). Both have revolutionized the way that we do software development, testing, deployment, and operations. For our purposes, we'll call DevOps and DevSecOps just DevOps to make it easier to follow. We accept that there is a difference between the two, in that one also focuses on security as well as holistic development.

Figure 4-7 depicts the general idea behind DevOps, both in the cloud and out. We set up a DevOps tool pipeline that consists of design, development, integration, testing, and deployment tools that we automate as much as possible. The objective is to change the design of an application on one end and have the pipeline almost instantaneously perform automated integration, testing, and deployment tasks. For example, if we find an issue with a software system at 9:00 a.m., we could have it fixed by 10:00 a.m., including testing and deployment. We can do the same with enhancements and changes to meet the "speed of need" for the business.

DevOps leveraged with cloud generates value through its ability to provide agility, which in turn allows developers to almost instantaneously build or change application solutions to meet the exact needs of the business. Thus, automated DevOps can bring a huge amount of value to the business because it provides the soft value of business agility, which was covered in Chapter 1, something that most businesses will value, allowing them to "turn on a dime," or expand innovation as needed by the marketplace.

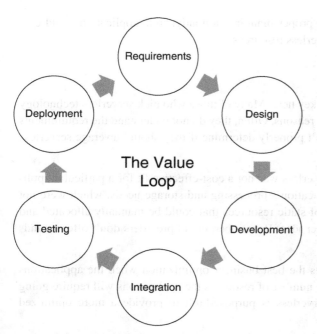

FIGURE 4-7 DevOps focuses on iteration, which means moving quickly and in parallel between one development task to another. The idea is to focus on speed, flexibility, and continuous improvement to obtain the most value.

Furthermore, DevOps can enable innovation. We can build innovative solutions at record speed that allow us to "fail fast" and drive innovation at scale. The company can quickly create game-changing innovations, such as providing an enhanced customer experience or other innovations that lead to increased business value for the company's shareholders, which is the end goal.

DevOps is a disruptive approach to development because it removes the wall between development and operations. Both parties are now responsible for building, testing, deploying, and operating an application solution. Both work together with open communications, and it's no longer "not my job" when it comes to ensuring the systems are fully optimized and meet the exact needs of the business.

DevOps accomplishes this state by removing much of the formality, structure, and processes that we follow with traditional software development. We no longer work down a set of tasks, where one task must be completed before the next starts. We no longer sit in a silo and wait for others to do their jobs before we can do ours. This creates a culture of teamwork, which removes many impediments to productivity and ensures that speed and agility are valued attributes. The result is the timely ability to build net new systems or alter existing systems to meet the changing needs of the business.

There are plenty of books and courses on DevOps, if you want to learn more about this concept. Here we examine the value of DevOps, including when it's useful and when it's not. Again, we get the insiders' view of the true value of DevOps technology and processes.

No Cloud DevOps

Until recently, most DevOps toolchains existed outside of cloud providers. This was true even if the deployment of the applications at the end state of the process occurred in the cloud. Why? DevOps tools began as open systems that ran within data centers, prior to any need to put DevOps on public clouds.

Although cloud-based DevOps is a thing now, it's difficult to create a cloud-only DevOps solution. The standard requirements for DevOps tooling are all over the place, and there are many tools to pick from. You may end up going from a design system on the cloud, to development on the cloud, to integration, testing, and deployment that occur in the data center. Then you could end up deploying to a public cloud provider as the end-state platform. Although most seek pure cloud DevOps toolchains, this often proves impossible, depending on the specific tools required by your use case or preferred by your staff. Thus, most DevOps in the cloud encompass hybrid, cloud, and traditional systems. At least, that's the case at the time I'm writing this book.

All Cloud DevOps

Most public cloud providers offer a mix of their tooling along with third-party tooling that can be leveraged in the cloud, specifically on their cloud. These tools generally work fine but may not be optimized for your project's specific needs if you prioritize "on the cloud" over "fully optimized." As with anything I discuss here, if you prioritize the platform over the core business requirements, cloud or not, you will end up with something less than optimized.

Some-Cloud DevOps

Most DevOps is *some-cloud DevOps* (see Figure 4-8). This means that some of the DevOps tools within the toolchain run in the cloud, and some run on traditional systems in the data centers or even on the desktop of the developers or operators.

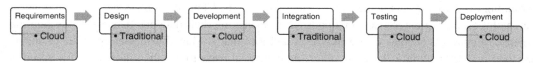

FIGURE 4-8   DevOps toolchains can run on public clouds or traditional systems, and they can work together when they run on both. This leads us to some-cloud DevOps, or a hybrid approach where you pick the best tooling and run it on the platform where it makes the most sense.

Of course, you may need to add more tools to the chain, or remove tools, based on your requirements. What's important is to design your toolchain to provide a fully optimized DevOps solution and run those tools where they can provide the most value. DevOps engineers often end up with a hybrid some-cloud solution as their best DevOps solution. The core message is to find the most optimal DevOps tools for your use case, cloud or not.

Finding Business Optimization

DevOps is an easy place to find business value. It provides faster and more agile development and enables teams to work together more effectively. We've needed this improvement for decades. The benefits of DevOps are easy to measure; it promotes both business agility and speed, with the outcome being more innovation.

Are there any downsides? DevOps can be taken to an extreme, which can result in negative value to the business. This often happens when people leverage DevOps as a religion and put more value on moving quicky than software quality, or what the business specifically needs. These DevOps-driven shops don't spend enough time on tools and processes to ensure the stability of their systems, and they accept unstable systems as a natural outcome of agile development. When confronted about the stability/quality issues, many will push back with the fact that they are "agile"; thus, the trade-off will be some lack of design and testing integrity. These people should be retrained or fired.

DevOps is not about moving fast to the detriment of application quality; it's about enabling application quality to happen fast. There is a huge difference, in that one leverages automation to become a better developer who produces better tested and configured systems versus being a developer who uses Agile as an excuse to skip steps that ensure system quality and adherence to business objectives. DevOps is a great practice, great set of technologies, and a huge value to the business…if it's done correctly. Otherwise, it can do a lot of damage that businesses typically need to hire someone else to fix.

Analytics

Analytics is the ability to understand the meaning of data and business processes, and support helpful automated processes in terms of trends, insights, and monitoring of business events so those charged with running the company can make better business decisions. Cloud computing became important in this arena because most enterprises do a poor job of managing their data and data assets, despite the emergence of concepts such as data warehouses and data marts. Many businesses continue to under-utilize their data, or they lack the vision to create beneficial ways to use their data. Cloud was and is tagged as a technology that could exploit these fallow opportunities.

The trouble comes in when considering the as-is state of data in most enterprises. Most enterprise data is scattered throughout the existing thousands of databases, without a single source of truth for important entities such as customers, sales, and inventory. In many cases, CIOs kicked this mess down the road when they realized that the costs to correctly fix the problems were far more than their budgets would allow.

Much of this "asset scatter" arose when different groups built systems for different purposes, and because very few people, data, or systems within an enterprise interact or share resources. Each group picked its own development and database technology, and, in many cases, these groups just created new databases to store information that already existed.

I would assert that cloud made the asset scatter problem worse. These diverse groups can now pick and choose different application development tools and data assets because today's cloud-based tools are far less expensive to acquire and easy to access. So, how do we retrofit good data analytics over a flawed asset scatter model?

First, undergoing a major renovation to consolidate the use of enterprise data is beyond the scope of virtually all enterprise budgets, although most enterprises need to do it. The reality is that money, staff skills, resources, and time to properly fix asset scatter issues don't exist. Instead, we must fix this problem on the fly as we move to cloud, and then find ways to lessen the damage moving forward.

Although most of us can't afford to eliminate asset scatter in one fell swoop, all of us should consolidate scatter patterns as we migrate systems to the cloud and never create new scatter problems. That's the name of the game.

Connecting the Data Is Key

The first step? Understand that it's all about leveraging existing data assets in optimized ways by adding value with new systems (such as AI) that can abstract the data we need. All of this can happen without major surgery. We can avoid remodels to the back-end databases, which is where the most money and risks come into play. Instead, we can use virtualization and abstraction to connect the data for analytics.

Figure 4-9 depicts what this connected model looks like. We deal with data, either old or new business data, that may exist in many different physical data stores, both within the cloud and out. Rather than replicate the data, we ensure that it can be efficiently read using data virtualization and abstraction to create the structure that makes the data most useful. This technology has been around for years and is often used to work around bad data designs and structures, both in and out of the cloud.

There are new concepts to consider as well, including data fabric and data mesh, just to name a few. Data fabric is an approach to data usage that employs a set of data services that provide similar capabilities for data access across endpoints. In other words, data fabric abstracts the physical data structure to consistently leverage data services, and it provides data and data analytics to give consumers a consistent array of services. Typically, data virtualization is the core mechanism behind data fabric. Although a detailed discussion of these approaches to connect with data is outside the scope of this book, if this is an issue you will or do deal with, you should look at other resources to take a deeper dive.

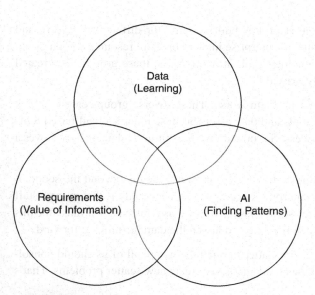

FIGURE 4-9   When we are dealing with data analytics, it's important to understand that data unto itself is not as important as how it can teach AI systems to provide useful insights and thus deliver value to the business.

The requirements in Figure 4-9 mean that we must look for the business value of the data that's recast using a more usable structure and view, as well as what the business can do with the data. Underutilized data means that it's there to be read, but there are other, unrealized uses of the data that could add value to the business. For example, I can see that certain data is related to a single sale of a product, or even a grouping of sales, such as finding the total sales for a given period. Other insights might be more useful, such as the ability to determine who, what, where, when, and why sales trend higher or lower by relating sales data to other data sets, such as seasonal trends for specific products. Obviously, in-depth analysis of sales data is useful for sales planning and production adjustments, and even how the company markets its products to optimize sales.

Finally, AI is related to all connected data. As we covered earlier in this chapter, AI is most useful when there is data around that can be leveraged for machine learning/training that can, in turn, enable the AI system to find patterns. You could instruct the AI system to look for specific patterns, such as transactions that may indicate fraud based on attributes that you provided. Or, more valuable are patterns the AI might detect that you didn't know existed. For example, a specific product that is marketed equally to both men and woman may have stronger sales trends around women buyers who also fit into a specific demographic, perhaps those who live in cities. These are patterns that create deeper insight into the data via data analytics.

Analytics Over and Under

Some businesses overapply analytics technology, whereas others underutilize data analytics, which is true in most use cases I see.

Overutilization of cloud-based data analytics typically occurs when someone overstates the value of analytics services, and/or it's used for incompatible tasks. Examples include a demand for planning around a specific product or service when there is not enough data to determine any specific patterns. I recall one case where a company invested in promotional marketing campaigns based on analytics that lacked any historical data to spot true trends. Analytics based on junk data or missing data cause too many businesses to put too much stock in analytics. In these cases, you need to consider the solution holistically. Can the analytics be correct within a certain margin of error? It's this belief in "magic data" that often gets companies into trouble. This is not the fault of the technology itself, rather the fact that the technology is being misused.

Underutilization of analytical technology is a far more common problem. The data exists; data analytics could derive information of value from that data. However, the data goes untapped. Indeed, some companies make mistake after mistake around sales and marketing trends when the information that would have saved them was an API call away. The trouble usually exists when enterprises look at the data itself rather than the potential ways to look at the data to find patterns or combine the data with other data sets to determine other meanings—for example, comparing sales data with economic data to determine how sales align with key market indicators. In some cases, you'll find that sales go up when the market goes down. This is the case with discount stores, which traditionally see an increase in sales during an economic downturn. Other less obvious analytics would be the ability to compare demographic behaviors with sales data to determine the best ways to advertise to the people most likely to purchase a specific product or service, based on what we find in certain demographics.

AI Convergence

As we stated earlier, the concepts of AI, data, and analytics are tightly coupled within the cloud. Figure 4-10 depicts this relationship and the understanding that business value for analytics can only be created by connecting AI, business processes, and raw data.

AI can find patterns in the data as well as learn day to day, which provides even more AI knowledge about how to use the data. No matter if this is general business analytics, or how an AIOs (Artificial Intelligence [AI] Operations) tool will deal with operational data to learn how to resolve problems over time, the fact that we're including AI means that the analytics system can learn ongoing. It does so from the data and applies that knowledge to find deeper understandings about what the data means for the business. Often, the business learns something about its data that becomes game changing.

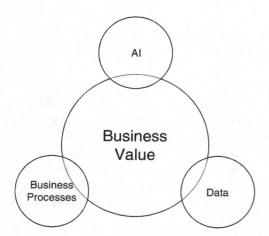

FIGURE 4-10 To find the true business value of cloud-based data analytics, we need to leverage a few key technologies that include the data itself that's housed within a database, analyze how that data is provided to key business processes, and then determine how that data can teach key AI systems. All of this is interconnected to provide the core business value.

For instance, analytics could determine that an improved customer experience versus an improved product generates more real value. The system might forecast that certain improvements to the customer experience will return 15 times more than an equal investment in product improvements. Very few humans would connect those dots, but AI can help businesses identify and pursue opportunities to generate more business value.

Business processes are often overlooked as a consumer for analytics, but they play perhaps the most important role. Let's say we support a core business process, such as a product sales process, and now we can embed analytics to allow this process to become more valuable for the business. For example, we add the ability to look at the sales history of a specific customer, understanding that this type of customer often closes after receiving a small discount on the price. The AI system can determine that the best target discount rate for this customer is 5 percent, and that this discount often results in an order quantity increase of three times the initial order. Building these analytics into the process, we'll understand how much of a discount to provide to which customers for the highest chance of closing the sale right away, while still maintaining margins. This process can even be automated so that the system offers the discount without human intervention, which removes any latency caused by manually doing the discount procedure.

Finding Business Optimization

Business optimization for analytics is the ability to provide the right information at the right time and provide insights into the business that are greater than the raw data itself. Raw data unto itself is largely meaningless. If we can look at the data with a different dimensional understanding and allow external data to be compared with that data, we can determine the raw data's higher and more valuable meaning.

So, this is about understanding the value that analytics technology can bring. We must determine how to successfully apply it so the cost of analytics implementation in the cloud returns the investment back to the business in terms of direct value understood, typically within a few short weeks. Typical cloud-based analytics systems are not that expensive. You integrate existing data with cloud-based AI engines and leverage models that were created for other purposes. Often these existing models are provided by your cloud analytics vendors that can be modified to meet your specific needs, which significantly reduces development and deployment costs. Some of the low-code and no-code solutions that are now a part of analytics can get us to a state where setting up our analytics models is just a matter of dragging and dropping objects on our screens—no programming skills required.

Edge and IoT

Edge computing is just another architectural approach where we place some of the data and processing outside of the cloud, closer to where the data is consumed, and where the processing needs to occur. Edge computing rose in popularity as those who build widely distributed systems realized it was highly inefficient to transmit data from its point of origin, say a factory robot, back to a centralized cloud-based system where it processes and then returns the information to the data source, in this case a factory robot. A "dumb terminal" type of device that requires unbroken communication with a "mainframe" or cloud system via Wi-Fi or Bluetooth is a recipe for disaster. If the Internet goes down, data processing would not occur. In some cases, the remote device or remote server could stop processing until communications were restored with the centralized storage and processing systems, often on the cloud.

As greater numbers of distributed systems emerged, we saw the rise of the Internet of Things (IoT) that opened the market to devices such as "smart" thermostats, TVs, watches, phones, and locks, with "advanced" capabilities. Those advanced capabilities are typically rudimentary when compared to full-fledged computing systems, but many of today's smart devices surpass the capabilities of a 10- or even a 5-year old desktop computer. With more virtual assistants (Alexa, Siri, Hey Google) and appliances coming online, smart devices now account for more than half of the Wi-Fi connections in our homes.

We can define edge computing as an architecture in which varying amounts of processing and data storage exist on some device outside of the architecture's centralized processing systems (which typically reside on a public cloud). IoT devices all leverage edge computing architecture.

Edge computing also includes sizable software and hardware systems, such as edge clouds that exist in data centers. These smaller versions of public clouds operate autonomously, away from public clouds such as AWS and Microsoft. Most edge clouds include a subset of public cloud providers' cloud services. Public cloud providers and others offer autonomous edge cloud services to enterprises. The enterprises themselves use edge clouds when they need to keep data in sight to meet some legal requirements, or if they're just paranoid that they will lose control of their data. Again, this is also edge computing.

So, edge computing is an architecture that applies to many things, and the term itself is so overused that it's become a buzzword. However, edge computing is designed to put processing and data storage in a place where they can operate with the most efficiency. This means eliminating or removing latency, because the smart device is at the origin of data collection. Also, the edge system can continue to support an attached but independently operating system, such as a factory robot, even if communications with the central server become disrupted. Your watch still tells time and counts your steps. Your thermostat continues to operate manually or on its set schedule. The IoT devices continue to collect data that will automatically upload to the edge cloud when the connection reestablishes itself. So, edge computing provides the architectural advantages of reliability and performance.

Edge and the Cloud Realities

In the early days of edge computing, some people thought edge would replace cloud computing. That will never happen. If you think about it, edge computing must be on the edge of something. So, edge computing itself can't exist without the "something" related to centralized storage and processing, which is typically found on a public cloud.

More and more edge computing services rely on public clouds to provide development, configuration, and management services. In other words, they have a symbiotic relationship, meaning that if you do edge computing, you will be working in the cloud as well…in most cases. This is a good thing, considering how complex edge computing can be, and especially when you consider the challenges around edge operations and configurations. Centralized control of the cloud makes edge computing work.

Cloud Controls the Edge

As alluded to in the preceding section, edge and cloud are tightly coupled. When you look at a list of the top 10 edge computing solution providers, the major public cloud providers appear first on that list. Public cloud providers support edge development, deployment, and edge computing operations by creating "digital twins" of the edge computing server or devices and by managing the twin of the device in the cloud. Thus, you automatically sync those changes to the deployed remote edge computing device or server.

As you can see by Figure 4-11, this structure provides many more advantages than if we managed each edge device one at a time. We create a single configuration that is automatically replicated as many times as needed, to as many devices and/or servers that the edge configuration needs to run on. This is very handy when it comes to operations, where the configurations need to be updated to fix issues or repair problems. The mechanism to roll out changes to the operating systems, databases, or other runtime utilities is in one place on the public cloud. Those changes are then replicated out to the edge computing systems, as are updates to any databases or specialized systems that may be out there.

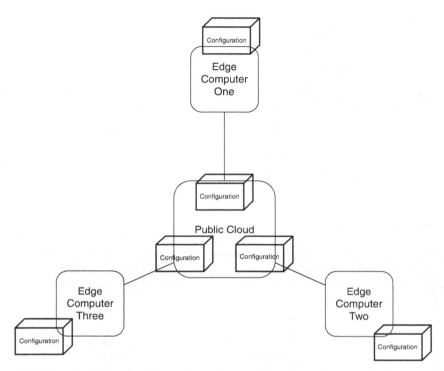

FIGURE 4-11 When looking at cloud computing and edge computing, you'll find that cloud computing is where many edge-based software systems are developed and deployed. In many cases, a copy of the edge computing configuration is kept on the public cloud, allowing configurations to be updated or fixed when needed.

Edge Computing and IoT Realities

Edge and IoT come with their own set of challenges, and you need to figure them out before you go all-in with edge computing and IoT in general. The main challenge is one of scale. As you can see in Figure 4-12, the number of IoT devices can be significant. There can be so many devices that your ability to effectively manage them becomes more of a challenge than building the devices themselves.

We've all experienced the sight of our smartphone updating its operating systems to provide fixes and new features. Even smart watches get occasional updates, as do our smart thermostats, as does the software within our vehicles. Large companies drive those updates, with the resources and ability to build specialized systems to deal with the scale of IoT devices purchased by their customers. Normal enterprises that want to leverage edge and IoT may not have access to the same capabilities. How do they efficiently and cost-effectively leverage edge and IoT when it comes to operational realities?

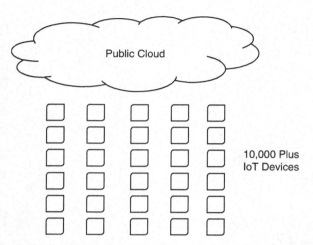

Public Cloud

10,000 Plus
IoT Devices

FIGURE 4-12 Public clouds are needed to manage the tens of thousands of IoT devices that might be needed to support a business. These devices must be centrally configured and managed, with scaling to support this number of devices. Scaling still presents problems for many of those moving to edge computing/IoT.

Let's say you're a small oil company that is looking to remotely manage pumping stations within South America, where the number of stations will soon number over 1,000. Because these systems need to be individually customized for the type of pump and the operations of the pump, AI is needed to monitor pump health and efficiency. AI introduces the ability to remotely fix issues and monitor the overall efficiency of the pumping systems. These fixes can be applied to an individual system, or all pumps at the same time.

The reality? This oil company has little to no chance of creating a scalable, cost-efficient edge-based application from scratch. If it wants any chance of building something usable, it'll need to leverage an edge computing development platform provided by a public cloud provider or other third-party providers. Most companies are sized at or below the oil company example. Clearly, the ability to leverage edge building tools and platforms is a force multiplier to jump onto edge computing, and it's the only realistic way for most enterprises to edge at scale, especially for enterprises that want to build edge-based systems for internal use.

Finding Business Optimization

When looking for business optimization of edge computing and IoT, you need to consider these realities: While many enterprises will leverage edge computing architecture, many will not. Many won't need to. Your first step is to consider if edge computing is even needed and then to verify that a business case exists.

In my experience, many enterprises intend to leverage edge-based systems with systems that exist within data centers; those are not low-powered remote devices or computers. That's not edge computing.

Other companies try to leverage edge architecture for a variety of odd reasons, such as a desire to push processing out of the cloud to an edge-based device or server to distribute the processing load.

Edge computing is of value only when there is a need to put the gathering and processing of data close to the source of that data. If you build jet airliners, there's a huge benefit if you put the engine processing technologies inside of the aircraft, which eliminates the need to deal with satellite communications latency or network outages to resolve problems with the engine in-flight. In that instance, edge computing is not only a smart move, but it's really the only move.

However, the use cases for most enterprises are not as compelling as they should be for edge computing. At the very least, edge computing will increase development and operational costs threefold. There needs to be a good use case to justify that level of complexity and expense.

Emerging Technologies

In covering innovative services, we're looking at a list that increases monthly, in terms of new service offerings that have the potential to provide more business value. The list of innovative services I reviewed in this chapter covers only the services that I feel are important to understand, as well as to put into proper perspective. My blog provides updates to developments in thinking around the uses of this technology, and I look at it through a skeptical eye rather than jump on every hype-driven bandwagon.

The advice I'm giving you here is simple. Every technology that you encounter needs to justify its existence, no matter who's writing about it, or the purpose it's serving for other enterprises. If there is no clear business case to use it, then it should not be used.

Call to Action

Understand any technology you want to leverage, in the cloud or out. This is not a race to determine who can build the coolest and most innovative systems the fastest; it's a race to see who can provide innovation that results in the most value to the business.

We need to deal with all technology a bit differently than many of us do today. Technology needs to be evaluated on its usefulness and its ability to bring value to the business. Often, this is easier said than done.

I realize that many of you are often put in positions where the crowd chooses to do something in specific ways, using specific technologies that they believe are innovative and game changing. The use of AI, for example.

AI is useful for many use cases; it's not useful for all use cases. The misapplication of AI bleeds millions of dollars from enterprises each year. The technology fails to bring any value, and it's often misaligned to the needs of the application or system. Even more often, the mistake is never caught until after (or long after) the system is built and deployed. It becomes something that is likely considered a "success," but is underoptimized to a point that it bleeds millions of dollars each year, and no one is the wiser. Don't be those people.

Chapter 5

Containers, Container Orchestration, and Cloud Native Realities

Please give me some good advice in your next letter. I promise not to follow it.

— Edna St. Vincent Millay

In this chapter, we take on the concepts of containers and container orchestration, which currently refer to Docker-style containers and Kubernetes container orchestration for the most part. Today's *containers* definition is closest to the way Docker defined them a few years ago, which came from the concept of containerization that has been around for decades. *Container orchestration,* simply put, is the ability to take groupings of containers and run them in parallel so that they can do more at the same time. Kubernetes is currently the most popular mechanism for container orchestration and clustering.

We define containers along with container orchestration in greater detail later in this chapter. We also review the term *cloud native*, along with the varying definitions that have confused me and many others. However, the fundamental concepts of containers could prove invaluable when all is said and done.

There is more hype around containers, container orchestration, and cloud native than any other topic at the time of writing this book, so I suspect many of you turned directly to this chapter. I also suspect these concepts will outlive the hype and become foundational to how we build and deploy cloud solutions. We're further down the road with container technologies, developers like them, and we're successful with them.

However, there are several issues to consider, trade-offs that many have not yet encountered. This book continues its role as the dissonant buzzkill around issues we'll soon face, again giving you the full and complete story rather than just blindly chasing the hype.

Containers

Let's skip yet another comparison of containers and virtual machines (VMs); you can find that information in many other places. Instead, let's look at specific values that containers bring to the cloud computing party and why you might want to leverage containers along with container orchestration. Keep in mind that containers are nothing new. Like most current technology, they're built on past technological innovations and use cases that led to the industry trusting today's containers as desired application development and deployment mechanisms.

The definition of containers started with a few PhD theses and IEEE articles, and then J2EE containers as the Web and Java grew to allow Java to scale. J2EE is an open standard based around the Java programming language that defines how containers are to be created and executed using any J2EE application server. Many of the benefits of J2EE technology are in the containers you see around today, including the ability to provide clustering for scalability and reliability benefits.

As mentioned earlier, the Docker set of Platform as a Service (PaaS) products most closely follow the current definition of containers. So, the core benefits of containers as they exist today include the delivery of

- **Consistent and isolated environments.** You create a platform within a platform that is the same no matter what platform or what cloud it runs on. Because the applications and sometimes the data are isolated, they can be consistently leveraged without regard for the native operating system host where the container runs (see Figure 5-1).

- **Cost-effectiveness.** The open-source evolution of containers and container orchestration along with economical tools and processes make containers more cost effective versus other technologies that provide the same features, such as portability and scalability. Note that cost effective does not mean less expensive. We cover more about costs later.

- **Fast deployment.** Containers and container orchestration provide consistent ways to test and deploy containers on cloud and non-cloud platforms.

- **Portability.** This is the big selling point. Containers can run across different platforms that support containers. Thus, you should be able to write an application once, deploy it as a container or set of containers, and that application should be portable across many different cloud-based platforms.

- **Repeatability and automation.** The development process is consistent from container to container, including many of the same tool types of skills.

- **Flexibility.** The platform is very customizable, allowing developers to take containers in as many different directions as needed to accommodate the requirements of the business.

- **Wide support.** Containers have a huge ecosystem of third-party providers for everything from container-based databases to container-based security. You can almost always find a solution that you don't need to develop yourself.

Containers are not very difficult to understand as an architecture. Consider Figure 5-1, which defines the basic structure of a Docker container. This includes the application that resides and runs in the container, binaries and libraries (Bins/Libs) that support the runtime, and even an OS within the container that provides basic services that it passes on to the host operating systems.

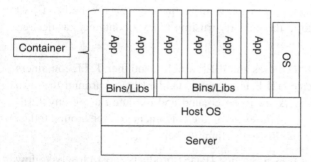

FIGURE 5-1 Containers leverage a wide variety of architectures. However, most provide isolation, meaning that they can operate as a separate operating system and platform inside of several host operating systems, such as those provided by cloud platforms. Of course, leveraging container orchestration layers for clustering operations can provide scalability and redundancy.

Containers need a host operating system to run, which can be on a cloud provider or not, and some sort of processing to support the host operating system, including basic infrastructure such as storage, compute, or networking, anything that traditional processes require to function. The idea of a container is to provide a layer of abstraction between the native operating systems, the native cloud provider, and the application and data that define the business solution.

This container mechanism supplies a consistent and isolated runtime environment that allows for portability, which was the initial selling point of containers. However, this portability soon led to the understanding that containers could be much more. Indeed, they can provide an enhanced runtime environment for applications that can be better than a standard OS, including the ability to cluster containers using container orchestration layers, such as Kubernetes, that provide automation and the ability to scale. And that's why containers are popular today and will be long after this book is published.

What Works

For the most part, containers deliver good support to the development community during the move to cloud computing. With containers providing a base architecture, they changed the way we think about software development in the cloud as container orchestration and Kubernetes provided mechanisms for scalability and reliability. The encouraging part is that containers were more of a grass-roots movement built on open-source origins. Thus, there were no big-name backers of containers trying to sell them as "their solution." However, some of the larger brands did jump in feet first to promote container and container orchestration. Those were the smarter players. Others saw no obvious way to make money and ignored containers. Those players ended up doing serious catchup later in the market evolution, mostly by selling containers and container orchestration as public cloud services.

Containers now provide a sound development and deployment technology for the cloud, which in turn promotes the use of cloud-based platforms. Given their impact on the marketplace, we can consider containers a success. Indeed, the "cloud native" movement, as we discuss later in this chapter, was largely built on containers, container orchestration (Kubernetes), and micro services. All are tightly coupled technologies.

So, the core list of what containers make work includes

- A standard development and deployment platform for applications.

- Built-in application portability approaches. While not perfect, containers seem to provide better portability.

- Cost-effective solutions. Containers are usually less expensive than traditional development and deployment technology.

- A large ecosystem of technologies that support containers such as databases, storage, backup and recovery, and security, many of which are now several generations old.

Containers: What Doesn't Work

The downside of leveraging containers includes issues around their rapidly increasing popularity, and thus the hype that surrounds containers. Like any other technology, containers are not right for all applications. Existing systems need to be carefully analyzed before they get "containerized." Remember the old adage: Just because you can doesn't mean you should.

Today the core downside of containers is the overapplication of container development and the over-porting of existing applications to containers. The reality is that containers are contraindicated for many applications and application types. However, to date, some businesses saw their way clear to spend twice as much moving an application to containers as they spent to develop the application in the first place. They also chased the benefit of portability when the application was unlikely to ever move from its current host platform. Moreover, they did not understand that to truly take advantage of what containers have to offer means a complete rearchitecture of the application, which they typically didn't do.

Of course, the mistakes extend to net new applications as well, or new applications that leverage containers as their development approach of choice. Again, many applications won't find advantages with container-based development. As we cover in the next section, enterprises could spend as much as four times the money to build the same application if container-based development and deployment are used versus more traditional methods. Moreover, the end product could cost more to operate by using more cloud-based resources, such as storage and compute. In many of these situations, containers were force fit due to the decision makers being motivated by the hype surrounding containers, not understanding the business problems, or not caring about the problems, or all three.

So, here's what doesn't work (or rarely works) with containers:

- Listening to hype reasons, and not business reasons.

- Overstating the benefits, such as portability.

- Not considering the operational costs.

- Underestimating the amount of time and money needed to move an existing application to a container.

- Not designing an existing application or a net new application as a purpose-built containerized application.

- Being able to forecast future costs based on the short life cycle of a container.

- Failing to account for the increased price of container development, deployment, and operations talent due to its popularity.

Container: Cost Considerations

The obvious key to figuring out what will and won't work is to determine the cost of leveraging containers. This includes the cost of development, deployment, and operations. Consider these costs against more traditional and commodity-type costs for similar development, deployment, and operations. The gap between these two choices is the "container tax." It's the additional money you'll spend just to leverage containers.

Make sure the benefits outweigh the costs. Containers are a good architectural choice for the right projects. However, consider the benefits you want versus the benefits you need with a clear eye. Are the odds high, medium, or low that your business will use a hyped tech's costly but nice-to-have features? There should be at least a medium to high probability that the enterprise will see a return on its investment in any technology.

Portability, for example, is something that many believe is a great feature to have in their back pocket because it removes the risk of provider lock-in. Let's say you leverage a cloud provider using an application that's tightly coupled to the cloud provider's services and APIs. If the cloud provider raises prices, or lowers the quality of services, or if the platform is no longer a good fit for other reasons, a tightly coupled application will require additional costs and development time to port the application, and that translates into business risk.

An application that runs within containers and is actually built using containers provides better portability. That puts the application in a better, more portable state that can be easily and cheaply moved to another cloud provider.

However, it's rarely a clearcut choice. Applications that leverage containers cost about 40 percent more to build. Container development prices are higher, as are the tools and technology prices, and, on average, it just takes more time to build an application using containers compared to more traditional approaches and tooling. Moreover, containers cost about 20 percent more to operate on a public cloud provider. These are costs you hope will be justified due to the lock-in risk they avoid, which should provide the ability to quicky move from cloud to cloud without a great deal of cost. But you must weigh these extra costs against the likelihood of that move ever occurring.

The cost issues with containers are not only around the costs to build them; they're not that much more. It's the increased costs to operate them ongoing. That means you need a solid business reason to leverage containers in the first place.

When I'm called into projects after containers are preselected as the development and deployment technology of choice, I usually discover that few if any of the team's reasons to leverage containers justify their use for either net new or the "containerization" of existing applications. This leads to many frowny faces when I make the unpopular announcement that containers are contraindicated for the project. Unfortunately, in many cases, the teams move forward with containers despite my feedback and just ignore the extra cost of development and operations. Of course, containerized or not, the application works just fine. However, one approach costs the business 20–40 percent more for the same application with ongoing cost overruns. Obviously, that expenditure could shortchange vital developments in other areas of the business.

More often, enterprises evaluate the use of containerization on an application-by-application basis, as it should be. Some applications will cost justify the use of containers, either net new or existing. Many will not. You need to cost justify every architectural or development decision to meet the core objective of supporting the needs of the business. The day we put technology trends over business needs is the day we should look for another job. Next week, next month, or next year, at some point you will be asked to cost justify your decisions. "All the cool kids were choosing containers" is the wrong answer.

Containers: Make the Tough Choices

Containers are an amazing technology and a concept that keeps evolving. It's an architectural pattern that allows us to compartmentalize applications and data for portability and design simplicity. It comes with the added benefit of providing "cloud scale" capabilities, which means we can scale to any number of users or processing loads and we can perform almost any number of operations.

But containers and container orchestration are not always slam-dunk choices. The business case must justify the need to leverage containers and include how it will benefit the business ongoing.

Although the trends will become a bit clearer as time progresses, containers are or will become a part of all cloud computing architecture. However, we should leverage a technology such as containers only when there is a definable business benefit.

Container Orchestration and Clustering

Again, let's not get into the details around container orchestration, which we typically refer to here as Kubernetes container orchestration. You can go other places to find more detail on the topics of containers and container orchestration, or even entire books written on these topics. Instead, let's have a pragmatic discussion about the issues you need to consider with the use of this technology. However, know that references here to container orchestration include Kubernetes clustering services.

Initially, there were a few container orchestration players. Now, almost everyone is on the Kubernetes bandwagon, and for good reasons. As mentioned earlier, the Kubernetes platform is also open source, providing core services for container scheduling and creating and operating container clusters; it's well designed, tested on public cloud providers that need to scale; and it has a large ecosystem of third-party products that provide everything from databases to security to operations administration.

My intent is not to push a specific container orchestration tool here. It's more important to understand the concept of container orchestration and how it may or may not fit before even considering its use. Kubernetes provides a backdrop for the explanations of that concept, and it's currently the container orchestration tool of choice for today's container development projects.

Too often cloud architects move to technologies such as Kubernetes because of good press and popularity. Kubernetes is even offered by most cloud providers on demand. However, they end up spending more money and time than required, and that hurts the business. Worst case, you get found out and fired. The more likely scenario is that you just built something that diminished the value of the business. Pull off many more of those mistakes and you'll end up looking for another job because your enterprise will sink under excessive IT spending and the lack of value returned to the business. Remember our teachings from Chapter 1, "How 'Real' Is the Value of Cloud Computing?"

For all practical purposes, container orchestration (which includes the use of nodes and clusters, see Figure 5-2) provides each container with the ability to virtually execute in its own private operating system rather than leverage static hardware and partitions. Many people compare containers with virtual machines, such as those offered by VMware and others. However, they are very different animals. Containers do not require a static partition of compute, storage, and memory to function. Consequently, the administrators are able to deploy a bunch of containers on servers without having to concern themselves with the limitations of physical hardware such as memory.

Kubernetes uses container orchestration and clustering systems that can launch, manage, and kill containers with ease on any number of platforms (see Figure 5-2). Although we're talking about container orchestration and clustering in the abstract, common patterns are beginning to emerge and will likely continue to emerge, such as

- A slave and master relationship between a control node or nodes, which are often called the master nodes and the slave nodes.

  - The master nodes oversee the container clusters, such as clusters that deal with scheduling and provide API access to the master node, which basically oversees the nodes that do the work.

  - The slave nodes carry out the execution of containers and manage them during the operational state on the platforms they are assigned to run on. In the slave nodes, containers are launched and killed based on support requirements from the master node. Slave nodes functionally allow the many containers in the cluster to work together around a programmed task.

- A container cluster is a dynamic system that places and manages containers, grouped together in pods, running on nodes, along with all the interconnections and communication channels. You can consider a cluster as a grouping of containers that together carry out a task by either replicating containers that do the same thing, allowing for scalability by distribution, *or* they may do different things. Of course, this capability depends on the needs for the application/solution you're looking to build using this technology.

- Other services such as security, databases, and governance are carried out inside and outside of the container orchestration layer. This capability provides developers with the advantages of plugging in whatever service they believe is the best fit for their container orchestration solution.

- This model supports (of course) fine-grained distribution. Indeed, containers can execute on any number of platforms; you could run 10 container instances on one platform and perhaps 4 on another. The number you use depends on what you need those containers to do, and then you can mix and match the containers and platforms to meet your exact needs.

- Scalability and resiliency are another benefit of this architecture, enabling technology, and deployment approach. You can program orchestration layers to automatically launch additional slave nodes and containers within those nodes to handle a dynamically increasing workload. The same mechanism can also work through partial outages by failing over to another slave node, or it can launch additional slave nodes to replace the nodes in outage.

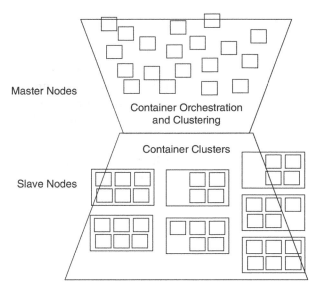

FIGURE 5-2 Container orchestration provides the ability to run many different or like containers in clusters that provide better scalability and flexibility. Container orchestration can support most platforms, most clouds, and most application development requirements. However, as with any technology, there is a right and wrong time to leverage orchestration. Understand the trade-offs before you embark on a business problem-solving journey with this technology.

Figure 5-3 looks at how a container orchestration system functions as an architecture. You can see that they all use a hierarchy of master nodes that manage slave nodes, which manage the container instances, including those that are running the business solutions. The solutions can include databases, applications, and security, and can operate across any number of platforms that support the execution of the containers.

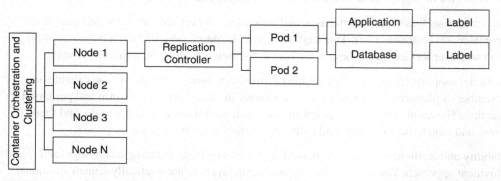

FIGURE 5-3   Container orchestration and clustering typically work by using a hierarchy of nodes or actors that can work from the higher-level controllers, the masters, to the lower-level slaves that carry out the work at the direction of the master. Although you'll see variations of this structure (depending on which technology you leverage), most container and orchestration solutions (such as Kubernetes) work in much the same way.

You also need to consider the value of declarative infrastructure programming. Declarative programming approaches just worry about the "what" we want to do or carry out in the program. This is you, the developer, declaring the desired state that is to be reached, which thus defines the output of the program without worrying about the steps needed to get to the desired output. In other words, you don't worry about "how" something is done. The steps needed to make it happen are abstracted from you, thus making your programming tasks much easier to get to a desired output and state.

This approach contrasts with imperative infrastructure programming, which, simply put, describes "how" an object state should change and the order in which those changes should execute to get to a desired output and state.

Container orchestration tools allow you to declare what the end state and output need to be, and they work out how to get to that state and solve problems they might encounter along the way. You can focus on "what" you need to solve a business problem and not "how" specifically to solve the problem.

Container Orchestration: What Works

Containers and container orchestrations generally live up to the expectations and hype. They offer cost-effective ways to build highly scalable and reliable applications on cloud or non-cloud platforms, and they provide portability within and between platforms. Vast ecosystems have grown around container orchestration, including security systems, databases, governance systems, operations systems, and other systems needed to meet specific requirements of an application that leverages this technology.

The ability to run containers that leverage redundancy, meaning either running cloned containers within a cluster manager or running more than a single cluster, provides both scalability and resiliency. Developers use containers to define an application that can solve business problems and then leverage container orchestration and clustering to effectively execute the containers and manage most aspects of the execution. Those magical capabilities are why most enterprises now choose container orchestration and clustering to build net-new cloud applications, as well as to redesign and rebuild applications to function on public clouds.

Of course, all this magic comes with trade-offs. Traditional development may still have more value over containers or container orchestration. Figure 5-4 depicts what most enterprises encounter when they adopt containers. The first trade-off is that, as mentioned earlier, containers cost more to build and deploy than traditional development approaches. It doesn't matter if the application is net new or an application that must be refactored to move to a public cloud platform. There are exceptions, of course, but they are not the rule.

On the magical side of the argument, the longer the containerized applications exist, the more business value they can create. This is often preceded by a dip in value for the containerized applications as enterprises go through an initial learning curve. Eventually, the enterprise will find the value drivers of the containerized applications, such as portability, scalability, and resiliency, and the recognized value inflects as you can see with the value curve container-based development in Figure 5-4. At the same time, traditional development-based applications slowly reduce in value over time, much as they did in the past.

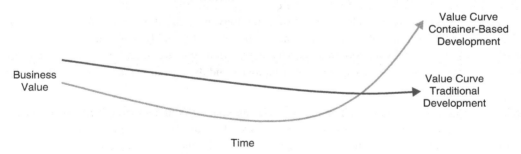

FIGURE 5-4 When comparing container-based development with or without orchestration and clustering, we must consider that the initial value is much lower due to the additional costs needed to build well-designed containerized applications. Over time the value increases and greatly surpasses that of traditional development approaches on clouds.

If you're sold on containers and the value they can bring to the business, first consider the added costs and then the longer-term benefits container-based development will likely bring. Many just assume that containers will be the best way to go. Perhaps, but the value this technology can bring will not be consistent from application to application. The values of portability, scalability, and resiliency are not the same for each application.

As a rule, container-based application development costs more and takes more time. You'll need skilled developers and architects to do a container-based application right versus more traditional approaches that we've leveraged for years. Do you have that talent on staff? One skill set is new; the other is not. New skills are usually more expensive to find, develop, and/or hire, and this is no different.

Keep an eye on the values when you do a business case. The additional build costs, staffing requirements, and learning curve of container-based applications remove value. Be prepared to put specific values on the benefits of scalability, portability, and resiliency. The value curve will determine if containers are worth it for your specific application or the enterprise itself. If you find the value, then containers will work for you.

What Doesn't Work

In two words, what doesn't work: operational complexity. Containers bring additional complexity, and that means you need abstraction and automation tools to deal with the complexity. This is not an unsolvable problem, but you need additional resources to run most containerized applications versus those that are more traditionally created.

Why? Containers and container orchestration systems are new platforms that must be managed in addition to existing platforms that may or may not reside on public clouds. Container systems are not more difficult to operate; many could be easier to use when you consider the available operations tools. It's that you must operate them in addition to the traditional systems, processes, and applications that still exist. This makes operations more complex, thus more involved and expensive to carry out.

In other words, containers are typically an additive technology, meaning it doesn't replace an existing technology. The containerized solutions require new skill sets and possibly new staff to operate and manage the new tools that will support containerized applications that are usually net new as well. As the numbers of moving parts rise, the amount of complexity and the cost of managing this complexity increase ongoing.

As the boom in container-based development and the number of container orchestration instances continue to rise, additive system issues will continue to fall away. However, today's containerized applications make things more complex; thus, operations will be more difficult and more costly for now.

Obviously, the complexity impact on your specific applications and business requirements will vary. Here we're talking about what's generally true without illustrating the myriad of exceptions. I urge you to do your own business cases to determine your specific impact. It's a wide variable.

Figure 5-5 shows what we currently see when it comes to complexity and the use of containers. As the number of container-based applications grows, with or without the use of container orchestration, the amount of complexity and the costs incurred from increased complexity rise as well. At a certain point between three to six years of operation, the complexity curve levels out and even begins to decline.

Again, this will happen as enterprises become more adept at managing their new container-based solutions, or when the traditional applications that must also be maintained retire and are removed as an operational responsibility. That's the good and bad news here: You must first endure the bad news on your journey to containerized solutions.

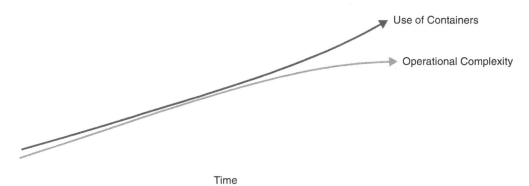

FIGURE 5-5 The more containers an enterprise leverages, the more complexity costs they must endure. Eventually, the enterprise learns how to deal with the additional complexity, and operational complexity levels out.

Other things that may be a downside of leveraging containerized solutions include finding the skills you need to build, deploy, and operate these solutions. Building containerized solutions correctly requires training and experience to make the right calls as to what technology to leverage. If they can't find the talent, many enterprises either settle for not-as-qualified developers and designers, or they delay moving to containers until the skills can be found. This approach often leads to additional costs and risk. In many instances, the skills acquisition issues around containers are not even considered as part of the cost/benefit analysis to determine whether the technology is a good fit for the business. That's not the way to find value for the business.

Container Orchestration: Cost Considerations

Much of what we called out earlier in the "Container: Cost Considerations" section of this chapter is applicable here as well. This includes the costs of skills, tools, and the time it takes to design and deploy a containerized application versus more traditional approaches. Your "container tax" may or may not be significant. Regardless, leveraging containers and container orchestration will cost you more than a traditional path.

So, let's look specifically at a few interesting container orchestration trends that affect costs. As you can see in Figure 5-6, as enterprises leverage more container orchestration such as Kubernetes, the costs are initially very high, but they decline over time.

It typically takes two to four years of container orchestration use until the costs decline enough to make it easier to define the hard values of using containers. As you may recall from Chapter 1, these hard costs are easy to understand, such as direct costs associated with operations and security. However, just as we defined in Chapter 1, the true benefit to the business is aligned more to the soft values, that is, the business abilities gained from the use of container technology. These new abilities include agility, compressed time-to-market, and innovation. These are all common soft values enterprises find with the use of containers and container orchestration.

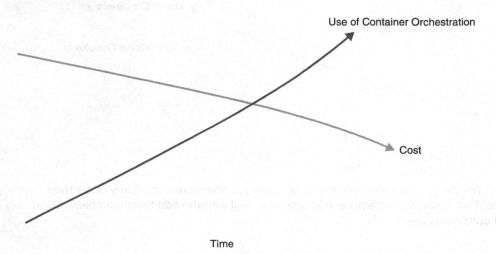

FIGURE 5-6 As the use of container orchestration increases, the relative costs should significantly drop.

It's important to understand the costs and the trade-offs of using container orchestration technology, which are depicted in Figure 5-6. The curve angles will vary depending on the type of business involved, the types of problems to solve, and the hard and soft values benefits for a particular business operation. It's the old "it depends" answer when it comes to costs, and how costs align with business value for each enterprise. This is an individual journey, but your best jumping-off point is to understand what's generally true, as outlined here.

Container Orchestration: Make Tough Choices

Following the crowd is often the easiest thing to do, but it's rarely the correct thing to do. Consider why IT exists in the first place: to bring value to the business. However, I've been in IT for a very long time, so I suspect that many of you are already off to containers and container orchestration and have not yet considered the business benefits of doing so. If that's you, you're not alone. In the old days I called this "management by magazine." Others call it "chasing the hype" to a technology because it's popular, without first considering the desired outcome.

It takes a bit of courage to understand the core purpose of leveraging any technology and how that technology stacks up with your business and technical requirements. If that technology does not fit, it takes more courage to push back on the hype and look for better solutions that will bring more value to the business.

Containers and container orchestration and clustering are valid solutions for many purposes and should always be considered not only for their direct value but also the value that they are likely to bring in the future. In many instances, they are the correct and optimized solution to leverage, but in some cases they are not. It's all about doing the up-front work to ensure that the right decisions are made, and your cloud solutions are as optimal as they possibly can be.

Cloud Native

Cloud native computing (or *cloud native*) is a buzzword term that means slightly different things to different people.

At first, most people referred to proprietary services as cloud native: If we leverage storage and compute cloud services on any public cloud provider, then those cloud services are native to the specific cloud provider that hosts those native services. Or, a native cloud service runs on a specific public cloud provider and nowhere else, and you must leverage that specific service under the terms provided by that public cloud provider.

With that interpretation, cloud native applications are applications that leverage native services on a specific cloud provider. The services are optimized for that provider by using the native cloud services. Applications that use those services are pretty much locked into that specific provider given that they leverage services that don't exist elsewhere on other clouds. So, in this context, cloud native allows us to create cloud native applications that are optimized for a specific cloud provider. The trade-off is easy portability to other providers. Let's call this the classic definition of cloud native.

As the term *cloud native* started to take off, several cloud and non-cloud vendors "cloud-washed" their marketing and proprietary products to hop on the cloud bandwagon. Confusion naturally arose as they stated that their products were either cloud native or could build cloud native things. Personally, I believe search engine optimization (SEO) was the real reason they used those cloud-washed terms without regard for the confusion that arose, or the reality that their technology often met no one's definition of cloud native. I call this the cloud-washed definition of cloud native.

A wider definition of cloud native recently emerged that seems to be the new normal. The Cloud Native Computing Foundation (CNCF) defines cloud native as "technologies [that] empower organizations to build and run scalable applications in modern, dynamic environments such as public, private, and hybrid clouds."[1] Or, perhaps better put, cloud native applications can be deployed across multiple cloud environments, which is core to the CNCF cloud native proposition. I call this the CNCF definition of cloud native.

I pulled a direct quote above, which I don't do often in this book. The purpose here is to show you how others define cloud native and allow you to come to your own conclusions. The goal is to define cloud

---

1 https://github.com/cncf/toc/blob/main/DEFINITION.md

native and its value in ways that you may be able to weaponize. Or, how to leverage cloud native to a pragmatic end when building and deploying cloud-based solutions.

What's the Right Definition of Cloud Native?

What concept should we be casing as solution developers when we build and deploy next-generation cloud computing systems? Or: What the hell *is* cloud native, and why should we care?

Given the way the term has evolved, and how it will likely continue to evolve, what definition describes the value that you can employ, and what technology stack does that definition promote? The original and cloud-washed definitions are still out there, and they're probably not what you're looking for when you consider cloud native development for your enterprise. Be sure you know exactly what you sign up for. Just as in the early days of cloud computing, where we experienced "cloud-washing," what is called cloud native may not be what you're seeking. It's perhaps the most overused and multimeaning term that I've seen in this industry.

Today's CNCF cloud native applications are built around containers, container orchestration, and microservices, and focus on the architecture of the applications more than the clouds they will deploy on. CNCF cloud native commoditizes public cloud providers by building applications above the clouds and then leveraging the public clouds as mere service providers to support the applications. This approach stands in contrast to the classic definition of cloud native that required building walled gardens within one provider's cloud that limits the types and selection of services you can use.

We'll use the CNCF definition of cloud native for the remainder of this chapter. It works with the larger idea that CNCF cloud native applications provide dynamic and scalable application attributes, functioning on many platforms that include public cloud providers, private clouds, and even traditional computing systems (legacy). The enabling technology stacks that CNCF cloud native promotes, as we stated previously, are containers, container orchestration, and microservices. The objective of leveraging this technology is to avoid cloud and platform lock-in.

The platforms in this CNCF architecture are foundational. However, foundational clouds don't typically provide services directly to the applications. Instead, you'll work through well-defined APIs that allow the underlying platforms, both cloud and traditional, to be abstracted away from the application. This provides better portability and should do so with very few trade-offs.

Figure 5-7 is a good representation of this idea. The top of the stack is where development, delivery, and deployment occur. Or, where the developers leverage a cloud native architecture. Moving down the stack, you'll notice that developers and applications communicate with the container and container orchestration layers using microservices. These microservices define discrete interfaces that developers and applications can consistently leverage. They also remove the applications from any dependency on a specific proprietary service because they consistently use the same APIs for any service the application may need. Containers and container orchestration services (clustering) carry out the heavy lifting of application processing, and they leverage the underlying platforms (cloud and not cloud) to provide the primitive platform services (storage, compute, databases, networking, security, and so on).

With this architecture, the public cloud providers (all platforms really) are no longer at the center of the architecture but are mere compute and storage service providers.

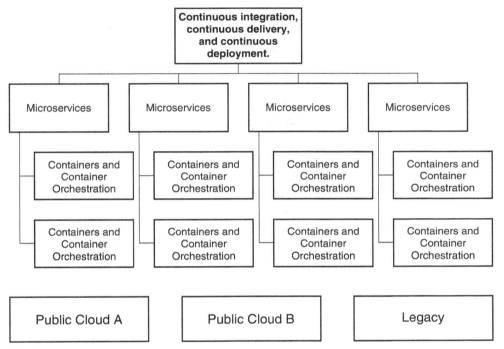

FIGURE 5-7 CNCF cloud native moves the application architecture above the public cloud, public clouds, and legacy systems to promote the best performance with better portability. This architecture is conceptual but promotes the use of "open" application development and deployment using a DevOps process and toolchain that leverages continuous integration, delivery, and deployment. In turn, DevOps processes leverage microservice interfaces with containers and container clusters that carry out the application functions using underlying cloud platforms.

This version of a cloud native architecture is nothing new. When containers and microservices came onto the scene several years ago, developers and application designers figured out that this version of a cloud native architecture was the best path. Thus, before this was labeled as a cloud native architecture, it was a best practice. There is no magic here, and this version of a cloud native architecture does come with certain advantages, including

- The use of open systems throughout; thus, this solution tends to be more cost effective.

- Portability is built into this version of a cloud native architecture; you don't have to constantly worry about leveraging vendor proprietary features that will officially lock in your application.

- Scalability is built into this architecture as well, allowing container orchestration to scale the applications as needed, without changing the underlying architecture to accommodate scalability. It's always there.

- The use of public clouds as just services providers that are largely decoupled from your application deployment means you can switch out public clouds that do not provide the best pricing and/or do not behave in the best ways. While this makes cloud providers a bit nervous around the future impact of this version of a cloud native architecture, the reality is that the cloud providers will likely sell more services without having to invest in their platform's customer interface. The cloud providers no longer deal with the user interfaces, but instead the cloud providers deal directly with the APIs that are native to a specific cloud provider.

Portability Argument

The portability benefits of being cloud native and building cloud native applications are the first things you'll hear about from those who support this type of cloud native architecture and technology stack. As I mentioned previously, because we abstract the cloud providers from the applications using a layer of technology that deals with the differences, the applications are truly portable. We can move them from cloud provider to cloud provider at will, when needed, and this architectural approach supports whatever business needs to do.

There are a few downsides to this argument.

First, few applications ever leave the platforms they were developed on. We like the potential of built-in portability, and this benefit usually comes up many times when we design applications and pick the architecture. However, for all the time and money we will spend to avoid lock-in, that benefit may never materialize.

Second, is the cloud native (CNCF version) stack not a platform unto itself? We define portability as the ability to move between cloud providers by leveraging a cloud native stack to abstract the cloud providers from the application. Although we can indeed move our applications between cloud providers somewhat easily by not being locked into the provider, we're still locked into the architecture we selected, in this case, a cloud native architecture. If you need to move to another architecture, say a proprietary architecture that provides some new key features that would bring value to the business, you'll need to rewrite most of the systems and subsystems built for your cloud native architecture.

Most would chuckle at this scenario, considering this CNCF architecture is built to be portable across cloud providers and the original goal was to avoid lock-in. However, having done this for many years, more than once I've made application design and architecture decisions to avoid vendor lock-in only to find that the architecture and development approach I chose led me to a configuration that was hard to move to another vendor's configurations.

Finally, it costs more to avoid lock-in. I cover this later in greater detail, but portability does not come cheap. A term used among developers is a "portability tax," or the extra money you'll spend to get something that minimizes lock-in. Note: We use the word *minimize*, and not *eliminate* because lock-in can never be eliminated, just reduced, no matter what architectural approach you leverage.

Optimization Argument

Optimization of this CNCF architecture, or other architectural approaches, will provide the best performance and functionality with the smallest price tag. Thus, we need proof that this architecture is the best approach with the understanding that it's the closest we can get to being fully optimized.

There is less historical evidence around optimization related to cloud native architecture. However, we know enough about optimization itself that cloud native costs in time and or money should factor into the decision-making process to determine whether a cloud native architecture and cloud native applications are truly the best choice for the enterprise. Business value is always the top objective.

Figure 5-8 shows our optimization curve again, this time with the added dimension of cost in the curve moving up and to the right. Note that we typically have a sweet spot of investment being made. Too little investment shows less optimization, and thus less value is returned to the business. On the optimization side of the curve, we can see that too much investment reduces the value returned to the business because we spent (and often continue to spend) too much on the technology and that dilutes the value. Thus, you want to target a point in the middle where the investment made at a specific level optimizes its business value.

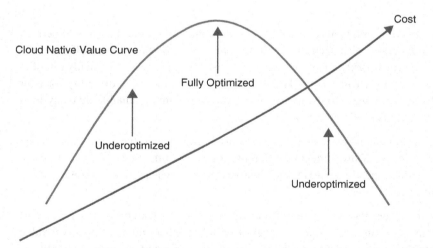

FIGURE 5-8 When considering the value of any architecture, including a cloud native architecture, you need to look at optimization as you increase the investment. You'll find a point along the curve that's close to being fully optimized. Obviously, that's where you want to be.

Although this value curve relates specifically to cloud native architecture and application development, it can be applied to any number of technology solution patterns. It's not about finding where technology is fully optimized when compared to the investment, but how does the curve compare against other development and architectural options, even proprietary cloud provider development that leverages proprietary tools and deployment platforms? Also consider architectures that are more in the center, with a mix of proprietary and open technologies that you can mix and match as needed. Most cloud-based solutions fall in the center. They allow you to mix and match technologies to find the right solution, but you must do so on a particular vendor's platform.

We can't really talk about optimization without talking about the cost of the overall investment (covered next). But the architectural choices really come down to your application requirements, as related to your business requirements, and how they should fit together to form a whole. There are a lot of technology and architectural choices out there, cloud native and many others. Don't fall into the trap of just moving along with the crowd, no matter how compelling the arguments are to use some hyped approach or technology. Doing so will quickly lead you to underoptimized solutions, and your decisions could easily end up damaging the business. Don't be that person.

Cost Argument

Believe it or not, cost is often overlooked when selecting the best development and architectural approaches. Or, should I say, we overlook the actual costs versus the known costs? It's easy to consider the hard costs, or what investment it will take to put an architecture and technology stack into production over the years. The soft costs often prove more valuable in the long view, but they are more difficult to identify at the outset.

For example, using a cloud native architecture to build a set of applications could provide 20 percent more agility over a five-year period. That scenario might translate into a $20 million windfall for the business because the business can quickly adapt to market and customer changes, and quickly retool to build products that are better aligned with the market. The trouble is that the value of agility for your specific business is rarely easy or simple to determine. However, this is more valuable than any hard value that you will define and thus needs special attention.

Figure 5-9 shows our friend the value curve again, this time looking at soft values over fully loaded cost. As we model different levels of investment, a different amount of soft value comes back to the business, values such as agility, speed-to-market, and innovation, that will peak and then bend the value curve at the point of overinvestment.

Several indicators determine where the value drop-off occurs as the soft value curve crosses the cost curve. First, the project hits the saturation point at a level of spending where no additional soft value benefits can be returned to the business just by spending more money. Second, if spending continues to rise, soft value drops significantly from that point. This is a classic case of tossing good money after bad. The chart displayed in Figure 5-9 follows the same pattern as the optimization curve in Figure 5-8. You'll see this pattern repeat as we attempt to define something that is nearly fully optimized. Also, remember that soft values can be 50 times that of hard values, in terms of what's returned to the business.

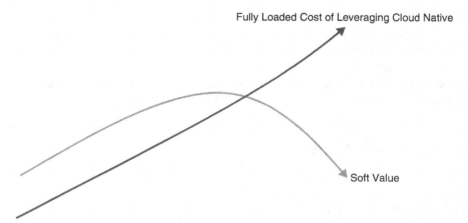

FIGURE 5-9 Again, you need to look at the behavior of the soft value curve over different levels of investment, cloud native as well as other architectures and approaches. There is significant soft value drop that occurs at a certain point in spending, and you need to predetermine that point.

Figure 5-10 looks at the behavior of hard value returned to the business at different levels of spending. Unlike soft values, hard values mirror the spending or cost curve with an increase in value at the end of the curve, likely from discounts the business receives by spending more on something. For example, our hard costs include the underlying cloud services that support a cloud native architecture. Most cloud providers offer volume discounts as those support costs increase over time, which is reflected in the "hard value" curve that becomes steeper about two-thirds through the curve.

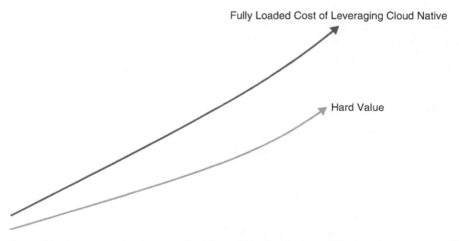

FIGURE 5-10 In general, when looking at the behavior of the hard value over different levels of investment, the more you spend, the more you save. Most technology investments embrace economies of scale with volume discounts.

Hard value is soft value's boring little brother. While you can track 10–20 percent savings over time in hard cost savings, soft value is the real core multiplier you need to consider. As I already mentioned, it often brings 50 to 100 times more value back to the business for the money invested. The trick is to understand how to model soft value for your specific use case and how to find the best optimized point for your particular type of business. You must also determine which solution offers the best optimization point of many possible solutions, including cloud native and other technology stacks.

Technology Meets Reality

It doesn't matter if the best optimized solution is the least popular solution. It's your responsibility to optimize value brought back into the business using whatever approach and technology will best fit the solution parameters. Keep this in mind as you drive through the more hyped approaches and technologies, such as containers, container orchestration, and everything that's employed using a CNCF cloud native architecture.

I'm often taken aback by those who make architecture and technology decisions before they understand what problems need to be solved. This trend seems to be getting worse as we're pushed to make faster decisions, and most solutions can be made to work at various levels of underoptimization.

The "It works" method of evaluating success is why many businesses can't find value in their technological investments, and why no one seems to understand how the "cloud thing" could cost more than originally projected, and or why it can't return its expected value. The cloud technology itself is not the issue; it's the fact that someone picked the wrong technology. The business requirements pointed to a different configuration and/or solution, so now the business must suffer through a fix or, more likely, just deal with the problems and inefficiencies ongoing.

Improper technology decisions with cloud migration or digital transformations will weaken the business over time, and eventually force a merger with or acquisition by a business that better understands how to do this technology stuff. This is where technology meets reality and where we need to focus most of the work to improve how we weaponize technology for the business.

Call to Action

Understand what you're getting into before you commit to a hyped technology like containers, container orchestration, and cloud native architecture and applications development. While the technology presented in this chapter represents only a fraction of the cloud technology you'll need to consider for future projects, the purpose here is to go through the value and costs of each technology, as well as learn how to apply this process to other technologies that exist now or may arise in the future. This knowledge will help you avoid the urge to follow the popular technology crowd like lemmings off a cliff. Moving with the crowd is always less important than first solving your specific business problems.

Again, this is about your business first and foremost. Nobody (not even me) can pick a solution for your business without first having a deep understanding of the problems the business needs to solve. This is about returning value to the business through the effective use of technology that best fits the solution patterns. You need to make that commitment now and have the courage to stand up to others who would rather chase the hype than the right solutions. I wish you luck.

Chapter | **6**

The Truths Behind Multicloud That Few Understand

Get your facts first, then you can distort them as you please.

— *Mark Twain*

Multicloud can make things much easier for a business, or it can become just another thing to be fixed, or it can be the thing that puts the business out of business. This chapter delivers factual multicloud information without the added spin from cloud and technology providers. We focus less on what multiclouds are but on what they should be, and less on what doesn't work but what does. We also impart some pragmatic advice about how enterprises can find true business value in these complex monstrosities.

The goal is to find the best business value rather than the buzziest technology. Although the best route to success could initially cost more, it can take you to a place where the business value is obvious. It could even change your business from fair to good, and then to great, and then to a disruptive innovator that can lead your market. The alternative is to become a fast follower, where mediocrity becomes the dubious reward.

The presence of multicloud in all our futures makes this perhaps the most important chapter in the book.

Hybrid Cloud Realities

To understand where multiclouds come from, let's look at the first complex cloud computing architectures that emerged back in 2008 in the form of hybrid clouds. Industry and government organizations initially defined hybrid clouds as public and private clouds paired to work together to provide the best of both worlds. You could have a private cloud running in your data center, perhaps hosting sensitive data or applications that required specialized processing. You could also run applications and store information using the exponential resources of a public cloud provider. The idea was that you could move applications and data sets in and between private and public clouds as a hybrid cloud configuration, and your hybrid cloud would ride off into the IT sunset, ready to deal with any business problems you tossed at it.

Unfortunately, that's not the way it worked out. Private clouds proved to be the Achilles' heel of hybrid clouds that eventually drove today's shift to multicloud. As you can see in Figure 6-1, interest in private clouds shrank relative to the growth of public clouds. This happened for a few reasons. Initially, both had parity of features, such as just providing basic storage and compute. Many private clouds were open-source systems that could not keep up with the explosion of features and functions in public clouds. Public clouds quickly grew to what they are today: one-stop shopping for most IT needs, including storage, compute, analytics, AI, IoT, management, governance, security, and…you get the idea. It just made no sense to move to a private cloud when all indicators pointed toward that becoming obsolete technology.

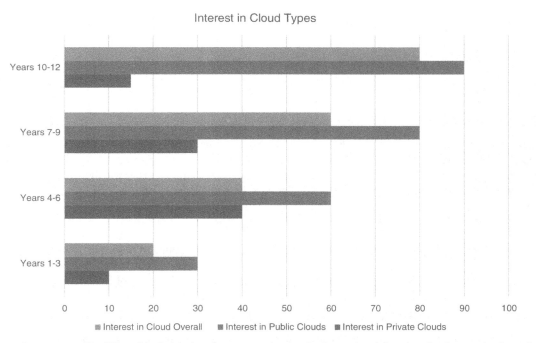

FIGURE 6-1 Traditional hybrid clouds were paired private and public clouds. An explosion of features and capabilities in public clouds caused interest to shrink in traditional hybrid clouds when the private clouds could not keep up. Meanwhile, the interest in public cloud computing continued its steady growth.

Of course, the old school naysayers pointed out potential public cloud security issues, claiming that in no world would their data be more secure running on hardware they did not own. That concern proved to be unfounded. As more R&D dollars were spent on public cloud-based security versus that of traditional systems or private clouds, it became less secure to host data within traditional data centers versus public cloud providers. Public cloud providers then and now get more R&D love from the technology providers and thus have the best of most systems, including security. So, with the security factor no longer working for the private cloud argument, interest in private clouds fell relative to public cloud growth that still dominates today (see Figure 6-2).

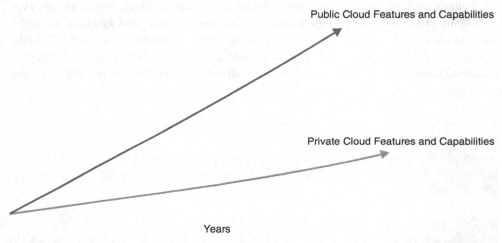

Public Cloud Features and Capabilities

Private Cloud Features and Capabilities

Years

FIGURE 6-2   Private and public clouds had feature parity when cloud computing first became a thing. Over the years, public clouds outspent private clouds on R&D. Most private clouds are open-source systems sold by integrators and small cloud companies, whereas private clouds are multibillion-dollar mega companies. Naturally, the momentum was on the side of public clouds.

Despite its decline, we did learn a few things from the use of hybrid cloud computing:

- The choice of services (private and public clouds) provides the advantage of flexibility. If one service does not work, the other likely will. One can back up the other, and we can also leverage them for different purposes.

- The ability to choose different services for different purposes means we're not locked in to one specific cloud platform. We can mix and match private and public cloud services to provide the most agility and flexibility.

- Hybrid clouds make operations much more complex. We needed to replicate tools across private and public cloud platforms, and we had to maintain two different sets of skills in the organization. Operations were more costly and complex.

Hybrid cloud computing is still around today, but it has evolved. Today, any local system that's paired with a single public cloud is called a hybrid cloud whether it's a true private cloud or a mainframe; it doesn't seem to matter. The idea is that a private and public cloud work together to process applications and store data. Although it's not like the earlier definitions of hybrid cloud, it's a legitimate architectural pattern that's perfectly fine to use today.

The Move to Plural Public Clouds

So, why the sudden move to multicloud? While it might seem as though multicloud suddenly showed up as a new cloud computing concept overnight, it's been steadily growing and evolving for years. Like most things that become famous, it didn't just happen overnight. People just finally noticed.

I have a saying about multicloud: Whether it's found on purpose or by accident, multicloud is an inevitable reality for most enterprises.

In its most simplistic form, multicloud leverages more than a single cloud provider, meaning two or more public cloud providers. While private clouds can be part of a multicloud, most multiclouds leverage multiple public cloud providers such as AWS, Microsoft, and Google. Or even those three and Oracle and Alibaba. Don't fall into the semantic arguments that are taking place around the definition of multicloud; it's just any cloud deployment that leverages more than one public cloud provider.

In the beginning of multicloud, many enterprises leveraged a single cloud provider and slid into multicloud almost by accident. There were always exceptions being made as developers and end users found some vital public cloud service that was not part of the preferred cloud provider's services for the enterprise. Ta-da. The enterprise became a multicloud user. In many of my clients' enterprises, IT denied that the other cloud(s) existed. A network scan will reveal other clouds in use on the enterprise network. Ta-da again. The enterprise has a multicloud.

Multicloud followed the same pattern of adoption we saw in the "IT Showdown" movement when employees used their company credit cards to adopt SaaS-based systems, typically to circumvent corporate IT because they were sick of hearing "No." This is how many companies first entered the cloud. IT got dragged in kicking and screaming when their outlaw users adopted cloud for them and then pushed the resulting problems back to IT when administration and security of those SaaS clouds got too hard and too costly.

Adoption of multicloud followed much the same patterns, but now IT is usually aware that it's happening, either on purpose or not. "Not on purpose" means that a series of exceptions were made to leverage cloud services from other IaaS cloud providers other than the IT-set standard. So, Cloud A could be an enterprise's primary provider, typically with many past press releases to promote the "partnership." The new normal is that the number of other IaaS public cloud providers in use is in double digits. Moreover, clouds are still being added to the mix because specialty cloud services are needed that the existing cloud service provider can't supply for one reason or another.

Okay, yes, it's safe to admit that we're all multicloud. Now what?

Obviously, "on purpose" is the way you should adopt any technology, multicloud included. It shouldn't just happen, but instead unfold around a well-thought-out plan that includes sub-plans about how to deal with security, governance, operations, and so on, across each cloud within a multicloud. If you fail to create and follow a plan, you'll likely have to solve the same problems twice. Once in quick reaction to an urgent need, such as a security breach or outage. Twice when you realize a comprehensive multi-cloud plan is required to deal with the complexity and heterogeneity that multicloud brings. We cover the downsides and the upsides of leveraging multicloud later in this chapter.

Best-of-Breed?

The typical battle cry of those who need to leverage clouds other than the approved enterprise standard is the fact that they need to leverage best-of-breed technology. This means a technology is identified as the most optimal solution for a specific problem or set of problems. For example, a special-purpose database built specifically for manufacturing that's needed to support a manufacturing application. Or a proprietary medical application and database that's needed for internal R&D. Or it might be a system built to provide current information about legal regulations and business requirements within certain territories and/or countries. These products are typically found within the walled garden of one cloud provider, but not others.

The pushback is, if we allow exceptions, then we'll end up with a "complex mess" of many different cloud services that must be maintained with the right staff skills to support them. They also need to be secured and governed to meet the standard of the company, and perhaps laws and regulations.

If the previous arguments and costs are presented prior to leveraging a "nonstandard" cloud, and the ROI proves the exception benefits greatly outweigh the costs, then the exception should be made. Unfortunately, most users who need the exceptions don't realize the domino effect of their choices, and they instead tend to ask for forgiveness rather than permission. Hello, complexity.

Because complexity is the primary downside of leveraging more than one cloud, this chapter suggests ways to mediate complexity and make multiclouds work in cost-optimized ways. This is perhaps the most important lesson that I can convey in this book.

To understand the reasons we leverage best-of-breed technology, it's best to look at two common problems and solutions, as depicted in Figure 6-3 and Figure 6-4. In Figure 6-3, it's assumed that those who build innovative solutions within an enterprise are limited to cloud services from one specific provider. As the need for innovation rises, the ability to leverage best-of-breed technology is limited to the cloud services included with the "preferred cloud provider." In turn, this limits the "Business Inno-vation Supported" and diminishes the level of "Business Value Created" as a direct result of limiting the use of best-of-breed technology—in this case, cloud services that are not offered by an enterprise's preferred cloud provider.

Of course, the preferred cloud provider may also offer the best-of-breed services needed by the innovator, but this will not always be the case.

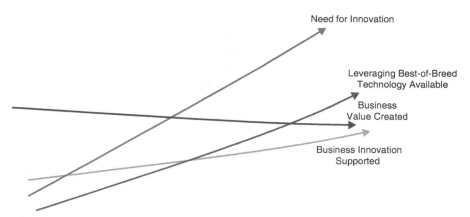

FIGURE 6-3   Leveraging a single public cloud provider limits the technology we can use. This leads to less optimized solutions than if we had access to more cloud services or best-of-breed technologies that could create more innovative solutions.

Figure 6-4 models a problem where the "Need for Innovation" is the same, but there are no limitations on the use of best-of-breed technology or, in this case, public cloud services from any public cloud on the market. This allows developers to find optimal cloud services for the problems they want to solve versus making do with services that happen to be available from a single IT-approved cloud provider. Thus, the ability to "Leverage Best-of-Breed Technology Available" raises the levels of "Business Innovation Supported" and, more importantly, increases "Business Value Created."

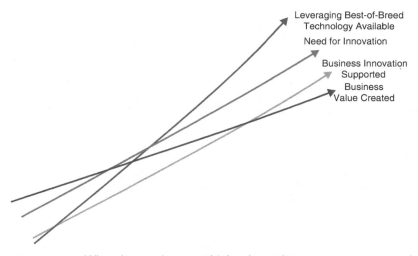

FIGURE 6-4   When leveraging a multicloud, you have access to more cloud services and thus more cloud technology, such as specialized analytics, AI, and high-speed computing. You can use whatever services you need to optimize your business solutions, which will support more innovation and thus grow business value. These are the primary reasons we leverage multicloud.

Of course, the specific business involved determines the amount of value available to create. Best-of-breed flexibility will result in the most benefit for companies that need unfettered innovation to increase business value. For instance, best-of-breed flexibility is highly valued by companies in the tech and financial services, where innovation can make or break an enterprise's ability to grow value in that sector. Best-of-breed flexibility will be less of a value driver for a tire manufacturing company that does not plan to change products or increase future capacity. Thus, we're back to the often-used answer: It depends.

Price

The price argument for multicloud is tougher to make. I've heard several variations of the rationale to leverage multicloud because of cost. They come down to

- **The ability to put yourself in a better position to negotiate with the public cloud providers.** Because there is an established relation with at least one other provider, you can threaten to give your business to that provider if the current provider doesn't come down in price or provide better terms.

- **The ability to leverage best prices for specific services as you need them, which allows you to compare prices in real time.** For example, if you need to leverage 100 terabytes of storage, you're automatically routed to the least-cost service that provides the same record of performance. Cloud service brokers (CSBs) automate this process for you. This can also automate specific cloud cost optimization, where an application load is rehosted with a mix of compute and storage services that are optimized cross cloud, which provides more possibilities for optimization because you're using two or more providers.

The reality is that most or all price benefits from leveraging multicloud are quickly eaten up by the additional cost of running a multicloud deployment. We cover that later in the chapter. The bottom line is that cross-cloud automation is not much of a benefit unless you have a specific way of leveraging multicloud to gain discounts that justify the time and cost of getting those discounts. Cost is a benefit that you should look at but is rarely the only reason enterprises move to multicloud.

Business Realities

As with any technology, multicloud needs to live up to some business realities. First, multicloud is more expensive than single cloud deployments for obvious reasons. As you can see in Figure 6-5, the more public clouds you deploy, the more it will cost:

- Operations require management of more moving parts (cloud services), so the cost of operations skyrockets as you obtain specialized skills and tooling.

- Cloud FinOps (Cloud financial management operations) also become more complex, and thus present missed opportunities for cost optimization across a multicloud.

■ Overly complex multicloud deployments increase security and outage risks, for which there is a clear cost.

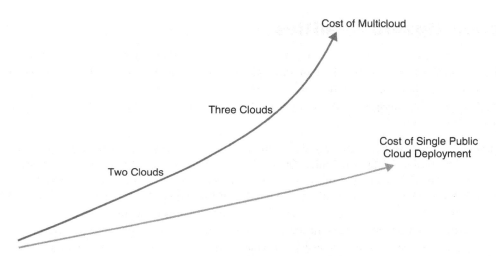

FIGURE 6-5 Even with complexity mediation, the cost of multicloud will always be higher. The added costs of operations, security, and heterogeneity also contribute to the cost of complexity. Base your case for multicloud on the soft values that multicloud can provide, such as support for innovation as presented in Figure 6-4.

Many are quick to point out that multicloud doesn't need to cost more if we properly account for operations, security, FinOps, and governance. While I agree with this statement in principle, the practical reality is that we can reduce the cost impact of multicloud, but we can't eliminate it. That's why I get concerned when I hear multicloud being promoted to save money. It doesn't. However, there are other factors to consider that can counteract or surpass the additional costs.

The ability to drive more innovation and speed within a business is the core reason to move to multicloud. Depending on the type of business involved, these benefits can return 20 times that of the investment. They can also offer a strategic advantage to a company that wants to become a disruptor, and not be disrupted. A good way to prove this business case is to look at the most innovative and successful enterprises in the marketplace. When asked, most will credit a culture of innovation, and few limits to the technologies the innovators can leverage. This means access to all best-of-breed, which results in multicloud 100 percent of the time.

The concern here is that business leaders will get sticker shock when they look at properly planned multicloud and may outlaw multicloud altogether to avoid the complexity and the costs it will bring. Although I can see the scary nature of the additional costs, I also see advantages that are too great to ignore. I've watched short-sighted executives avoid multicloud for the wrong reasons and then wonder why other more aggressive and innovative businesses beat them in the marketplace. These days, if you're unwilling to weaponize technology to take your business to the next level, you'll fail. Full stop.

Multicloud Upside Realities

Multicloud benefits should be beginning to form in your head at this point in the chapter. Now it's helpful to understand what's being said in the marketplace and talk about what's true and what's not, because the amount of misinformation in the cloud computing space is becoming a problem. Yes, cloud computing professionals can disagree on issues, but facts are facts. Instead, marketing narratives are taking over technology realities.

Let's look at some of the realities of perceived benefits and then the upsides, considering that they naturally lead to a discussion of the downsides. Indeed, most multicloud upsides become the downsides. How can this be true? It's a matter of understanding that most benefits and costs of multicloud are a set of trade-offs that need to be carefully considered well beyond the PowerPoint presentations of vendors and analysts who often have hidden agendas. Complicating this issue, the same people may get some of this right as they demonstrate some advantages of multicloud. Too often they fail to cite all the upsides and downsides that need to be considered. That oversight does not help build a multicloud strategy based on pragmatic reality. So, let's share some secrets here that are rarely discussed.

Lock-in Realities

"Multicloud avoids lock-in." That phrase is often sold as an upside to multicloud, and you can kind of see the logic here, but the reality is far more complex. If you have a multicloud that's made up of more than a single public cloud provider, then you have access to different native cloud services and can thus avoid lock-in. Right?

Wrong. There are shades of gray. First, it's easier to move from one cloud provider to another if that cloud provider is already onboarded as part of your multicloud deployment. So, if you build applications and databases on AWS, which is part of your multicloud along with Microsoft and Google, then it will naturally be easier to move those applications and databases between public clouds that your multicloud already supports. This is just a reality, and it's an upside, but not by much. You're not actively avoiding lock-in; it's just a by-product of preexisting relationships with other cloud platforms that makes moving applications and data a bit easier.

Second, you don't really avoid lock-in. If you use a cloud provider's native features to localize applications and databases, then moving to another cloud means the code and databases still need to be modified to accommodate another cloud provider's native cloud services. You're just moving from one walled garden to another. You must adapt application processing, governance, security, database access, and so on to accommodate the "new" public cloud provider's services. Of course, we can use more portable technologies such as containers and build applications that take a least common denominator approach to development, which allows for better portability.

However, containerization of more traditional applications costs more time, money, and risk. Leveraging the least common denominator approach means that your application will provide substandard performance on all platforms, albeit the application will be much easier to move between platforms. When given the choice, most will want native performance and not want to sacrifice that performance for platform portability that they'll likely never utilize.

There is always a way to toss money at an architecture to avoid lock-in, which will resolve parts of the problem. However, tossing money at the problem means that the business case for building portability takes a hit, considering that you're spending more resources to achieve it. Most applications and databases are neither business critical, nor will they ever move. This is how the upside of avoiding lock-in becomes a nonissue. We talk more about this when we hit the downsides of multicloud a bit later in this chapter.

Power of Choice

By far, the largest upside of multicloud is choice, which allows the use of any cloud service, for any reason, for any purpose. Although I already introduced this benefit earlier, it's helpful to have a deeper understanding of the core choice benefits.

Multicloud provides the ability to leverage unique services to create innovative systems that can take the business to the next level. Figure 6-4 depicted the relationship between access to the most types of cloud services with the ability to quickly build solutions that are unique and innovative. More access drives more innovation and thus more business value.

Leveraging these services puts volatility into a single domain, the domain of each service. As we learned back in the days of service-oriented architecture (SOA), and now the use of microservices, it's better to leverage reusable services than re-create the same service each time you need that function or feature. Multicloud can provide the maximum number of service choices, and it promotes the use of services by its ability to find specific solutions to problems. Thus, if we promote the use of services, we promote sound application development that allows us to get to innovations faster. That's the choice value point in a nutshell.

Of course, choice is an upside and a downside. Many CIOs point to the cloud's abundance of choices as the reason that heterogeneity and complexity become problems. Indeed, many short-sighted CIOs restrict the use of cloud services, both in a multicloud and even within single cloud deployments. These restrictions are their sincere attempt to deal with complexity issues and promote the use of standard services with easy-to-define levels of required support and skills. CIOs may feel good about this decision, but the restrictions could ultimately kill many businesses that require innovation to remain competitive. Although this might not doom the tire company in Ohio, a bank or health-care company that needs to leverage technology as a true force multiplier would see its value drop like a rock.

Figure 6-6 depicts a single cloud deployment, a simple structure that provides only those services that are native to the specific public cloud provider or third-party services that can run on that provider. Thus, you have access to a finite number of development platforms, databases, AI systems, storage services, compute services, and other services that are a part of the walled garden of that specific provider.

Single Cloud Deployment

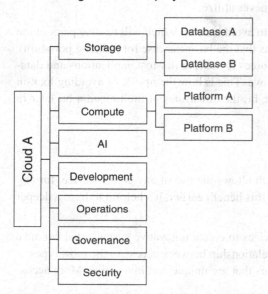

FIGURE 6-6 A single cloud deployment, while better than most traditional systems, limits cloud users and developers to a finite number of services. The impact of this limitation depends on the needs of the specific business.

An argument can be made that most major public cloud providers offer a wide-enough variety of choices to promote innovation. Indeed, when you add up the native services and those that can be found in the third-party marketplaces, you'll see an impressive number of available services. The trouble arises when you consider the true value of best-of-breed, where many of those public cloud services have unique advantages if they run on a specific cloud, such as AI, analytics, development, and other features that some clouds might do better than others. Limiting choice means an underoptimized solution, such as an application that uses a cloud-native first-generation AI system that is 50 percent less effective in forecasting market demand than a non-cloud native third-generation system. The application that's native to your cloud won't bring the maximum amount of business value back to the business.

Figure 6-7 is a multicloud that depicts some of its advantages and limitations. There are more boxes, thus more services to choose from. Moreover, there are more core services such as storage, compute, AI, and development services that we consider foundational to most applications that we use these services to build. This is not about one specific service, but picking services that have many interdependencies on the native cloud platforms that combine to provide value.

Multicloud Deployment

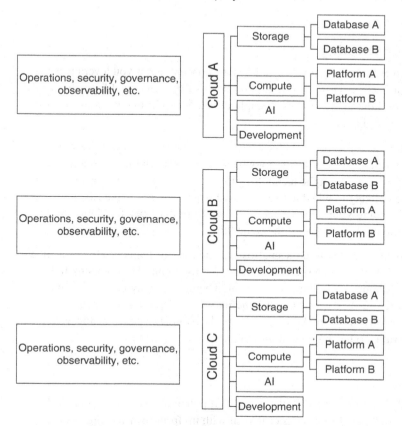

FIGURE 6-7 Choice relates to best-of-breed and thus the ability to enhance innovation. This is the single highest reason that enterprises move to multicloud. They have access to more services, including types of services, that are provided by different public cloud providers. However, if you must figure out operations, security, governance, and so on, for each cloud, that additional complexity costs more time and money. You'll see the connections later in Figure 6-10.

Let's say you have a database running on a cloud provider that is tightly coupled to the native serverless development systems and high-performance storage systems. All are native to a specific cloud. You measure the value of a service not only by the service itself, but by the collection of services that are part of a specific cloud provider. Remember that the same systems function differently on different cloud platforms. Although the same third-party vendor could provide databases, AI systems, and data analysis systems, their performance depends on how that cloud's services leverage native cloud services to work. The results range from "I can't tell the difference" to "This is a huge difference that will make or break the solution." Because the same technologies run differently on each cloud, they provide different value drivers.

The Need to Own Your Destiny

Another primary multicloud driver (and a secondary upside) is the concept that if you leverage a multicloud, you control more of your destiny. This need for control comes from some real fears that you're at the mercy of a provider if you bind all your IT to a single cloud. You will march along with their evolution and hope they make the right choices.

For example, if you leverage a single cloud provider for development, databases, and AI services, then you're stuck with where that provider takes that technology over time, and even their business success. They might make some dumb decisions about the technology to invest in or have some business issues such as a major lawsuit they are unlikely to win due to a security breach. You're on that ride with them. That is, until you invest in decoupling your applications and data from that specific cloud and move them to a new cloud that may end up doing some of the same things.

Don't go too Chicken Little here; these extreme scenarios are unlikely to happen. However, many boards of directors get unnerved when an enterprise is tightly coupled to another company that may end up deciding your destiny without your control or consent. Therefore, many enterprises move to multicloud without even considering the best-of-breed benefits we've already covered. If you need peace of mind that another company won't make key business decisions for you, owning your own destiny could be a core upside value to leveraging a multicloud.

Risk Reduction

Risk is a cost. It's time to analyze and commodify the actual and potential risks of multicloud based on each specific use case. The devil you know is easier to deal with up front than waiting to deal with inevitable problems down the road.

There are a few schools of thought here. First, multicloud is risk adverse for many of the reasons we just covered in the previous section. We maintain more fine-grained control over what services we leverage (or not), and we do not couple enterprise IT to a single cloud provider that could end up making bad moves and make the enterprise depend on a weak player.

For these reasons, many enterprises look at multicloud as risk adverse because they can take control of how and what cloud solutions are built, as well as manage major services such as security and governance using a layer that spans all clouds rather than use unique tools that work only for a specific cloud provider.

Of course, risk runs in both directions. Yes, we remove the risk that we're locked into a single company that may end up becoming a weaker player in the marketplace or do other things that make it less useful to the business. The other side of the argument is that the use of multicloud itself presents risk, which we cover in the next section. Again, look for the trade-offs. It's never one extreme or another, but shades of gray.

Security Issues

Multicloud is harder and more costly to secure than a single cloud deployment. However, it does have certain advantages that you need to consider as a true upside. First, to do proper multicloud security, you need to build a security layer that spans all clouds within your multicloud. Although this common service is more costly to implement and operate, it could end up being the better solution considering that you can also add your traditional systems under this security layer, and even edge computing systems.

This solution provides a net-new security layer that's typically better than your existing legacy system security. The net-new security layer solves the security problem for your multicloud and can span other enterprise IT systems as well. Indeed, I recommend that this always be looked at as an approach. The added expense could be offset by maintaining one rather than two separate security deployments. There's also the fact that cloud-ready security finds more R&D dollars from the technology industry, which means better security. Finally, a net-new security layer reduces security complexity because you use a single layer of abstraction and automation to deal with all security.

Governance Issues

Many of the same benefits apply to governance as well. Multicloud governance can include traditional systems under the same multicloud governance framework. In this case, multicloud governance maintains centralized policies and policy management, and again deploys a holistic governance framework using abstraction and automation that spans all traditional and cloud-based systems.

Ops Issues

Operations in a multicloud deployment present a few challenges, but there are upsides to consider as well. Again, we can extend our operations framework and technology stack to provide operations management to all existing systems, cloud and not cloud, that span the entire enterprise. This is the objective of most enterprises but is something that was unachievable in the past. Operations tools did not support enterprise-wide operations and management, although many said they would. Now we have better tools with better funded R&D. Yes, they focus on the cloud, but they also support more traditional systems. They can even support bespoke systems that many enterprises leverage for some critical business purpose, such as the AI systems leveraged by ride sharing application providers.

Of course, there are vast differences between a system or applications that run in a data center and those that run in public cloud-based systems. The idea is to leverage whatever native operation you may need by using those tools and abstraction and/or automation layers that can hide the complexity of all those native systems. This is a common theme: We control multicloud ops by dealing with complexity and heterogeneity via an automation mechanism that removes humans from the operational complexity that they just can't deal with at scale. If we successfully implement automation, then we have a better chance of making any complex distributed system work effectively, including multicloud.

Multicloud Downside Realities

Remember, for each downside there is a counterbalancing upside. Yes, complexity is an issue, but there are solutions to complexity that allow it to be easily mitigated and holistically managed. It's also true that multicloud costs more, but the costs can be managed by making better architecture decisions and weaponizing automation technology to reduce the human operator costs and the number of security and governance mistakes those operators will make. Of course, the benefit is more choice, thus agility and access to best-of-breed components to build the most business-optimized solutions.

Cost of Complexity

As you can see in Figure 6-8, complexity typically goes up by adding more systems to a deployment, such as a multicloud that may include traditional systems as well. Many multiclouds will reach a tipping point where the value of adding additional systems can't be cost justified because unchecked complexity drives costs up to an unaffordable level.

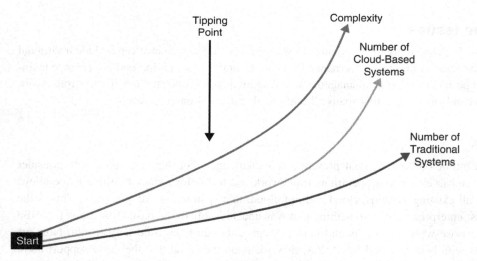

FIGURE 6-8   As we add more systems (and cloud services), cloud or not, the amount of complexity rises. This complexity adds to the cost of operations, security, and governance. Many deployments reach a tipping point where adding more systems generates more complexity than can be cost justified.

Unchecked or unmanaged complexity drives up costs (see Figure 6-9). The more complexity, the more those systems cost to operate and manage. A deployment will reach a point where adding more systems will drive complexity into negative values. Each dollar spent past that tipping point will cost more than any business value it generates. Negative values can be offset only by soft values such as agility, innovation, compressed time to market, and other attributes that provide true business value to your specific business.

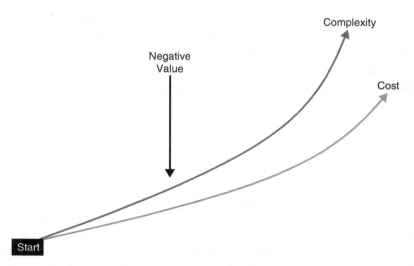

FIGURE 6-9 As we spend more money on computing, cloud and not, we increase complexity. At a certain point, complexity reaches a tipping point. From that point onward, additional money spent on cloud and other systems (hard costs) has a diminished or negative value returned to the business. Post-tipping point spending must be offset by soft value business benefits such as agility and innovation.

Here we greet the true downside of multicloud. The complexity increases with the cost of operating and managing that complexity. Multicloud leads to architectural complexity, which leads to more costs, which leads to a tipping point of value. However, complexity can and should be managed. Complexity is unavoidable, but effective management is the only way to obtain multicloud's potential value. We talk about this later in the chapter.

Cost of Heterogeneity

Heterogeneity and complexity are similar, but it's helpful to define how heterogeneity affects the amount of complexity that occurs.

For example, an enterprise may leverage 20-year-old LAMP (Linux, Apache, MySQL, and Python) stacks, and 90 percent of the enterprise's core business systems use that specific technology stack. Let's say you move the LAMP stacks and business systems to a multicloud deployment that spans AWS, Microsoft, and Google public clouds. The resulting multicloud becomes a complex distributed type of deployment, but it's much easier to operate because it's homogeneous in nature. You leverage basically the same platform on three different cloud brands. Of course, each version (in this case, a traditional LAMP stack) that runs on each platform operates a bit differently on each cloud, even though they are basically the same. The more homogeneous the applications' platforms, the easier it is to operate those platforms in a multicloud—for example, running the same Red Hat Linux version on each cloud platform and leveraging the same open-source database.

Sadly, the world does not always work that way. Most of the deployments you'll deal with involve very heterogeneous systems that support the application and data deployment and run across public cloud providers that are heterogeneous unto themselves. Thus, less homogeneous technology stacks that you deploy to a multicloud become more complex and costly platforms to operate once deployed. Both homogeneous deployments and heterogeneous deployments on multiclouds are complex in nature, but heterogeneous deployments will always outstrip homogeneous deployments in complexity and costs to operate.

Lock-in

Lock-in still exists within multicloud, albeit moving to other clouds is easier because you have a preexisting relationship with other providers via a multicloud deployment. However, those who think that a multicloud eliminates or reduces the downsides of lock-in don't fully understand their multicloud. An optimized application or data set deployed on a specific cloud provider will leverage the native features of that provider. A move to another cloud provider within our multicloud still requires us to refactor the code and change the data to work well on the new cloud provider. That's the definition of lock-in and is thus a clear downside of leveraging a multicloud.

As covered earlier, there are ways to minimize lock-in and make applications more portable. These methods include the use of containers and writing applications that do not take advantage of a specific cloud provider's native features. However, these options cost more money to leverage, depending on the applications themselves. So, the same downsides exist in some form if you leverage multicloud or not.

Security Issues

Security is more costly to operate for a multicloud because we must deal with more than one cloud platform, and the goal is to deploy security as a set of cross-cloud services. Multicloud security requires a common directory system to support identity and access management (IAM) security, common encryption services, and common systems to support multifactor authentication (MFA).

Complexity unto itself is a security limitation. Most deployment teams use whatever native security services are provided by each cloud provider to deploy multicloud security. Many of the same people must run those security services and multiplex between specific native security systems, which often leads to confusion about which native system interfaces they're using, which leads to mistakes that raise the risk of a breach.

We should also consider other issues, such as user access, as well as miscellaneous controls that may be needed. Also, the need for visibility and observability, such as having insights into what's going on now, in the past, and what will likely occur in the future. Also, application hardening, or the ability to bring security to the application level, thus fighting off breach attempts from within the application, not just on the platform where the application is running.

A common security service(s) that spans all clouds in a multicloud deployment is the best approach. However, this typically requires highly skilled security architects to knit together a solution that allows a multicloud to operate using a better security solution than a single cloud deployment, and it should certainly be better than traditional security. No matter how creative you are at building multicloud security, know that it will end up costing more money to build and operate than single cloud deployments. We touch on this issue more in the next section.

Governance Issues

Basically, the same issues that we should consider around security for a multicloud deployment apply to governance as well. Instead of managing authorization across a complex distributed deployment (that is, a multicloud), you must instead manage everything from policies that may relate to a single microservice running on a platform within a single cloud, to common policies that may span all clouds and all services.

The goal is to build a governance stack that provides service governance, resource governance, cost governance, and usage governance services that are configurable to enforce policies that exist for one service or 10,000 services that run across a multicloud deployment. Governance is obviously more expensive and complex for multicloud deployments. In the next section, we talk more about finding common ways to implement governance that spans clouds.

Ops Issues

Operations is a major downside of leveraging a multicloud for reasons I've previously covered. Complexity means many more moving parts. Those parts need to be monitored, maintained, backed-up, and updated. Those and many other operational types of processes need to work together to keep all the cloud platforms working with little or no downtime.

Multicloud operations are costly and risky. Seamless multicloud ops don't just happen. They require a lot of forethought and planning. Many teams approach multicloud operations in tactical ways, using whatever native operations tooling is available on each cloud provider. That approach will run your deployment into a complexity wall that will quickly lead to platform performance issues and outages because the humans who operate the vast array of native ops tools can't keep up.

This is another problem that requires a cross-cloud solution, an operations layer that sits above rather than within specific cloud providers. Abstraction and automation can hide the complexity from the humans, and they can leverage advanced features such as AI and automation of operational services to achieve a multicloud operational state that's pretty much hands off.

Key Concepts for Multicloud Success

Now that we understand the challenges of deploying and operating a multicloud, and some of the approaches that will likely overcome these challenges, let's dig deeper into specific approaches to a multicloud deployment that will optimize its use. The goal is to leverage a multicloud deployment using approaches and technologies that minimize risk and cost and maximize the return of value back to the business. Everyone will eventually move to a multicloud deployment, and most have no idea how to do this in an optimized way. In other words, the deployment won't be successful. Again, the concepts presented in this chapter are perhaps the most important in this book. Applied correctly, they will lead to successful multicloud deployments.

Remember that most enterprises won't increase their operations budget to support a multicloud. The key themes are to not replicate operational services for each cloud provider, which is the way teams typically approach multicloud today. That architecture won't scale, and you will just make the complexity worse. Eventually, you'll run into complexity issues such as security misconfigurations that lead to breaches or outages due to systems that aren't proactively monitored. If these issues go unresolved, chances are good that your multicloud deployment will be considered a failure in the eyes of the business, or more trouble than the cost to deploy it.

So, do not replicate operational processes such as security, operations, data integration, governance, and other systems within each cloud. This replication creates excess complexity. Here are some additional basic tenets to follow:

- **Consolidate operationally oriented services so they work across clouds, not within a single cloud.** This usually includes operations, security, and governance that you want to span all clouds in your multicloud deployment. Because it can include anything a multicloud leverages, it works across all clouds within a multicloud deployment.

- **Leverage technologies and architectures that support abstraction and automation.** This removes most of the complexity by abstracting native cloud resources and services to view and manage those services via common mechanisms. For instance, there should be one way to view cloud storage that could map down to 20–25 different native instances of cloud storage. Because humans do not need to deal with differences in native cross-cloud operations (security, governance, and so on), abstraction and automation avoid excess complexity.

- **Isolate volatility to accommodate growth and changes, such as adding and removing public cloud providers, or adding and removing specific services.** When possible, place volatility into a configurable domain (see Figure 6-10) where major or minor clouds and cloud services can be added or removed to meet the exact needs of the business.

As illustrated in Figure 6-10, move as much as possible above the clouds to work across the clouds. Typical services such as security, operations, and governance should repeat across public clouds, or any service that can normalize complexity. This approach removes services that can operate only on a single cloud deployment and instead deploys services that work across cloud providers.

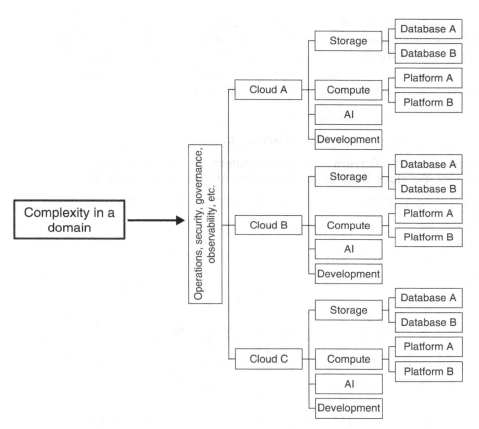

FIGURE 6-10 The only way to effectively leverage multicloud and not increase complexity (and the costs of having too much complexity) is to place complexity into a domain. Leverage cross-cloud tools to deal with mechanisms that were once native to each cloud, as depicted in Figure 6-7. Although difficult to accomplish, it's the only option to build a multicloud that provides best-of-breed services with the least amount of complexity. This approach maximizes business value and minimizes risk.

Figure 6-10 depicts what is often called a "supercloud" or "metacloud." A metacloud puts most multicloud complexity into a domain. Services such as operations, security, and governance, as well as a few other common services, are now in a single layer. The metacloud controls the lower layers. In Figure 6-10, you can see that all boxes are connected to Cloud A, Cloud B, and Cloud C. This allows us to control the multicloud as if it were a single cloud deployment. Many types of manual operations become automated in the metacloud, which leads to improvements that typically result from eliminating human errors.

Figure 6-11 depicts another way to look at a multicloud deployment. It's a good reference point when you build and deploy a multicloud for your enterprise. It's all about building the cross-cloud layer, a.k.a., the metacloud, which is where the magic happens. The metacloud layer pushes as much as possible into cross-cloud operations. These services include anything that can move from a service that's repeated within each cloud to a common service for all clouds.

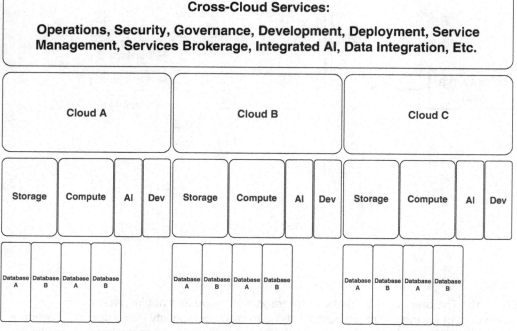

FIGURE 6-11 It's all about building cross-cloud services that eliminate specific native solutions for each cloud and instead leverage common services that run across all clouds through abstraction, or the metacloud. This is how multicloud works at scale.

Call to Action

What strikes me is that no architectural trickery or gimmicks are required to do multicloud the right way. The solutions described here involve good old-fashioned architectures that eliminate as much redundancy as possible. What may come as a surprise is that traditional approaches can solve the complexity problems introduced by multiclouds. The elimination of redundancy always was and probably always will be the best approach to reduce architectural complexity.

With that said, few multicloud design and deployment teams implement the forethought and planning processes necessary to deploy a multicloud that returns value to the business. They could be part of a "rush to the finish" culture, or key members of the team might lack the required knowledge, or the budget lacks the resources to hire the right team members. If any of those examples or other barriers describe your enterprise, someone must first understand the scope and implications of a multicloud deployment to justify the planning processes, budgets, resources, and staff required to do the multicloud job right the first time. If you're reading this book, you're probably that person.

A successful multicloud deployment requires careful planning and detailed research to compile a realistic "big picture" of a multicloud deployment. The new metacloud needs to eliminate redundancy by including cross-cloud approaches and technology that puts complexity in its place. Abstraction and automation should hide much of what makes the same or similar things complex.

Cloud computing will only become more complex over time. All enterprises will need to address complexity at some point as cloud computing becomes more widespread and becomes just everyday computing. Those who "kick the can down the road" to avoid solving the complexity problem until they can find a magical solution will spend at least twice as much time and money to redeploy and redefine the correct solution. Worse, the solution will become harder to define and harder to deploy as time goes by, and the deployment will ultimately hit a complexity wall. I would rather you and your business not go through that pain.

Chapter 7

Cloud Security Meets the Real World

We shall defend our island whatever the cost may be; we shall fight on the beaches, landing grounds, in fields, in the streets and on the hills. We shall never surrender.

— *Winston Churchill*

Why wait until Chapter 7 to get into cloud security? At this point in the book, you might realize that cloud security must now cover so many things that it's difficult to figure out where storage, compute, databases, AI, and cloud architecture end and cloud security begins.

In the past, security systems could be bolted on during or even at the end of an IT project cycle without too much trouble. In the case of cloud security, that's no longer true. Many enterprises will learn this cloud security lesson in hard and costly ways. My goal in this chapter is to help you avoid the hard way. But first, let's back up a step to see a bigger picture of the challenges cloud security presents.

A certain large insurance company uses their trademarked red umbrella in many of their ads to metaphorically represent how their insurance policies will protect you from all of life's potential disasters. In today's world of cloud computing, we need a cloud security umbrella that covers every physical and virtual thing that could be compromised, damaged, and/or destroyed in a cloud architecture. Our current cloud toolbox sometimes requires the use of a few different security umbrellas, but each day we get closer to full and comprehensive cloud security coverage under one umbrella. That's the good news.

To complicate matters, these are the adapt-or-die days of cloud computing with most enterprises implementing as many cloud projects as they can, as fast as they can. Our in-house cloud skills and expertise can barely keep pace with the advances in cloud specialties. This is especially true of cloud security knowledge and expertise. There are features available in some security suites, but we don't know enough about cloud security to realize that we need them. Or there are features in otherwise advanced security systems that we want, but it turns out those systems are incompatible with components we need to secure in our architecture. Or there are security services that sound great in theory (or in the sales pitch), but they don't perform as expected in actual usage.

"What went wrong?" It's the universal question I get asked when I'm called in to determine why a cloud security system failed to live up to expectations. The answer lies in my interactions with more proactive clients who call me in at the beginning of a project. Inevitably, someone in the meeting wants to or has already defined the cloud security solutions before anyone has a clear idea of what they need to secure.

Never start a cloud security plan with a list of potential security tools and toys. That's happening all too often right now, and it's why the number of data breaches on cloud computing platforms continues to rise even as cloud security technology continues to improve at the same time. Cloud security is certainly much better than the traditional solutions in most data centers. So, we can reach a security level unachievable in the past, but, for some reason, we can't figure out how to get it done. Hint: Define what you need to secure before you decide how to secure it.

The second drawback with today's cloud security leads back to the "red umbrella" example. Cloud security offers a narrow view of technology that solves specific problems such as encryption. But it also covers a wide area of technology that includes data management, networks, compute, applications, application development, and a lot of things that those who are trying to figure out cloud security would rather not consider.

> **TIP**
>
> A secure cloud needs a holistic security approach that systemically addresses cloud security. It's an impossible system to implement if you don't know how everything works or how everything needs to work together. Consider it all and figure it all out.

My goal with this chapter is to provide you with the insider's track on what's important and what's not, and what you should pay close attention to. I focus on what's not being said in other places that discuss cloud security. It's stuff you won't learn from cloud security technology providers with their mostly self-serving views about how cloud security works. Part of this insight is to look at the conflicts of interest you need to consider, and thus read between the lines of surveys and analyst rankings to understand what cloud security is and does. Finally, I give you advice about how to deal with cloud security now… and 10 years from now.

Let's get started.

An Insider's Guide to Cloud Security Fundamentals

First, know that cloud security is a simple process that many people make more complicated than it needs to be. The basic steps are to protect, detect, respond, and track (see Figure 7-1). Each step has its role, and the requirement is that you must do all four steps well, or the other steps won't matter. Think of this requirement the next time you hear of a breach where the enterprise spent millions on network security but spent very little on data security. After the data was breached, any good or bad part of security no longer mattered because they'd already been breached.

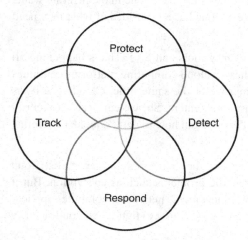

FIGURE 7-1   Cloud security has become a complex beast with many different takes on what it is and what's important. It boils down to four fundamental methods to leverage security. If you focus on these four steps, it will be much easier to understand security at the end of the day.

Step 1: Protect

Protect is a passive process because we set up systems to defend against threats using whatever security mechanisms are best for that defense—data encryption, for instance. Even if the data can be seen, it can't be understood; thus, it's worthless to the attacker. Data protected.

Of all the core cloud security attributes we cover here, protect is the easiest to pull off. What's frustrating is that the protections most cloud-based systems need are not difficult to set up. Also, remember that cloud security is the best computer security in the world. Cloud provider security and cloud security in general get the lion's share of R&D budgets, which means these technologies can provide the most innovative and thus the best security approaches and mechanisms available today.

What's missing is the people aspect. Most breaches can be traced to human error, which is unsurprising. After all, cloud computing is a complex technology that's still relatively new to most cloud practitioners. A certain number of errors are bound to happen in any learning curve. However, when you look at the incidents, it's the simple stuff that gets screwed up. For example, some breach postmortems show that security engineers worked around default security configurations (which are typically very secure) to expose systems and data that are difficult to expose. In other words, they worked extra hard to find a way to accidentally expose sensitive data and processes. Not that I'm asserting any malicious intent. It's just an example of people who know enough about cloud security to be dangerous who were promoted to their level of incompetence. With the current skills shortage, it's a more prevalent problem than management might realize…until it's too late. For instance, leaving outbound traffic unrestricted, which in many cases is the default. Or, some worse mistakes, such as disabling monitoring or logging, opening ICMP access, misunderstanding storage access configurations, or failing to manage credentials and keys.

Many of the cloud breach incidents I see are things that you can't make up, and almost all link back to dumb mistakes that someone could have easily avoided. Of course, cloud computing gets the blame. If there are major cloud breaches or breaches in general, I'm on speed dial for most business reporters who ask for SME (small- and medium-sized enterprises) quotes around a recent breach. The most common question asked is: "Does this [enter breach name here] call into question cloud computing as an option for enterprise IT?" I then explain (again) that cloud security uses a shared responsibility model, where everyone must be well trained and make a conscious effort to not make common errors. With cloud security being the best security available, the focus on cloud protection needs to be on the humans who oversee cloud protection. We seem to have some growing pains in that department.

Protect requires that you take precautions with all your cloud-based assets and don't do dumb things. Don't leave data exposed or misconfigure security settings or do other generally stupid but known things that cause cloud breaches. A security engineer certification from any public cloud provider will quickly get you a six-figure job because not enough people know how to configure clouds and cloud security systems to protect assets, including data and processes. Books have been written about how to protect cloud-based assets in general, as well as for specific public cloud providers. Invest in a few. Where cloud security is concerned, encourage learning, and invest in knowledge.

Step 2: Detect

How do you find and stop attacks on your cloud-based systems? The cloud security system must be smart enough to constantly monitor and interpret things that are happening, have already happened, or are about to happen and then raise the alarm that a breach attempt is underway and prompt the system and/or humans to take evasive actions.

Detecting a breach means being proactive. The system finds states and behaviors that may indicate a breach attempt, or it monitors the shady actions of potential bad actors who might do or be doing something to our systems and data. This could be the increased use of CPU resources as access attempts are made that fall out of set thresholds and then doing some additional detecting to determine whether the threat is real or just one of the hundred anomalies that occur daily on cloud-based systems. The detect step can also use observability as a defensive weapon for cloud security (we discuss observability later in this chapter).

Detect is becoming the best cloud security asset that most enterprises choose not to employ. Systems that detect are more costly to set up (such as observability, covered later) and require deep knowledge of all the systems you're protecting. You can't detect anomalies in a system or data store that you don't understand. The best insider advice I can impart about where to make cloud security investments is to invest in systems that can detect trouble or systems that can be proactive. It's the only means we'll have to stop new cloud security threats that will arise in the next few years.

Keep in mind that detection is more complicated in both hybrid and multicloud deployments. As you'll discover in this chapter, cross-environment observability is key, considering that many times, these environments are separate silos, and it is often time consuming to try to track down what is going on in one system and how it is impacting the other. Security breaches can exploit these gaps.

Step 3: Respond

How do you respond to a detected attack or threat? There are many options. The system could simply disconnect and block an IP address, then back up systems and data just in case they are breached, turn off systems and data storage to stop an attack, or, my personal favorite, take punitive actions to go after the system that's trying to breach. This means attacking back, which could become a more normalized approach than it is today.

Again, there are passive and proactive responses. For example, a passive response could automatically block an IP address, which seems more proactive. It's done without much forethought, and it acts on other areas that may be vulnerable to a detected attack. This approach is passive because it normally takes place outside of the security system; it's just something that's triggered at the firewall and may or may not communicate back to the core cloud security processes and mechanisms. It may not even know that it's responding to an attack or even let a human know that it's occurring. This is an old-school-style cloud security response.

Proactive responses are much more effective and fun. A proactive response takes direct action that can take the fight to the attacker. For instance, the system could respond by tracing the origin of the attack and then work itself around mechanisms that may be hiding IP addresses. Once found, the system observes how the attack is being carried out and can even provide "bait systems" that exist in a virtual sandbox to help further identify the bad actors. When a profile is complete, the system stops access (obviously), interprets the knowledge of how the bad actors executed the attack, and automatically adjusts accordingly, often using AI-assisted processes.

The results? We learn more about the attacker and the attack, and the system adjusts our defenses so future attacks that fall within the same parameters are more likely to be spotted and stopped. Of course, many types of responses can occur. The system can change the encryption key, back up core data, force password changes and MFA for the users and external systems, update firewalls, and do any number of security tricks (do an online search for "cloud security threat tips" for the most recent information).

Step 4: Track

Keep a detailed log of everything that happens, including breach attempts as well as normal operations. It's pointless to gather massive amounts of data unless we understand how to filter the data to work around the "noise data" or overly detailed data. The objective here is to provide enough monitoring and security operations data that it can be mined by observability systems, including some that may leverage AI. We discuss observability in more detail later in this chapter, but for now, understand that it's key to cloud security's future success. Observability can look at long-term monitoring data to denote behavior and identify patterns that can build better defenses for our cloud computing systems and data. As you learn later in this chapter, observability used with security is the key to taking security to the next level.

What Cloud Security Worked

Cloud security is well over 20 years old, believe it or not. Cloud computing security began its life as an evolution of website security because SaaS-based cloud systems were more like websites than enterprise resources in a data center. Cloud computing itself evolved to become a core enterprise resource that needs security equal to or better than traditional web-based systems.

As cloud security evolved, what worked and what still works today? The consensus is that cloud security did better than we thought it would. Many of the "Chicken Little" persuasion thought major breaches and outages would plague the cloud. In their minds, when the sky fell, everyone would agree that data and core systems needed to stay inside power-hungry data centers. Putting anything "important" within public clouds would just ask for trouble.

The reality is much different. Around 2015, cloud security quietly became better than most on-premises systems. Security professionals now have more confidence in cloud security than in traditional enterprise security. Again, if you look at the major breaches that make the news cycles, clouds are nowhere to be found. Here are the core reasons cloud security is better than traditional security:

- Spending on cloud R&D and innovation outpaced that of more traditional security for more traditional systems. Cloud security development received more funding, and thus more innovation, which equated to better security in the cloud. Pretty simple math.

- The best security talent moved to cloud security. Rockstar security leaders and engineers saw the future in the cloud and shifted their careers accordingly. Thus, the top security talent drove better security outcomes and innovations in the cloud.

- Enterprises moved to the cloud in slower and more methodical ways than many expected. In most cases, they were overly careful about securing data and applications, especially given the Chicken Little warnings that continued to ring out in meetings. Most enterprises overengineered security "just in case," which meant they used more security than they needed.

Let's get into some specific areas to learn from what went right.

Data Encryption

Encryption is fundamental to any security system. It hides stored or in-transit (in-flight) information and requires an authorized key for users to unlock that data. This is how we ensure our data cannot be viewed by anyone who breaches the cloud, although that's an extremely rare occurrence. Data encryption itself is not infallible, although it's a good insurance policy to protect data access.

Encryption is critical to cloud computing and cloud security because we physically place our data on a system that we don't physically control. If data encryption did not work, enterprises would not send their data to any public cloud.

Identity-Based Security

Second only to encryption is the ability to leverage identity-based or identity and access management (IAM) security. Everything and everyone receive a unique identity that allows or disallows access to specific fine-grained resources that also have a unique identity. Because users, APIs, storage systems, databases, data, and so on, have an identity, we have complete control over how they interact. We establish parameters to control how they work, what they can do, and how they function. IAM systems typically use directory services to track and manage these identities as a separate function from the security system.

IAM was not invented just for cloud computing, but they are complex distributed systems with many endpoints. You must configure cloud security systems to the specific needs of systems deployed in the cloud. Most traditional role-based security systems cannot deal with this kind of complexity.

Again, IAM is not perfect, but it's currently the best security model you can deploy to cloud-based systems. The core advantage is that it's extensible. The flexibility of IAM can deal with and adapt to complex cloud deployments such as multiclouds that manage three to six public cloud providers, thousands of applications, hundreds of databases, and hundreds of thousands of APIs.

Also, you should consider zero-trust network access (ZTNA). This cloud security solution provides secured remote access control policies. This approach and technology set differ from virtual private networks (VPNs) in that they grant access privileges to specific applications or services. VPNs, in contrast, grant access to the entire network, which can create more security risks. As the world becomes more work-at-home, this could be better technology to leverage, by cloud insiders.

Security Automation

Automation has always been a part of security, but cloud computing takes security automation to the next level. We can define behavior as well as status rules and policies. This capability is the only feasible path to success if you work with a dynamic set of systems in a constantly changing environment, which is the case with most cloud-based systems.

Again, the ability to react to security issues using automation becomes a game-changer for cloud computing security and security in general. Security automation allows us to harvest the powers of observability and AI. The three combined take security evolution a giant leap forward. We talk about security automation in more detail later in this chapter.

AI/ML Integration

Artificial intelligence and machine learning are changing the world. Cloud security is along for the ride. If you have trouble differentiating the terms, think of AI as a system that can teach computers to think like a human—for example, Siri or Alexa or Hey Google. ML is an application of AI that Siri, Alexa, and Hey Google use to develop their knowledge and intelligence ongoing.

Combined with security automation, AI has a special place in the world of cloud security. The ability to emulate learning, which is what AI does well, allows cloud security systems to proactively adapt and adjust to changes in security threats.

AI and ML were mostly science fiction for the last 40 years because they existed only in very advanced and expensive systems. I used them to create simulation systems in the 1980s. The price of AI dropped dramatically a few years ago, which put AI capabilities within reach for more pragmatic uses such as operations and security. These days AI and ML are feature-rich and almost free. Cloud security systems can now take full advantage of AI.

What Cloud Security Didn't Work

Now let's discuss what didn't work so well. This is an important conversation because many of these faulty or limited cloud security technologies are still around, and many are being sold as workable options. My advice is to stay away from these technologies or use them at your own risk.

The theme here from providers is making old stuff new again. Many of the legacy security players cloud-washed their security solutions by leveraging well-known and perhaps once competent security methodologies. However, this was akin to fitting an old round peg into a new square hole. Cloud security requires bespoke solutions that are purpose-built for the special needs of cloud computing. Yes, I'm sure I'll hear from a few of you who use older security approaches and technologies with great success, and that's fine if those solutions fit your specific requirements. My assertion here is that a one-size-fits-all security solution will not be available anytime soon. As always, the best system will result from an approach that works from the requirements to the solution and not the other way around.

Let's review a few of the failure points.

Remove Focus from Non-Cloud Systems

One of the biggest mistakes I see made is the failure to include non-cloud systems into security domains and frameworks. The result? Our public cloud deployments have great security. Everything is encrypted, we leverage identity-based security, we have advanced security observability systems in place, and we are sitting pretty. However, most of our company data and processes still reside on non-cloud systems such as legacy and traditional computing platforms that exist in corporate data centers. The systems running at the highest security risks are also the most neglected because all the good security thinking and technology went into the cloud-based systems. The non-cloud systems are the ones breached most often.

You need only look through the major breaches of the last 10 years to discover that clouds are rarely involved. Hackers found neglected legacy systems that presented much easier targets. I guess you can say that cloud made all systems less secure because it removed the focus from older systems to the point that they could be easily breached.

Figure 7-2 depicts how much native (isolated) security is done today, and I suspect this won't change much in the next three to five years. Note how each type of system (cloud, legacy, and edge) has its native security layers that only deal with that specific type of platform.

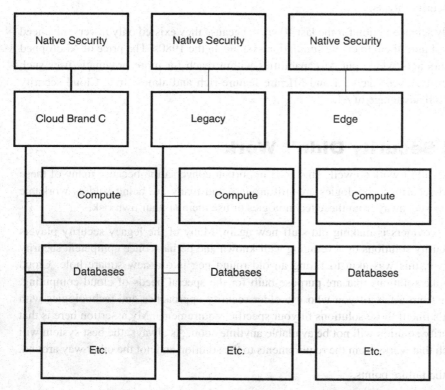

FIGURE 7-2 Cloud security is still an island unto itself. Most enterprises use whatever native security tools are available on the platforms they deploy on. This configuration won't scale and quickly becomes too complex to manage. Worse, it's prone to human error.

Of course, the situation is never as simple as Figure 7-2 depicts. There may be two to five different types of security for each platform. Multicloud typically deploys with native security for each type of cloud (AWS, Google, Microsoft, and so on). Native database security also introduces more complexity, as do brand-name native network security, native container security, and so on. Although you can certainly deploy native security systems for each platform based on best practices and recommendations for those platforms, the complexity and silos you create lead to higher security risks.

The solution is to consider security as a more holistic endeavor, which isn't easy. All parts of the architecture need to be holistically managed using cross-cloud and cross-platform security systems, observability, and orchestration that may or may not abstract native security (if needed). As we see later in this chapter, this dashboard-type security umbrella that covers all enterprise IT architecture is the cloud computing security evolution that will enable scalable security.

Failure to Manage Complexity

We've already beat the complexity issue to death in our discussion of multicloud, where complexity is the negative result. Security has the same systemic problem. The more platforms, systems, services, and native security systems that operate at the same time, the more complexity, which leads to more security risks. These risks come in the form of human and system errors because the sheer number of systems that need to be secured becomes more difficult to manage if you do them one-by-one or platform-by-platform, which is largely what we do today. More complexity, more breaches. Not good.

In Figure 7-3, notice how complexity, risk, and costs rise with more systems under management that must be secured. This figure depicts a multicloud deployment, but you could add legacy, edge, ERP, CRM, and other more traditional systems as well. The default response is to secure them using whatever native security is at hand, so the number of security systems and approaches builds more complexity and thus more risk and cost.

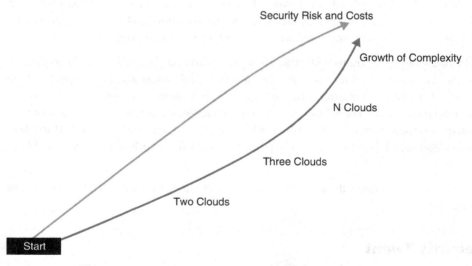

FIGURE 7-3 The most negative impact on cloud security, past and present, is that too much complexity now exists. Misconfigurations by humans cause most breaches because they have too much to humanly track and manage.

The reality is that complexity can't be avoided, so it must be managed. The trick is to deal with complexity by removing as many moving parts as you can, such as native security systems. Combine them into more holistic security that can leverage the concepts and approaches of abstraction, orchestration, automation, and observability. Do this cross-platform at a logical layer that exists above all the platforms that need to be secured that include cloud but not only cloud.

Little Focus on BC/DR

Business continuity and disaster recovery (a.k.a. BC/DR). An old IT supervisor of mine told me to "back up anything that you don't want to lose." In those days, we used mag tape storage for offline backups, and it took hours to back up a single gigabyte of data. Of course, the one time someone on my team failed to back up data at the end of the day, we had a hard drive crash. Over a day's worth of transactions were lost and had to be manually re-entered into the database.

These days, backup is an automated and seamless process. Indeed, as I write this book, each keystroke gets recorded on a cloud service, and I'm unlikely to lose anything if there is a system failure. BC/DR systems are cheap, but they often get left out of the discussion in security planning meetings, specifically cloud security planning meetings.

Many of the attacks these days will go after your data, and that fact makes backup a core security component. Ransomware attacks, for example, just encrypt your data in place and then demand that a fee be paid to buy the key that will unencrypt your data. Because many enterprises don't bother to back up data to safe data storage units, the only recourse is to pay the ransom. However, sometimes the backups are encrypted as well if they are stored where the bad actors can access them.

I often see good cloud security programs with state-of-the-art approaches that lack a well-planned and/or implemented backup and recovery function. In many instances, customers assume that public cloud providers take care of backup and recovery. Beyond some basic systems maintenance and recovery services, public cloud providers do not babysit your data. If you accidentally remove your data, or your data gets corrupted, or someone encrypts it and demands money, you're on your own. BC/DR needs to be systemic to all cloud security deployments. Unfortunately, it's often overlooked or deployed with fatal flaws.

The most common word that follows the term *BC/DR* is *plan*. As in, have a BC/DR plan. Make it as bulletproof as possible.

Lack of Security Talent

Back to the talent thing. Many enterprises build and operate cloud security systems without qualified talent. The argument I often hear is, "We can't find the right security talent, but we need to deploy the cloud systems." So, they deploy the cloud systems knowing they lack the cloud security talent who would know how to best protect their systems. An unfortunate follow-up to this argument? Too often it's some version of, "We were breached! Now what?"

There is a huge talent shortage when it comes to cloud computing in general and cloud security specifically. I suspect we'll have a few ebbs and flows around supply and demand, but too many jobs will chase too few qualified cloud security candidates for the next few years. The impact of this shortage is depicted in Figure 7-4, where the demand for security talent rises over time. When supply can't keep up with demand, the risk of a breach rises. More simple math.

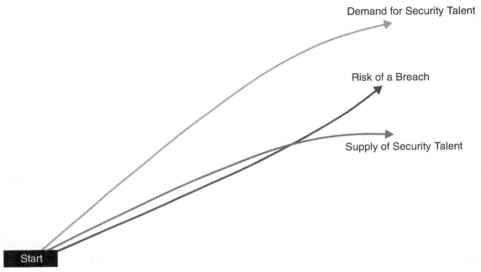

FIGURE 7-4 Few enterprises saw a cloud security talent shortage coming or understood its inevitable impact. Although the tools are getting better, most enterprises endure a much higher breach risk than should be allowable because they can't find qualified security talent.

We continue to build cloud systems that include cloud security (obviously), but we don't have the on-staff security talent to make the critical decisions during the planning and implementation phases, or to effectively operate these systems ongoing. What we end up with are cloud solutions that resemble Figure 7-2, the siloed security defaults offered by providers because no one on staff knows how to design a systemic security system. Often, security pros on staff have a certification in cloud security for a specific cloud provider, but they're lost when it's time to look at solutions for other cloud platforms or other platforms in general. Or the longtime security pro who understands little or nothing about cloud security attempts to force-fit their go-to cloud security solutions into cloud deployments. After all, most security providers now claim to support cloud deployments due to the massive amount of cloud washing. Why wouldn't it work?

My advice here is to get the talent you need. Either identify someone on staff who's looking for new cloud opportunities and provide the education they need to grow into the cloud security role you need, or wait for the right person to show up in the outside talent pool. Don't force forward progress without a good handle on cloud security, or all security for that matter. I understand that the inability to access qualified security skills will hinder progress while your timelines won't change due to the talent shortages. However, the alternative sucks. Poorly designed and implemented cloud security solutions must be fixed down the road. That is unless a major breach takes out the company before the massive overhaul can be done. Taking the time to train and develop in-house talent in cloud security internships or waiting for the right outside hire will cost less in the long run. Oftentimes, much, much less. This is the part where leaders need to make tough calls.

The Rise of Non-Native Cloud Security

Okay, it probably seems as though I've spent the first half of this chapter complaining and pointing out how many things can go wrong. Now let's look at how to succeed with cloud security. I purposely float general ideas here without specific technologies or specific solutions. Although technology will continuously change, good ideas should remain pretty much the same. I want the messages in this book to be valuable now and 10 years from now.

When I refer to "non-native security," I'm talking about security systems that are not purpose-built for a specific platform but designed to operate across platforms. This could mean across many public clouds, many legacy systems, edge systems, mobile systems, and anything else that you need to secure. However, the overall goal is to use security orchestration, abstraction, and automation that exist logically above all the platforms being secured. The resulting security system will share common security services such as identity management, encryption, directories, or anything else that provides common secure access across many different platforms that would normally promote the use of native security. This must be the approach if we're to provide the span of security that's required for modern platforms. And we must do so without added complexity, which just makes things less secure.

The Movement to Cross-Cloud Security

As you can see in Figure 7-5, the move to cross-cloud security is the crucial first step to mostly non-native security. The use of multicloud drives the need for this configuration (as we covered earlier in this book), which drives the need for cross-cloud operations, governance, FinOps, and security.

Figure 7-5 shows how this will work. Notice the common layer of security that hosts security orchestration, observability (discussed later), access management, and directory services. It can perform common tasks in the upper layer (on the left) but can also incorporate native security systems (if needed). This allows us to leverage the best of both worlds, native and non-native. However, the use of native security layers doesn't add complexity because we use them through abstraction and automation. We normalize security complexity using the cross-cloud security layer as well. The result of a successful supercloud/metacloud implementation is a command center that can control every part of the enterprise's systems architecture. Welcome to the new bridge of your enterprise ship.

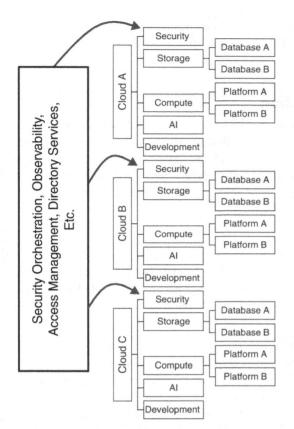

FIGURE 7-5 Security moves up to a logical layer that exists above the cloud providers, which could be security itself but is more likely part of a larger layer of cross-cloud services that exist in a supercloud or a metacloud.

Security Peer-to-Peer Authentication

The growth of blockchain and Web 3 concepts (which we're not going to discuss here) provides new opportunities for the future of cloud computing security. Blockchain successfully fueled the growth of the cryptocurrency market because it does not rely on a centralized technology stack and directory, but instead uses distributed ledgers that must agree with each other for a transaction to take place. A transaction must satisfy its peers before the transaction is allowed, which makes this pretty darn secure because the transaction trusts many through consensus rather than trusts a single entity that could be compromised.

I'm on many panels and podcasts that predict blockchain or something like blockchain will be the new standard for cloud security. Perhaps all security for that matter. Certain aspects of blockchain are already sneaking into cloud security systems, including new cross-cloud security systems that are available today. Many of the cloud security providers will likely replicate this model at some point. It just makes good sense. The peer-to-peer authentication approach seems to be the way to go for current and future cloud security.

Security Abstraction and Automation

We've talked a lot about abstraction and automation already, so the mention here is to make sure you understand that abstraction and automation have an application in cross-platform cloud security as well. Mostly we'll see both concepts employed in cross-cloud and cross-platform security systems that need to simplify complex security using abstraction and provide automation to remove as many humans from the processes as possible. These become the saving graces of how to make many things work better. We talk more about automation toward the end of this chapter.

Security Intelligence (AI)

We can weaponize AI for pretty much everything these days, and security is no different. AI enables security layers to learn as they encounter breach attempts (both at the native and cross-platform layers), learn security operations over time, leverage observability to determine insights, and employ AI to interpret what it all means.

The idea is to set up these security systems to learn from the data gathered ongoing. As the systems learn, they gain insights into how to deal with normal and abnormal events encountered during security operations. For example, they have the ability to spot breach attempts using nonstandard approaches such as looking for CPU saturation that could indicate a cloud-based system is being employed for an attack. Ordinarily, this "red flag" could go unnoticed because cloud operations typically deal with straightforward performance issues, but there are many observable cases where breaches can be detected using an overarching intelligence that considers everything and learns as it goes.

Security Observability

We cover observability in the context of cloud security later in this chapter, so we don't get too deep into it now. However, know that observability is key to cross-platform and non-native security. When we gather data for all systems in a security domain, which may span many platforms, we must pay attention to what that data means. Insights, trends, and analysis will help predict future security events that need to be managed or can provide raw learning data from past security events that may not have been detected at the time. As we learn how to figure things out in more proactive ways and focus on the intelligence-gathering features of systemic cloud security, observability will become the major league weapon for cloud computing security. We will no longer just react to events and hope to get to them in time. The crossed-fingers approach won't work long term.

The Rise of Proactive Security

The key to cloud security is what most cloud security pros already know and what most cloud security systems can't do well: Be proactive. Traditional security approaches and security systems are reactive. They wait for something to happen, and then they respond. It doesn't matter if it's a login system that rejects invalid credentials, or an IP address that's blocked during a DDOS attack. Something happens, and then the system responds.

Most cloud computing security instructors don't teach how to be proactive because proactive technology is still relatively new, and many instructors don't fully understand its capabilities. Most instructors focus on the reactive parts of security because it's easier to understand and follow the patterns of existing security approaches and technologies. When I lecture on cloud security and talk about the opportunities to be more proactive, I'm often met with confused looks and a lot of questions.

Proactive security is the most likely future of cloud computing security. Just waiting around for something to happen to launch a defense means it's only a matter of time before an attack is successful. The attacker will learn more about your defenses from each failed attempt. Just look at the postmortems on cloud computing breaches. You'll see that the attackers went at it many times and failed, but they used those failures to figure out what didn't work to figure out what finally did work.

Proactive security systems can deal with those types of security issues before they become issues at all. The system can identify likely attacks before they become actual attacks and set up proactive defenses that deal with attackers before they even understand that they are being dealt with. In other words, you proactively take the fight to the enemy and don't let them take a seat at your table. It's a much better strategy.

The Importance of Observability

Thus far, we've covered observability in the context of operations. The more we understand the insights we gain, the better we can do many things. This includes FinOps, operations, governance, and, yes, security. Observability for cloud security is the same as observability for anything else. We continuously gather data from everywhere and make sense of it by understanding any emerging security threats or those that may be more likely to emerge.

Figure 7-6 depicts an overview of observability and security, and the important features that allow you to put this concept to good use. These include

- **What's happening?** What's the current state of the systems? This covers security-related data and systems-related data as well—for example, the status of CPU saturation, I/O saturation, overall system performance, and network saturation. Anything that will lead to a trend, which leads to insights around that trend.

- **What's likely to happen?** Based on current and past data, what is likely to happen in the future? Deep analytics and AI can provide insights into this data.

- **How to defend?** Based on what the system knows is occurring, or is likely to occur, what are the best courses of action? For example, the system could deny an IP address or move data access from one cloud server to another to confuse the attackers.

- **How will it happen?** What are the likely attack vectors and mechanisms that will be leveraged? These are solid leads to educate AI-assisted guesses.

- **How can we stop this event in the future?** What did we learn about this event, and what does it reveal when we include past and current data? What can be done to stop this from recurring in the future?

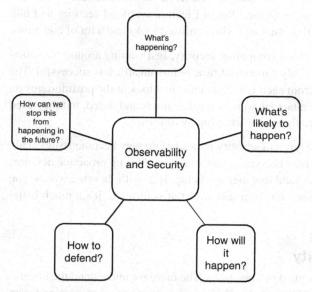

FIGURE 7-6   Observability becomes the tool that allows us to create a solid cloud security approach with systemic processes and deployments. Security observability will let us determine who, when, where, why, and/or how, and what to do about an endless array of events through complex data insights that leverage AI. This is the only type of red umbrella that can cover all the disparate parts of modern IT architecture.

It's interesting to see how observability works and why traditional security folks often avoid it when it's time to deal with cloud security. It's much more costly and time consuming to set up security observability systems, and the cost is often higher than the perceived cost of risk. Again, the ability to be proactive and leverage the concept of observability to defend your cloud-based systems is the only productive way cloud security will evolve. If you can't afford it now, build it into the next budget and keep the focus on security observability goals. You're looking at the future of cloud security.

Pattern Searching

Observability and proactive cloud security approaches find and track patterns. These could be patterns that indicate normal operations or patterns that indicate something is about to happen—for example, a breach attempt. Deep analytics and/or AI can find patterns and create insights to build appropriate responses to the patterns. Observability as a security tool provides the ability to monitor data and create actionable patterns, which is foundational to proactive security.

Most of today's cloud security systems don't search for patterns. This is something many other CloudOps tools and cloud operations teams now do, looking for the same proactive benefits. In this instance, cloud security teams could learn something from cloud operations teams regarding how data can become patterns and what those patterns mean to core cloud security systems. It's most important to learn how to find patterns and understand what they mean, and then determine what can be done to avoid negative events that may occur as a result. The result of effective pattern searching will be proactive cloud computing security that continuously learns and improves.

AI

AI is now systemic to all that's proactive. Yesterday's too-expensive technology is today's most efficient and effective key to all proactive security systems that must monitor and interpret mountains of data. One of the huge advantages of leveraging AI is that we don't have to deal with data on the data's terms. It's humanly impossible to use manual processes to find patterns in the amount of data our systems gather and track these days. The patterns are difficult to understand even with advanced data analytics. AI can find meaning in data that we humans can't see or sense. AI can then learn from the data and become better at understanding the data as time progresses.

AI still needs to be regarded with its limitations as well as its usefulness. AI systems don't come to conclusions on their own; they must be trained. This training is done by humans who point the AI systems at data that can teach the AI system how to spot the patterns and trends they need to be proactive.

Things can also go wrong if you don't understand how to properly train an AI system. Improperly trained AI could result in erroneous conclusions that fool the system into believing it's protected when it's very much not. Humans require a certain amount of expertise to properly train and drive AI systems. You and your team must navigate a clear learning curve to understand and implement effective AI-enabled cloud security.

The Rise of Security Automation

Human involvement in day-to-day security operations causes most breaches. Study after study reveals breaches caused by misconfigurations and misunderstandings about how security systems work. These are just normal human errors, but these errors can cost the company millions of dollars. It's a fact that most of our security problems breathe air and walk the earth.

A sound security system must do many more things in automated ways and remove all human interactions that can be removed. This might sound mean, but these changes will rarely result in the loss of someone's job. The demand for skilled cloud security professionals is so high that newly freed staff time will usually be reassigned to other cloud projects such as the design and deployment of cloud computing security automation. It's a win/win: We can staff empty cloud positions or send reinforcements to overworked cloud staff and remove humans from most day-to-day security operations, which is how we get into most security trouble in the first place.

Figure 7-7 follows a standard breach attempt to show what automated security should look like. The system understands what's going on in detail and tells our AI-enabled security system how to defend itself. A defensive posture is set, perhaps moving data, backing up data, blocking a specific IP address, or any number of things that ensure the attack is stopped in its tracks. Because we learn from the unsuccessful attack, the system can better defend itself from this type of attack in the future.

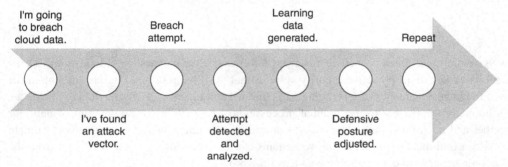

FIGURE 7-7   Let the computers battle each other. As security evolves, the objective should be to remove human interactions from cloud security as much as possible. When humans get involved, things go wrong.

What's unique about the process laid out in Figure 7-7 is that all these steps were once or are still managed by humans. With AI systems in place, all observability, automation, and data pattern-matching processes may take just a few seconds to execute. Then it's just a matter of monitoring the automation and reviewing the outcomes.

We have some automation available today, but it's automation around standard structured decisions that don't leverage observability and AI. Therefore, humans must monitor most of this automation, and many times humans must step in to manually solve the problems. These half-measures won't work. Security automation has access to near-perfect information to support proactive intelligence that is constantly improving. If your cloud security relies on human involvement to solve problems, you're doing something wrong. Automated cloud security systems should remove humans from the process *and* always be better than humans.

The insider advice here? Automation is the only way to provide complete cloud computing security and allow cloud computing security to scale.

Call to Action

I understand that automation is a leap of faith. The first time I sat behind the wheel of a self-driving car, I was nervous (bordering on panicked) for the first hour. However, the car could see 500 things going on in and around us while I could see only a few. The car could avoid obstacles or respond to traffic conditions with zero reaction time, and it did not get tired or angry.

When set up correctly with sound technology, automation can do things better and provide us with a better path forward, which results in a huge risk reduction. As trains, planes, and automobiles incorporate more extensive automation features, enterprise IT systems must keep pace as well. I suspect that need will become painfully apparent when today's lack of cloud security skills becomes tomorrow's rise in successful cloud breach attempts.

It's a fact, cloud security systems are better than traditional security systems. It's the humans who set things up and/or insist on running them in manual mode who cause problems. That approach won't work or scale and is bound to fail.

It's time to look more than two to three years into the future and start building security systems that can carry out complex actions and processes better than humans ever could. Those who don't understand what's coming need to catch up fast. Remember, bad actors have equal access to AI tools. AI-powered ransomware is just one example of how they've already turned AI tools into weapons. If you don't have an equal or higher generation of defenses in place, it will be akin to defending the enterprise with bows and arrows against an enemy armed with cannons.

Bottom line: It's time to adopt cloud security automation, observability, and AI.

Chapter 8

Cloud Computing and Sustainability: Fact Versus Fiction

The nation behaves well if it treats its natural resources as assets which it must turn over to the next generation increased, and not impaired, in value.

— *Theodore Roosevelt*

This chapter does not focus on climate change. You bring your own beliefs to the table with that political football, and it doesn't really matter if you consider yourself "green" or "anti-green." Right, wrong, or indifferent, it's time to set aside what you think you know about the topic to focus on the factual business reasons to pursue sustainability goals.

The concept of sustainability comes down to perception versus reality. The perception is that we all want to do what's right, which is to lower our carbon output to stop or slow down climate change. This balancing act translates into many heated discussions about which paths a business should take to achieve these competing goals: good for the planet, or good for the business.

A happy coincidence is that doing things to make a business more sustainable often saves money as well. Plus, if businesses promote their achievable sustainability goals, they gain PR credibility. Finally, the environmental, social, and corporate governance (ESG) scores being assigned to companies can make or break your enterprise's ability to obtain investments and new customers. Those are facts.

Figure 8-1 shows how public interest in sustainability accelerated over the last 10 years, which happens to be the same time interest in cloud computing grew. Cloud now approaches the 50 percent mark in the way that we do computing. The world began to focus on limiting carbon output around the same time cloud computing began its rapid growth. A frequent question soon arose: Is cloud computing green?

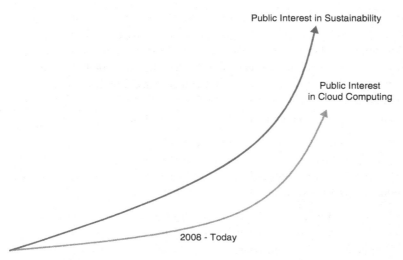

FIGURE 8-1 Public interest in sustainability grew at the same time cloud computing grew. The obvious question became: Is cloud computing good or bad for the planet? The answer, as usual, is, "It depends."

IT in general outputs a significant amount of carbon and has for a long time (see Figure 8-2). IT's heart beats on electricity, and fossil fuels still produce most of our power. Voila, carbon output. This will likely continue in the short term because renewable energy sources (such as wind and solar) are unlikely to become efficient enough to overtake traditional means of IT power generation until the long term.

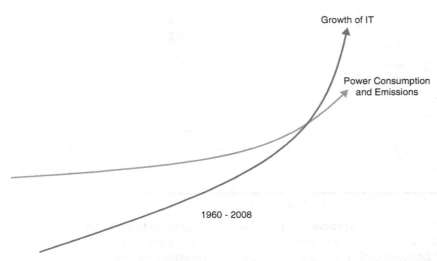

FIGURE 8-2 IT has a huge impact on carbon emissions. Although there are green benefits to IT systems, this chart depicts the actual relationship between computing and sustainability from 1960 to 2008.

Figure 8-2 depicts an aggregation of trend data over the time period of 1960 to 2008, or the start of cloud computing, including the growth of IT and the corresponding rise in IT energy usage. This period starts when businesses, educational institutes, and the public started to use mainframe computers until 2008 when computers and technology became systemic to everything we do. The year 2008 also happens to mark the rise of cloud computing, for all practical purposes. Of course, SaaS clouds predated 2008, and time sharing predated SaaS clouds. However, 2008 is when the industry saw the value of cloud technology shift and began to track it as a new technology thread, which leads us up to today.

There is some good news, such as the fact that today's servers are much more efficient than servers of 20 years ago. Today's power supplies, processors, and storage systems are engineered to use less power. The problem is, we're using much more of them. If you use 100 times more electronics than you did 10 years ago, power consumption will go up despite the devices being more "power optimized."

Traditional in-house data centers also continue to leverage more and more servers, where hardware capacity is typically purchased well ahead of the need for that capacity. In-house data centers usually operate and power servers at 5–10 percent utilization. Thus, we run on hardware that is underutilized by default (see Figure 8-3). Yes, the utilization will increase over time, but it will never reach full utilization. In-house servers use the same amount of electricity at 10 percent capacity as they do at 99 percent. Therefore, every percentage of underutilization is a waste of power.

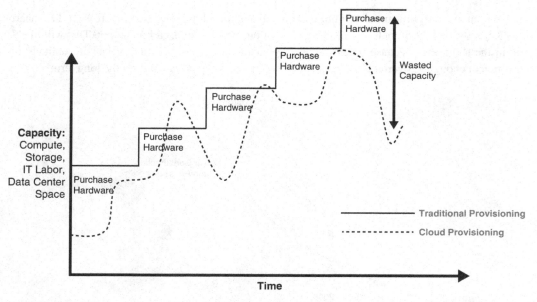

FIGURE 8-3 When using traditional approaches to computing, you need to purchase hardware well ahead of need. As you can see in this chart, those are the square lines, when capacity is raised by purchasing hardware outright. Thus, the hardware is running and using power, and the unused capacity is wasted.

You're probably guilty of this yourself, if that desktop computer or laptop on your desk runs idle 80 percent of the time. Perhaps you use only 20 percent of storage and perhaps as much as 50 percent of your processor and memory. That extra capacity exists because you'll need it at some point. Until then, those nonutilized hardware resources consume power to function, but you're not leveraging that much of the capacity that you're powering.

Initial Thinking: Cloud Data Centers, Bad

In the early days of cloud computing, representatives from various environmental organizations often contacted me. Because I am a cloud computing subject matter expert, they wanted to express their concerns that a massive amount of data center construction was underway to support emerging public cloud offers by the major cloud computing providers. They claimed that these new centers created higher power consumption, which would lead to more carbon and thus more climate change.

In some respects, they had a point. For decades, we built in-house data center after in-house data center to support the pre-cloud growth of enterprise IT. Now, the cloud providers were doing the same thing. Yes, those new cloud data centers will make things worse. However. Although the explosion in data center construction projects alarmed the environmental people, they often overlooked the big picture.

The purpose of this chapter is to explain what the growth of cloud computing means for sustainability.

More Data Centers, Bad

Let's back up about 60 years when computing emerged as an acceptable business tool. Few businesses could afford to have their own data centers, so they accessed data centers owned by large tech firms (IBM, Oracle, and so on) or universities via time sharing, serverless "dumb terminals" that emerged in the 1960s and 1970s. Enterprises used these computing systems as a utility and paid only for the time they leveraged the computers (and, of course, the power to access the systems).

Because this was a time-sharing service, businesses usually tapped into these services along with many other enterprises via a shared multiuser server.

This "old days" multiuser configuration is a bit different than multitenant, which is the model that public cloud computing services employ. An enterprise's cloud computing services can share coarse- and fine-grained IT resources such as storage, compute, AI, databases, and so forth, as if the enterprise owned these resources.

Conversely, traditional multiuser time-sharing services leveraged dumb terminals that provided a view of the computing system, typically as applications, that a few mysterious people in IT used to support business operations like customer databases. Those systems now seem quaint when compared to the processing power of almost any smartphone.

We were good at sharing computing resources in the early days of computing because we consumed less power per computing user. In other words, we started the computing journey greener than we are now because we were much better at sharing powered hardware resources.

So, what happened? Figure 8-4 shows the trend we dealt with for almost 50 years. We went from extensive time-share resource use to owning our own hardware for the exclusive use of an enterprise. This trend drove the growth of data centers to house and operate these new hardware resources that were solely owned by an enterprise. At the same time, the use of time-sharing systems diminished to almost nothing. Today, we've come full circle, as time-sharing systems are back in vogue with the use of cloud computing.

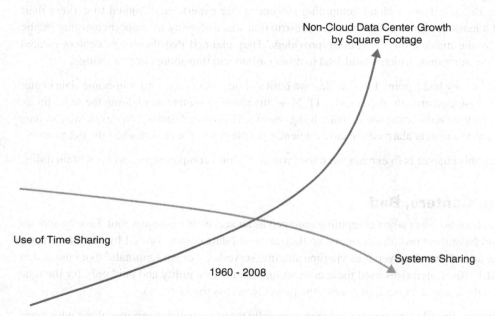

FIGURE 8-4 History repeats itself. We went from a time-sharing model in the early days of computing when data center costs were beyond the reach of most businesses. Then we shifted to privately owned equipment and data centers. Since 2008, we have gone back to sharing in a different way with cloud computing.

As the number of in-house data centers grew, most ran grossly underutilized hardware resources that consumed power and produced carbon. Remember our discussion of 5–10 percent utilization? You can see that cloud computing had a perception problem in the early days of cloud.

In comparison, data centers that are built to house cloud computing services can be shared by tens of thousands of users from hundreds of companies. A single company could use 10,000 times the power and space for an in-house data center than the equivalent usage in multitenant cloud computing services. This is what makes cloud computing truly green: sharing.

It's like the services we see today that enable excess capacity sharing for underutilized vacation homes, private car usage, and more. Cloud computing's capabilities to easily share and manage resources allow us to do more with less. In the case of enterprises, cloud allows more computing and storage and other types of business processing with fewer hardware resources and much less power. Yes, public cloud providers may have more data centers to house their cloud computing services and offerings. However, they operate at many times better power efficiency than traditional approaches to in-house data centers where everything is owned and nothing is shared.

More Shared Data Centers, Good

Figure 8-5 depicts two very important past trends. As the number of systems and the number of enterprises that owned data centers grew, we got a lot worse at utilizing those resources.

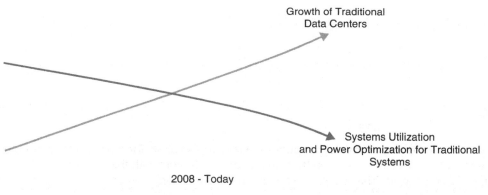

FIGURE 8-5 As we increased the number of owned systems and expanded data centers, we became very bad at system utilization that led to underoptimized power utilization.

Virtualization is another tool enterprises use to better utilize in-house data center resources. The capacity utilization problems remain with virtualization, in that we must purchase computing assets well ahead of need, as discussed earlier. However, it was a step in the right direction. Indeed, virtualization benefits were often confused with cloud computing, with the solution patterns being similar. However, multitenancy is more efficient than virtualization considering that more than one user, or one organization, can use the same resources at the same time.

Conversely, public cloud services can adjust utilization around changing needs. Many enterprises need additional compute power at specific times of the year, say, end of quarter/fiscal year, or during seasonal/holiday usage spikes. A public cloud service can provide an enterprise with what's needed, when needed, and then remove those additional resources when they are no longer needed.

Cloud computing will not save us from climate change. However, it's a step in the right direction. Cloud can at least turn the tide of wasteful enterprise computing operations.

Figure 8-6 illustrates the growth of public clouds from 2008 to today, which leads to higher system utilization through shared resources and lower use of power per cloud user and per enterprise.

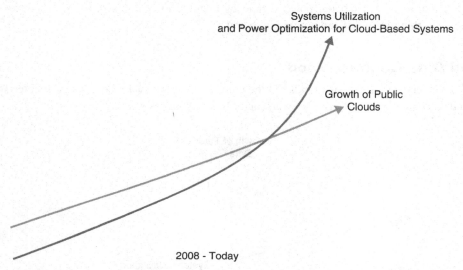

FIGURE 8-6   The multitenancy models that public clouds employ allow for much better compute and storage resource utilization, meaning that we can do much more with the same amount of power-consuming resources. This is a huge step in a more sustainable direction.

This is not rocket science. We have always understood that our ability to share resources leads to less waste. The prevailing wisdom was that everything needed to be owned and not shared for security reasons, and that any other approach was risky. It turns out that cloud computing is typically less risky than traditional approaches, with the added benefit of being greener as well. Let's break this down a bit and look at all aspects of cloud computing for sustainability, including the good and bad aspects that need consideration.

The Politics of Sustainability

So, who said this wasn't a fun topic? The political aspects of sustainability mean that those who try to create a sustainability path using cloud computing (or other technologies for that matter) can end up with a solution diluted by so many different opinions and debates that the white noise pushes any sustainability progress offtrack. Here's how to manage a path forward.

First, don't get into dumb arguments. Sustainability for the enterprise is not about who said what, it's about facts that follow along with many of the ideas presented in this chapter. Don't just provide an opinion; provide data to support your opinion. If there are other ideas, they should be considered if they also come with legitimate data.

Second, out of all the presentations I do and articles I write that discuss sustainability, the audiences or readers often focus too much on the topic of sustainability as a concept. I really don't care what people's opinions are on the concept of sustainability. Instead, we need to discuss strategies to reduce power consumption and better align power consumption to capacity needs.

That's why I typically don't get involved in discussions about the politics of sustainability and suggest that you don't either. Focus on reality, and objectively consider the negative and positive aspects of cloud usage for sustainability.

Power consumption optimization leads to the by-product of sustainability, which in turn saves money as much as it saves the planet. We must progress toward that objective for many reasons.

Finally, Sharing Is Possible

The current practice of building private data centers to house hardware that we may eventually use is itself unsustainable. Having those systems standing by and consuming power is not a good use of resources (again, see Figure 8-3). We shouldn't pay for power that doesn't create any business value. Incidentally, it's also not a great thing for the planet to waste power.

Cloud computing is not the ultimate answer of consumption-side sustainability, but it's a much better alternative to power-hungry compute and storage services running at 5–10 percent capacity. Those of you who run data centers, I urge you to look at the utilization reports for your standard and even virtualized servers to directly see the capacity and power that's being wasted. Remember, these reports do not account for the power needed to cool the data center, lighting, or the fact that people must commute to the data centers to maintain this equipment.

Data centers are necessary, but they are a huge power draw. Most consume as much power and water as a small town. It's better to have hundreds or thousands of enterprises use one public cloud data center than it is to have hundreds or thousands of individual data centers.

Once upon a time, we were very good at sharing compute and storage. We moved away from shared services when our data needs grew more sophisticated and compute resources became cheaper. We wanted complete control of our compute resources from the software to the hardware.

Cloud takes us back to the economies of scale with shared resources that are now better than solutions we leverage on owned data center resources. Also, R&D investments made by technology companies have shifted to cloud services over the last 10 years. Some enterprise software providers have already "sundowned" in-house data center services, and others continue to set expiration dates, which means you will soon have no choice but to move to cloud-based systems.

There is no bad news here regarding sustainability. Cloud moves to a more efficient technology consumption model, with additional applications and resources that are (or will soon be) far superior to those in an in-house data center.

The Greenness of Multitenancy

Multitenancy is what makes cloud computing sustainable. Simply put, it's the ability to share IT resources using mechanisms that allow for better sharing approaches, where the resources are as close to 100 percent utilization as possible. Although the multitenancy systems employed by each specific cloud provider are a bit different, they all have the same basic objectives:

- Share resources but disguise all sharing aspects from systems and humans who leverage those resources. Although this seems obvious, some multitenancy systems are very bursty and thus don't function well as sharable cloud services.

- Protect from other processes that you don't own. No other process is allowed to affect your processing such as a program running in memory or sharing a processor.

- Share all I/O resources including storage, such as databases running on shared storage, memory, network, and anything else that may consume and produce data.

- Allow scaling to occur without interruption; more resources are automatically allocated as needed to support a greater processing load. Those who use a multitenant system (typically a cloud provider's system) don't have to think about when and what to allocate to obtain greater scale.

- Return resources to a resource pool after use. For example, at the end of a holiday season, we can automatically eliminate excess capacity usage on a shared storage system, and that resource is returned to the public cloud's resource pool where it can be shared by other processes and humans.

Figure 8-7 illustrates a multitenancy model's nonlinear use of physical servers and workloads. Again, the core advantages here are resource sharing and offloading ownership, operations, and maintenance of hardware and software from enterprises to cloud providers. The use of excess capacity in a multitenant system drives more power efficiency out of the same number of physical servers. Yes, virtualization could create a multitenant structure for one enterprise. However, those who believe virtualization can replace public clouds often miss the bigger picture when it comes to efficiency of scale, including power consumption, considering that cloud computing makes resources more sharable and thus more efficient in terms of lowering power consumption across many different companies.

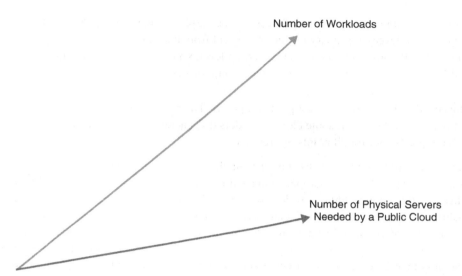

Number of Workloads

Number of Physical Servers
Needed by a Public Cloud

FIGURE 8-7   Multitenancy models use fewer power-consuming servers, which means that public clouds knock sustainability out of the park.

Not All Clouds Are Equal

A dirty little secret in the world of cloud computing and sustainability is that all clouds are not created equal in the race to sustainable results. Even different data centers owned by the same provider can be at different levels of carbon efficiency, or the same centers at different times of the day or week or year. This happens because each cloud provider must deal differently with load requests from cloud computing users depending on

- The current load the cloud provider is experiencing. Other centers in different geographical locations and servers within those centers may be activated to deal with increasing loads. Those centers and servers could use more carbon-producing "dirty" power than the provider's primary centers.

- The availability of green power around the location (point of presence) of the cloud computing data center you leverage. A provider might show you a wind farm and solar-powered facility that drives some of their data centers.

  However, in many areas it's still impossible to provide renewables at sustainability levels; thus, you're left with fossil fuel–generated power. Cloud providers do not try to hide that fact from you or the public. But if you choose a certain point of presence that's close to a major factory your enterprise owns, the provider could have few opportunities to create renewable power in that location.

- Most cloud providers cannot control the kind of power being placed on the grid. During off-peak hours, you might leverage primary power on the grid from nuclear power, which is as green as renewables. If consumption moves to a certain level, your power sources could also include fossil fuel–generated power to augment the cleaner power sources.

  In most instances, the cloud providers just purchase power. The power companies still control the source of that power. However, some cloud providers do generate their own power using renewables, but typically not for all points of presence.

A simple way to measure if or how much a cloud is sustainable is to consider Figure 8-8. Answer the power consumption questions with yes/no and percentages if possible, and this decision tree will help you figure out whether your public cloud provider supplies sufficient carbon-neutral computing to meet your sustainability goals. Also, assume the enterprise data center and the public cloud provider will hold at an average utilization rate of 50 percent. This means that 50 percent of the hardware will be utilized for workloads. Note: This is just for the sake of this example. In the real world, enterprise data centers average less than 20 percent utilization, and most public cloud providers are north of 90 percent utilization.

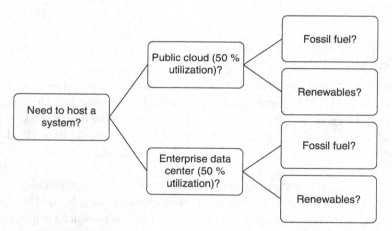

FIGURE 8-8 When it comes to development with an eye on lowering power consumption, there are many issues to consider.

It would be remiss of me not to mention that we can often fool ourselves with a binary rating. It's almost never completely carbon neutral or completely free from the use of dirty power. Instead, it will be somewhere between the extremes of more green or less green.

Continuing with our example in Figure 8-8, we have two location choices to host a system: public cloud or an enterprise data center. (For now, let's ignore the fact that the choice is never that simple.)

From there, we can find a path through other factors that determine if the place we host our computing and storage services is green. Does the data center (public cloud or enterprise) leverage fossil fuel or renewables? An owned data center that uses 90 percent renewables would win out over a cloud provider that uses only fossil fuel–generated power, or vice versa. Know what you're using.

Figure 8-9 shows an example of a path through this decision tree that determined a less sustainable conclusion with a public cloud provider that powers their data centers with fossil fuels.

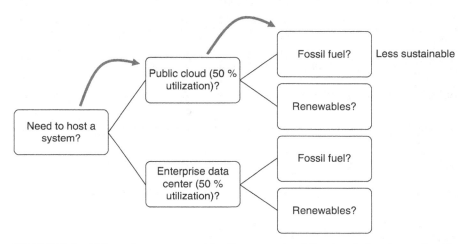

FIGURE 8-9 Although many consider the use of public clouds to always be the most sustainable choice, in this scenario the public cloud burns fossil fuel for power. The public cloud route in this instance is not optimized for sustainability.

Figure 8-10 is an example of a more sustainable outcome, even though you leverage your own data center that happens to be powered by renewables. So, this non-cloud solution ends up being more sustainable than some cloud solutions.

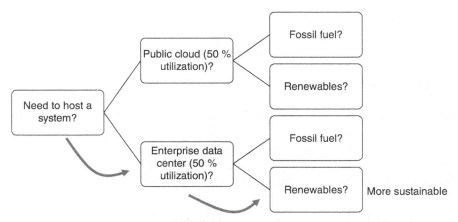

FIGURE 8-10 Although it may seem counterintuitive, data centers that employ renewable power could be the best choice for sustainability.

If this approach seems overly simplistic, you're right. However, it's the way most enterprises evaluate their deployments for sustainability, cloud or not. This kind of static analysis is helpful for basic decisions and to understand what's sustainable. However, it's often unrelated to the real world, and actual results will be very different, especially when using actual utilization versus an equated average.

A better model to consider is Figure 8-11, which has an added dimension: utilization. The reality is that utilization is not static. Ever. Although we can assume static utilization for some models, a more realistic model would be to look at different levels of utilization for different approaches to computing (cloud and enterprise data centers), and for different types of power being supplied at different levels of utilization. This example uses 25, 50, 75, and 100 percent levels to consider.

At higher levels of utilization, more will get done on a single, powered piece of hardware. The higher the utilization, the greener the deployment. Remember, cloud computing is typically the more sustainable solution because it can share hardware resources and thus do more with less. This is the most important point in this chapter.

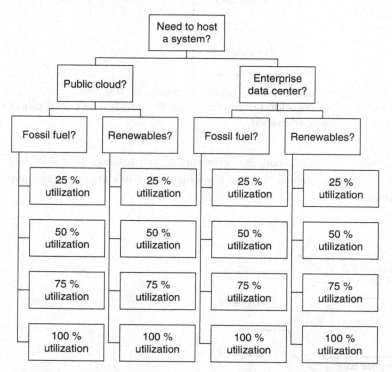

FIGURE 8-11   In this example, we look at utilization of the hardware to determine if a deployment is sustainable. This model more closely resembles the real world.

What's interesting about this model are the very different conclusions made from different levels of utilization that are more reflective of the complexities of these decisions. For example, an enterprise data center that leverages renewables at less than 25 percent utilization may have a larger carbon footprint than a cloud solution that leverages fossil fuel at near 100 percent utilization. Why? It takes carbon to build the hardware (more than you think), and to build the data center as well. Just using renewables does not mean a data center is fully carbon neutral…and very much not carbon neutral if utilization is suboptimal. Indeed, some enterprises can achieve near 100 percent utilization with cloud providers that use dirty power and end up with a more sustainable solution than a deployment that uses renewable power sources.

Here are a few things to keep in mind:

First, sustainability is often not what it first appears to be. Public relations and marketing campaign claims of sustainability can be incorrect for both cloud providers and traditional data center real estate providers. You must consider all variables in your modeling. Account for the carbon impact of building a data center, the data center infrastructure, and the impact of building all the hardware that will be contained in the data center.

Second, sustainability is a dynamic process. What's true today may not be true tomorrow. Literally. You must reanalyze the true carbon impact of your cloud and non-cloud deployments on a regular basis. Not every day, but perhaps annually. For example, the source of power that supplies the grid often changes based on increasing demand. While you might brag about how green your cloud deployment is in 2025, that may not be the case in 2027. If cloud computing sustainability is an ongoing concern for your company, then it's a wise call to add a sustainability monitor to your cloud operations (CloudOps). This is especially true if your enterprise is graded on sustainability by outside regulators, or if it's monitored by the press. The enterprise could end up with a huge PR problem if you're outed for using dirty power, no matter if you meant to or not.

Resource Optimization and Sustainability

Much of the sustainability effort concentrates on ways to reduce our carbon footprint by using more sustainable compute and storage methods such as cloud-based resources. There are more obvious things to consider as well. The big one is to reduce the number of virtual or real server assets required. This means doing the same (or more) with less. Better optimizing the number of resources reduces your need for power. Let's explore this a little.

A hiding-in-pain-sight secret of enterprise computing is that we always use more compute and storage resources than we really need. This comes mainly from a lack of architectural planning that leads to inefficiencies, that in turn cause more resources to be deployed than needed. For instance, that old data warehouse system that was built in the 1990s using 500 terabytes of storage because the same data is replicated a dozen times during processing. If redesigned, it could do the same or a better job with only 50 terabytes of storage.

The system works and nobody wants to reopen that issue, so the problem gets kicked down the road. When this old data warehouse system is lifted and shifted to the cloud, we'll pay a much larger data storage bill than we should. Although that's bad enough, we must also understand that this top-heavy system has an impact on power consumption as well. If you're green, the old data warehouse system isn't. If you're just a pragmatic businessperson and good corporate citizen, the system is also unoptimized for its business value. Fixing this dinosaur could kill two birds with one stone.

The average enterprise has between 100 to 400 systems in dire need of better optimization for the resources they leverage. What's likely to happen to these systems is that the cloud will shine a new light on their inefficiencies. In the past, resource-hogging systems installed within enterprise data centers did not seem to be a problem. We had to power and operate those dedicated systems anyway, so it didn't matter if we leveraged 67 percent capacity versus 22 percent. The bill at the end of the month was the same.

When these systems are moved to the cloud, the inefficiencies become much more visible. That's when you get a surprise $20,000 storage bill for a specific system that will generate many more questions about how to reduce that cost. Eyepopping cloud bills like those are the drivers of the current trend toward FinOps, which can monitor and optimize cloud costs. FinOps encompasses a dedicated set of people, processes, and tooling that will ask the hard questions until some sort of better optimization occurs. The good news here? When you solve the efficiency problem to save money and make the finance team happy, you'll also reduce carbon output. Win/win.

Green Application Development?

Being an old developer, I recall having to deal with fewer resources. Memory and storage were expensive commodities back in the day. Thus, we were forced to conserve the number of resources we could leverage, which led us to build and deploy much more efficient applications that used a minimum number of resources. We didn't even consider developing applications that used power more efficiently; that outcome was simply an unplanned by-product.

Now we want more sustainable computing platforms to run our applications and store our data. We're also finding that the applications themselves can be optimized to burn less power and thus become more sustainable. This is known as green development (or similar terms), which means that we focus on the optimization of applications and data storage to burn much less energy than unoptimized applications. It's a huge paradigm shift for a generation of developers who looked at resources such as CPU, memory, and storage as cheap commodities. Beginning with the application bloat that began in the mid-1980s, application developers just kept growing the number of resources that software needed to operate, which drove the need to upgrade to larger and more power-hungry hardware resources (pre-cloud). Just try running a modern operating system on an older PC and you'll see that it's almost unusable. Those who built the operating systems in those days operated with the understanding that additional resources were cheap and readily available. That's why they created software systems that were much less efficient than those built in the 1970s and early 1980s.

"Bloatware" is what many now call it, which refers to the fact that many developers got lazy when it came to resource optimization. Bigger and better CPUs and memory systems could always accommodate the resource-hungry applications that were created over the last 20+ years. What we also failed to notice? Bloatware applications also require larger and more powerful resources that burn more power…perhaps a lot more power.

Today there is a new focus on green development, both on public cloud platforms and traditional systems. The idea is simple. A check is done during development, typically within a DevOps toolchain, where the applications are tested for security, performance, reliability, stability, power optimization, and many other things. A code analyzer scans through the code and analyzes the behaviors of the executables to determine how optimized the application is around power consumption. There are huge sustainability gains that can be made here that will also lower your cloud computing bill.

Green development has several benefits. First, it puts the burden on the developer to write and deploy more efficient code. Doing so will also optimize the resources used. Note the word *optimize* versus *minimize*. Developers must learn to do more with less by using proven approaches to lower the number of resources leveraged by a single application and to do so in a way that nothing else is sacrificed. Developers should not feel obliged to sacrifice performance and usability to optimize resources. If that's what happens, the developer is not doing "green development" right. Creative approaches and tooling are now available that allow us to program both better and more optimized code. The bigger objective is to build and deploy applications that provide the same or better business value with fewer resources and less power.

When optimized applications and systems are operational, FinOps should monitor resource optimization for ongoing sustainability. Remember, in optimizing our cloud spending, we also optimize power consumption, and thus we can monitor both at the same time using many of the same cloud operations tools. Another win/win.

Multicloud as a Sustainability Weapon?

The use of multicloud to find greener cloud and traditional computing solutions is an emerging area of discussion. If done correctly, multicloud can leverage any number of providers and services that we consider best-of-breed. We can pick solutions that leverage green power sources and thus provide a boost to sustainability.

Figure 8-12 depicts how this works. In this multicloud deployment example, we have three different clouds that run under our single layers. This may include cross-cloud security, operations, governance, FinOps, and other common services that holistically manage the multicloud deployment. I discussed this in Chapter 6, "The Truths Behind Multicloud That Few Understand," so we won't dive in too deep here. The important thing to remember? When deployed correctly, a multicloud can use any number of services for any number of reasons and leverage the best services for the job, including best for functionality, performance, cost, and, yes, sustainability.

Multicloud Deployment

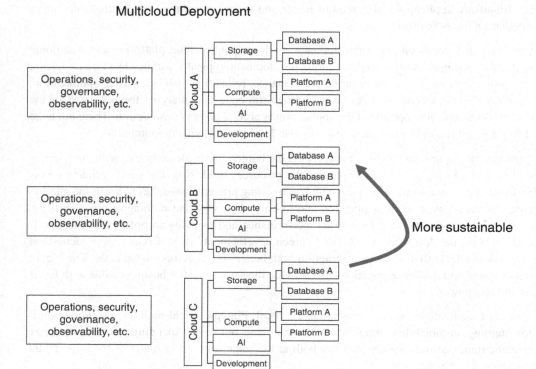

FIGURE 8-12 Multicloud deployments can leverage cloud services that provide the best sustainability rankings. Cloud service brokers are beginning to track sustainability as a ranking for services that can be promoted over less sustainable services.

Related to what you see in Figure 8-12, let's say we leverage a database from a point-of-presence where only a fossil fuel—powered energy source is available. However, another cloud provider supports the same databases but runs within a special cloud computing data center that only leverages renewables, including a well-publicized wind farm that was created specifically for that cloud computing data center.

Multicloud allows you to capture a sustainability advantage by using that specific database, running on that specific cloud provider, over the other cloud brand that does not offer a sustainable solution. Of course, you need to consider cost as well, including the ability to support the core business requirements, which could include growth, scalability, and reliability. Don't make the mistake of leveraging one cloud provider over another for sustainability reasons only to realize that specific provider is less reliable and less cost effective. You need to consider all factors when selecting a cloud provider and cloud service for a multicloud deployment. Sustainability can't be the only evaluation criterion.

What Is Your Real Impact?

Sometimes I think we focus so much on sustainability that we miss more important issues that need to be addressed, such as the ones listed in Figure 8-13. We must approach sustainability with a holistic understanding of what it means to be truly sustainable and recognize when we're working toward the wrong objectives.

FIGURE 8-13 Sustainability is not just one thing; it's many. People, culture, and technology must work together to make sustainability happen. It's more complex than many understand, and the danger is that all the focus on sustainability will have unintended consequences.

For instance, we might focus too much on the power source for our system deployment and not consider the true business impact. I've seen enterprises move to more sustainable deployments, typically in search of a better rating from outside agencies, and at the same time give up reliability. That solution could cost the company more in bad PR due to the cost and stress of dealing with system outages and outraged customers than any green advantages they gained.

Sustainability needs to be a change in culture more than a change in technology. We need to educate everyone in the company about doing things that are more sustainable, and best practices and approaches that work for other companies. For anyone who grew up in a household where a parent figure constantly harped about turning off lights when you left a room until it was second nature, you know what I'm talking about.

In the enterprise, teach the mechanisms staff can leverage today to make more sustainable choices for the business, such as cloud computing itself. This also means looking holistically at the business, knowing that a few sustainability gains may not justify other negative impacts on the business. The law of unintended consequences often arises if you make sustainability the main goal. Recognize when you may hurt other areas of the business and even cancel out any sustainability benefit by being penny wise and dollar foolish.

For example, let's say you move all data storage to a single public cloud provider for their sustainability benefits. When audited, you discover the provider is violating several data privacy regulations and just flunked an audit during the first month it hosted your data. Aside from the numerous fines the provider may incur on your behalf, the carbon output required to fly enterprise executives and a legal team to that jurisdiction to clean up the legal and PR mess will remove any carbon benefits you should have received from that move for the next 100 years. But at least your heart was in the right place. Remember, in that and many cases, moving to sustainability can backfire in ways you can't anticipate. If my suspicions are correct, we'll see many of these types of sustainability case studies in the next 10 years.

Sustainability is a hot topic right now, but we can't blindly chase a politically correct ideal that ends up hurting the business. Enterprises tend to move quickly when a regulatory requirement will also provide good PR and save money. However, they will find that sustainability is much more complex and less forgiving than most people realize. The name of the game here is to find a trusted path that is sustainable with a net benefit to the business.

Hopefully, you got the overall sustainability message in this chapter, even though we focused mainly on sustainability's impact on cloud computing.

Call to Action

When it comes to cloud computing, we need to weaponize automation to provide better sustainability. Rather than rely on humans to shift workloads and data stores to get the best carbon impact, we must leverage automated tools to dynamically make those decisions. Those tools can use advanced approaches such as AI to ensure that we're as optimized as we can possibly be, with all things considered in terms of what the business needs.

Figure 8-14 shows the rise of automation along with the rise of cloud computing. Automation provides us with mechanisms that can support more sustainability—for instance, the ability to dynamically move workloads from cloud provider to cloud provider in response to better sustainability rankings, as well as lower costs and improved reliability. These automated processes need to consider everything about the business to make the right decisions. If we focus them solely on ways to be more sustainable, they're likely to inflict unintended consequences that can remove any benefits.

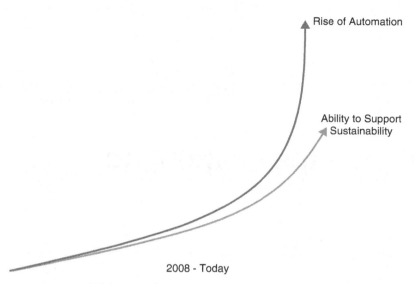

Rise of Automation

Ability to Support
Sustainability

2008 - Today

FIGURE 8-14 Widespread automation manages decreasing and increasing uses of cloud and even traditional IT resources, as needed, as demand ebbs and flows. By not under- or overserving the enterprise with resources on-demand, automation provides the most sustainable path available today.

Automation provides an even further benefit. We can leverage automation to find the right number of compute, storage, and databases instances that need to be launched to support our enterprise IT needs. These needs will likely grow and contract day to day and month to month. Automation can better align need with the number of resources leveraged. It's this kind of automation that's often overlooked. We need to consider what's running versus where something is running to gain sustainable results with long-term benefits to the business and the environment.

This effort is about more than just sustainability. This is about being more efficient, which will naturally lead to cost and environmental savings.

Bottom line: Efficiency should always be our goal.

Chapter 9

The Evolution of the Computing Market

Advertising is legitimized lying.

— *H. G. Wells*

Where is cloud computing today? Where is it going? This chapter answers those questions.

The answers do not include a bunch of obvious, generalized statements, such as "The cloud will expand in the enterprise moving forward," or "Data will continue to grow in the cloud." Thanks, Captain Obvious. Nope, in this chapter we focus on where the cloud market is now, how it will likely grow, and point out trends that are more difficult to perceive. In many cases, we may push back on the business plans of some cloud providers while validating others. Let's get started.

First, understand that cloud is the next phase of computing, which means it will pay off to get cloud done right the first time. Some enterprises already got a few (or many) cloud things wrong. If they don't correct course, companies that do cloud wrong will see costs go up while the quality of their services and products goes down. Meanwhile, more innovative companies will step up and take their market share. These disruptor companies will learn how to effectively leverage cloud computing technology and cloud services such as AI. Companies that provide better customer experiences using better technology will displace the companies that don't understand until it's too late that cloud adoption is life and death.

So, how do you get on the right cloud track? It's not about understanding the details of what I'm about to tell you, it's about understanding the general trends of how I see the market evolving. In some places, I make educated guesses as to what will likely happen based on existing data and trends. Some patterns have already emerged, so it's not a question of if they will occur; it's an educated guess as to how they will play out from here. The most important aspect is to get the gist of what will probably happen, its relationship to how and when you adopt the technology, how the technology works in the enterprise now and moving forward, and ways you can weaponize the technology for your own business advantages. This means spotting trends that many others don't see and leveraging them as true force multipliers.

Again, I provide an objective take on each topic. I'll talk about the good, the bad, and ways you should consider the topic from the viewpoint of your own business requirements. Of course, you should also consider your own life experiences and interpret what I'm saying from your point of view. I never claim that I'm always right, and I always welcome challenges to my thinking from those who read my books or articles, take my courses, or follow me on social media. I recognize the fact that anyone who does not want to hear other points of view or gets inordinately defensive about their own should perhaps be reconsidered as a reliable source of information. With that disclaimer out of the way, let's get to it.

Forced March to the Cloud?

It's Monday, you're visited by two "suits" who insist you must move faster to the cloud, and they give you a deadline to get more applications and data moved over to public cloud providers. If you do not meet that deadline, they explain that your systems will be at greater risk and the costs to maintain those systems will skyrocket to the point that they put your business in jeopardy.

What did you do to deserve this? Are these strong-arm tactics from a tyrannical government that wants to control the future of your business? The local mob?

No. This is what happens when an industry shifts its resources to an emerging technology (in this case, cloud computing, in which you're only partially invested) and rapidly removes resources for the technology that runs your business day-to-day. You end up with fewer maintenance updates to those systems, little or no innovation, and eventually you have no choice but to move onto the new platforms. If you don't, your business will "die the death of a thousand cuts." The lack of support and innovation from your existing business systems will erode your IT footprint to the point that your business will lose a great deal of value.

Is this fair? No. However, we've seen this play out before. You don't see many 30-year-old computers around, even though they would likely work to spec with their original software and operating systems restored. Technology providers eventually "sunset" the technology you're using, which will force a move to newer and hopefully better technology.

We saw these shifts during the rise of PCs in the 1980s, then the rise of distributed systems, and now the rise of cloud computing. How the supply side of the industry makes investments in R&D and new innovations will move enterprises off older technology, no matter whether enterprises want to move or not. The provider shift to cloud investments will force your shift to cloud consumption at or around the same time frame. If you don't shift, you'll be stuck with undermaintained technology. This could be a security system that does not get consistent updates to do battle with new and emerging threats, or an operating system that does not receive driver updates to support new hardware, and so forth. It's time to ask yourself, Where is your business positioned on its forced march to the cloud?

The Shift in R&D Spending

Let's just get this out of the way: You can't really put the R&D spending shift at the feet of cloud providers. Having been a technology products and services CTO for years, I know the name of the game is to focus on emerging markets and investments in those markets to support the growth of a technology business. The larger technology players (certainly the enterprise technology providers that have been around for decades) are acting in their own best interests by shifting R&D investments to technologies that focus on the cloud computing market and away from traditional systems that are found in data centers. What's most interesting is that many of these companies still make 80 percent of their profits from traditional or legacy business, but they are not pushing more investments into improving that technology. Instead, their focus is on shiny new objects that promise better growth because the industry, technology press, and investors are laser-focused on cloud computing.

Figure 9-1 depicts how this shift played out since the start of the cloud computing boom around 2008. That's when spending on R&D and innovation for core enterprise technology companies shifted from traditional to cloud-based systems, no matter what aspect of technology they provided, including databases, networking, security, and operations. Most R&D is now focused on cloud computing, which the industry views as the next evolution.

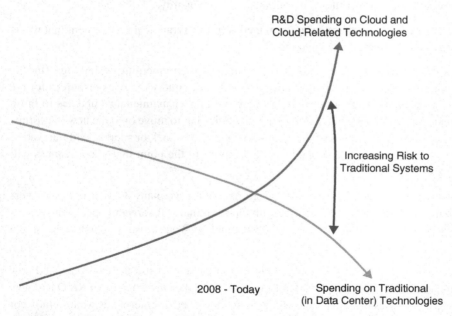

FIGURE 9-1   There is a vast difference in the money now spent to develop cloud-based technologies versus traditional computing technology. Approximately 80 percent goes to the development of cloud computing–focused products and services while 20 percent goes to more traditional systems such as mainframes. Traditional systems are being left behind as R&D focuses on cloud platforms.

Of course, companies that maintain more traditional technology incur mounting risk, as you also see in Figure 9-1. As the gap widens between investments in traditional technology and newer cloud-based technologies, the risk and cost of maintaining traditional systems shoot up. Those who maintain this technology will see fewer updates to key system components and fading technical support with fewer talented support staff taking longer to respond to requests. Those who maintain these systems are already starting to notice.

At the same time, you may leverage cloud-related services from the same company at deep discounts, with exceptional support, and you're typically dealing with the top talent. Again, this may account for only 20 percent of the provider's business, but it's getting 80 percent of their time and talent.

Leaving Systems Behind

So, how do you deal with the need to move into cloud computing and still maintain many existing systems for the foreseeable future? It's all about learning to manage risk.

Figure 9-2 depicts the three levels your existing systems will probably move through, and the timing depends largely on how your technology provider invests in their technology. The bottom level is "Production Ready," where the technology is near or at production quality. It might not be the focus of growth and innovation by the technology provider, but it's considered good enough to sell and service. When the technology does not receive the investments needed for continuous operations and improvements, it will move to "Limited," which means the system does not live up to expectations. Problems such as performance and stability issues go unaddressed, or there are huge delays to address them. Finally, "Obsolete" sounds like what it is: Your technology has been sunsetted by the provider. No further investment will be made, and the vendor plans to remove it from support and maintenance, regardless of your opinion on the matter.

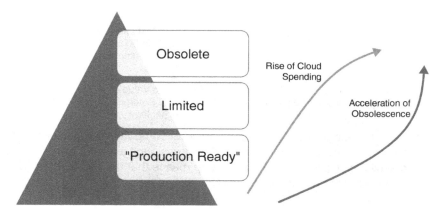

FIGURE 9-2 As money spent to build and maintain cloud-based solutions increases, the obsolescence of non-cloud systems accelerates until risk and cost inflect for enterprises that chose to maintain more traditional systems in data centers.

Customers do not have much recourse, assuming the technology provider still follows standing agreements. Normally, the vendors will work with you in good faith to move to other systems, such as those based in the cloud, and perhaps provide migration services to make the transition. Hopefully, you'll get a discount on the new cloud services, but this normally comes with a new set of agreements. A new cloud service-level agreement (SLA) will usually lean in the vendor's favor, perhaps more than the agreements provided for traditional systems.

You should also note in Figure 9-2 that we're dealing with two shifts. First, the rise of cloud spending, which shifts focus to other technologies in the marketplace. Second, the effect of the rise of cloud spending, which pushes the market to make an older technology obsolete.

This is nothing new. The technology market evolves. At the same time, we evolve the products that are being sold within these evolving markets. Again, the movement to PCs, smartphones, the Internet of Things, and other waves of technology are obvious examples of this phenomena. We just see a more obvious shift with the vast differences between traditional technology that ran within a data center and cloud-based technology with its very different consumption, billing, and value models. Clearly, it's more noticeable. Enterprises are starting to worry about how cloud will affect their IT footprint.

Figure 9-3 depicts how this shift will likely affect the market. We'll see more cost and risk from 2022 to 2023, and onward. The business need for traditional computing will diminish over time as more and better cloud computing alternatives become available. The value of traditional computing technology will drop much more significantly as a cost and risk gap widens for enterprises that leverage traditional technology.

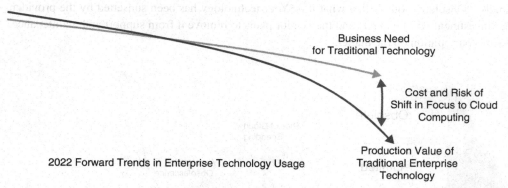

FIGURE 9-3   The business need for traditional technology over cloud computing will diminish as fewer investments are made in traditional computing systems areas such as security and operations than are made in similar cloud technologies. This gap means that the cost and risk of technology quickly shift to those who chose to maintain traditional systems.

Can enterprises do anything about this shift? Not much. Some of you will feel the shift impact much more than others, depending on what core technology your business has in place, and the speed of the providers' and your enterprise's move to the cloud. The key here is to understand your technology provider's sunset plans for your systems, or to recognize if your provider is on a path to be put out of business by the cloud or (more likely) absorbed into another technology company. Those last two possibilities are not great outcomes. You'll have even less control of the technology you leverage today. It's still better to have a plan in place that takes those possibilities under consideration. Yes, it will be a plan that makes some assumptions and calculates the path of least risk and cost for the enterprise, understanding that you might make some wrong guesses, and you'll need contingency plans in place to get back on track.

More Consumption, but Prices Stay Static

Other issues seem to be artifacts of a changing market. For example, more enterprises now leverage public cloud providers, but the prices remain static. Yes, you can show me instances where prices have gone up or stayed the same or gone down, but it's unlike the early days of cloud computing when prices fluctuated mostly downward to the point that it looked as though the public cloud providers were on a race to the bottom.

Figure 9-4 shows how cloud providers moved from a relatively new and innovative market where price cuts were more common to a point where the cost of development becomes more optimized, which is all in contrast to the early days when more innovation and inventions were needed along with low pricing to entice customers into cloud computing brand loyalty. The result is a market where service providers' costs to develop and maintain cloud services continue to fall while enterprise IT organizations' costs for specific services remain relatively the same. However, overall enterprise cloud costs continue to significantly rise through the increased use of cloud services.

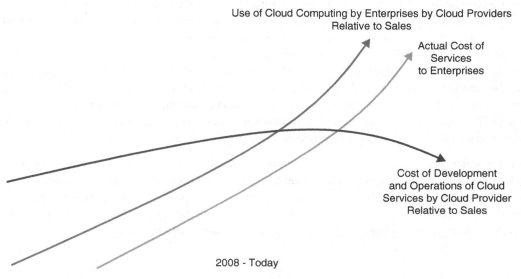

FIGURE 9-4   Cloud providers are enjoying a relatively mature market with the cost of development relative to sales going down as time progresses and as the use of cloud-based resources continues to grow. However, per unit prices remain relatively the same for their customers.

Cloud providers explain this to me as passing on the cost of innovation from the market's formative years back in 2008–2012. Much like the traditional software market, cloud profits appear in the later stages of the market when growth inflects, and the maturity of the services leads to better margins. At the same time, the relative cost of development and operations falls while market prices remain much the same.

Again, this behavior is something you see in most technology industries, where the entrance into the market produces loss leaders and there are limited or no profits. However, management speculates that current investments in innovation will reap future rewards when the market matures. That's why I don't often complain about higher provider profits now that cloud computing is a full-fledged technology market. By the way, there was risk that cloud computing would make a big splash and then come to nothing, which was also risk the providers had to manage.

I suspect there will be downward pressure on the price of cloud services going forward as some of the more common layers become somewhat commoditized, such as storage and compute. Also, the movement to multicloud and other higher layers of service that run across cloud providers will make it easier to switch between services, and thus put more competitive pressure on specific cloud providers that may have enjoyed a functional monopoly. For instance, some companies leveraged only one public cloud provider and were more of a "captive audience" when it came to their choices of cloud services. That's no longer the case, perhaps for good economic reasons.

The Power of a Few Players

We also need to address the elephant in the room: A handful of public cloud players dominate about 90 percent of the market. This is not considered a monopoly because three major players compete against one another. But there were dozens of players in the early days of cloud computing. Some concerns arise that the big three will act as one when setting prices and gang up to drive upstart competitors out of the market. All these price fixing and collaboration activities are very illegal in most countries, so they are unlikely to make formal agreements or put plans in writing due to the penalties. But the potential is there. They could coordinate and control the market, and they will already control most of enterprise IT at that point. It's a concern I've heard often from CIOs who must put their trust in public cloud providers. For now, let's just hope it doesn't happen.

Figure 9-5 depicts how the market has changed over the past 12–15 years. There were dozens of cloud provider upstarts in the marketplace when cloud began to form into its own market, typically around the rise of IaaS clouds. Basically, every telecom company, enterprise software company, and even hardware providers had public cloud and private cloud startups at the genesis of the market. Today we have only six to eight relevant public cloud providers. What happened to everyone else?

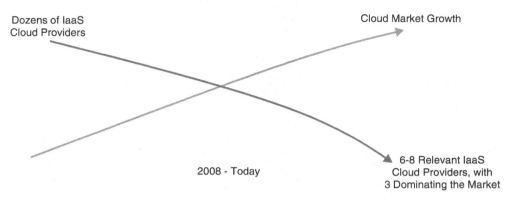

FIGURE 9-5 In the early days of cloud computing, there were dozens of public cloud providers started by telecom companies, software companies, and startups. Today, we're dominated by just a few key public cloud players that needed to spend billions of dollars to provide services that enterprises would leverage. However, this does lead to just a few providers making up much of the public cloud market, which comes with its own set of concerns.

It became a matter of how much money could be spent by any given cloud provider. If you look at today's major players, the top three had to invest billions to begin to capture significant market share. The larger players were the only companies in position to get to the scale and innovation level that cloud computing required to provide a viable public cloud platform. The companies without access to resources, or ones that did not have investors willing to take the risk, simply bowed out of the public cloud market and conceded defeat as they sought other ways to play in the cloud market. Some became managed services providers (MSPs), some focused on cloud networking, and many just focused on technology to work with cloud technology, such as operations and security.

For someone who had many of those companies as clients, both those able to build a significant public cloud provider or those that had to settle for second place, these were tough decisions. These decisions will likely need to be made again as we move on to other technological shifts, but they probably won't be as significant as the shift to public cloud.

It's interesting to note that there will surely be another evolution of public cloud upstarts that will try to enter the market. These will be cloud providers that serve a special purpose, such as focusing on a specific industry to create "industry clouds." These clouds will provide services that are purpose-built for a specific vertical such as health care, retail, or finance.

They will stand up a public cloud to provide specific services that will most likely be mixed with the services from larger public cloud providers. Perhaps they'll leverage multicloud deployments and/or use one of the existing mega clouds as their operations platform. We'll have core storage and compute services from a major public cloud provider, but secondary industry-specific services from these industry clouds. There is a viable place in the market for providers that offer a limited number of services that work with public cloud providers to offer products that are custom-built for specific businesses. Of course, the larger cloud providers could enter this market as well, but they are unlikely to have the speed and agility of the smaller players.

Beyond industry clouds, the "micro-cloud" market has been evolved over the last several years as those aligned with larger public cloud providers seek to augment their core public cloud services and thus provide a viable and growing part of the services market. The likely evolution will be micro-clouds that stay away from areas that the larger providers will likely enter, which will be a common pattern as the cloud market becomes more saturated and existing cloud providers look for avenues of growth. Look for the growth of very innovative industry- and micro-clouds that can take public clouds to the next level by providing additive services.

This Is About Market Capture

Let's go back to the competition between the larger cloud providers and how that competition will likely progress. While the market expands for public cloud services, there will be an aggressive dash to obtain as much of that emerging market as possible.

"Once a customer, always a customer." That old marketing adage still holds true with cloud computing. Enterprises, organizations, and even specific systems are unlikely to change providers, although they may shift investments to other cloud providers, such as in the case of multicloud. However, after a system is coupled to a specific cloud provider, that marriage typically means a costly divorce. Captured market share remains durable for many years, which is why public cloud providers aggressively go after the same customers, basically selling many of the same cloud services.

Although one public cloud provider dominates the market right now, the overall market seems to be normalizing. Other cloud providers (including two of the top three) or the other second-tier players will accelerate their market share acquisition to gather a larger percentage of the market. Considering the rapid growth of cloud computing in general, most of the cloud players will experience rapid growth with some growing faster than the others. This process should continue as far as 2030, when we'll see an equalization in the market for most of the major cloud players. A few of the smaller players will fall out, meaning they'll be purchased by another larger player.

Yes, I hear all the antitrust concerns around cloud computing, and speculation about the likelihood that a single cloud provider will control the market. However, the most likely outcome will be 8–12 major cloud players, with 100 or fewer second-tier players (those that provide additive technologies such as security) with most of the market shares equalizing over time. That equalization will hurt some of the larger players that initially captured a large share of the market, but everyone will end up making a lot of money. The market will eventually be evenly distributed among the first- and second-tier players. I don't think equalization will result in as much drama as most expect.

Why They Don't Work and Play Well Together

Here's a question I get a lot: Why don't the major hyperscalers (large public cloud providers) work together to closely coordinate enterprise technology and platforms? The short answer is that there is nothing in it for them. They don't run charities; they run massive businesses that depend on them to innovate and grow their businesses as rapidly as possible by using that innovation. As businesses, their objective is to return as much shareholder equity as possible. That means capturing more market share than the competition, and not sharing any secrets that will allow the competition to do something as fast as they can. Yes, there are some partnerships and coordinated standards activity, but don't expect them to work together on your behalf when it's contrary to their own.

Figure 9-6 depicts how this scenario plays out. Any major cloud provider will have their own set of business objectives (make money and capture market share). Because they want to capture the same market share, they work at odds, even though the goals of making money and creating value are very much the same. Therefore, you can't count on any significant coordination to build common or other cross-cloud services, unless you can successfully present a mutually beneficial business case to the public cloud providers.

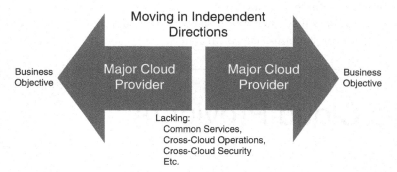

FIGURE 9-6 It should surprise no one that the major cloud providers operate with their own sets of objectives. They have no incentive to coordinate common services that could prove helpful to customers now that multicloud deployments are much more common.

What about the emerging multicloud market, where the game will shift to cross-cloud services? With a few exceptions, the larger cloud providers understand the shift to multicloud, but they do not plan strategic shifts of any significance to accommodate multicloud. When speaking at public cloud computing conferences sponsored by specific providers, I'm even "discouraged" from presenting multicloud topics because these topics conflict with their "existing messaging." The bottom line is that they have yet to see multicloud as an opportunity, but it's a clear risk to how they position and sell public cloud services. This situation will likely change as the market reality overcomes strategic shortsightedness.

Will Public Cloud Providers Become Like Video Streaming Services?

The comparison with streaming services is an apt one, given the way the market is evolving. Right now, most of the public cloud providers are building the same types of services that provide the same types of functionality. This compares to how you can stream *The Office* on several different streaming services with prices that range from free to $5.99 per episode. The version of *The Office* that streams on streaming service A versus streaming service B is the same, although the price, speed, clarity, and amount of advertising could vary (or not). Shows that exist on streaming services are one of the reasons people unsubscribed from cable and satellite services over the last few years.

Of course, cloud providers will quickly point out that you cannot apples-and-oranges compare their services to shows on streaming services because their services are unique and provide better functionality than the same types of services running on their competitor's cloud. It's true; providers typically use different interfaces, APIs, security systems, operations systems, and so on, but they still provide overlapping functionality. Storage systems store stuff, processing systems process stuff. With a few native differences, it's pretty much the same with public cloud computing resources; they provide the same functionality across many of the core public cloud services.

Figure 9-7 puts this functionality into perspective. Sets of overlapping technologies are very much the same from cloud provider to cloud provider (storage, compute, databases, containers, container orchestration, and so on). Major cloud providers offer their own versions of core cloud services such as object storage. However, many of the other services they offer are the same brands and technology, such as popular databases, application development platforms, and AI/ML.

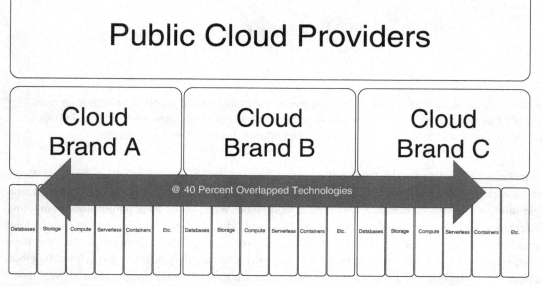

FIGURE 9-7 Just as you can watch the same episode of a TV show on streaming services like Netflix and Amazon Prime, today's public cloud providers offer overlapping services that provide the same or similar customer experiences.

If you think this sounds like commoditization, you're right. Much of the evolution of cloud technology will be to solve the same solution patterns. Thus, you can purchase access to the same or similar technology from many different cloud providers. Of course, the public cloud providers continue to push back hard on this analogy by offering more innovative and unique services. Think about how services such as Disney +, HBO, Netflix, and many others create movies and content that aren't available on other streaming services. However, they still offer "stock" content like the exact same classic TV series and movies that many other streaming services provide. In the case of cloud providers, their "stock" business has the same core resources such as storage, compute, and databases, which are the same or similar across cloud providers.

Next, we discuss how cloud providers supporting basically the same cloud services across cloud brands leads to some commoditization of the cloud computing market.

The Emergence of Commoditization

Commoditization is defined as the concept of products that have economic value and are distinguishable in terms of their attributes that become simple commodities in the eyes of the market or consumers, or something that's common and thus has less value. Commoditization occurs in most markets as technology and products mature. If you think about flat-screen TVs, calculators, even hoverboards, they start their life cycles pricey and limited and then end up plentiful and cheap. This is how a product moves from limited use as it gathers market share and then moves into wide use where the market share is gathered and mature.

Cloud computing is not yet a commodity, but it's moving from one side of the market to the other with some signs of its commoditization. One sign is that core cloud services are beginning to look alike on the major public cloud providers (hyperscalers). Also, they are selling many of the exact same cloud services such as branded databases, open-source systems such as Kubernetes, and popular AI systems that function the same across all cloud providers. These services are common, and thus they push the cloud providers into commodity territory.

So, cloud providers are made up of many things such as services (storage and compute) that are becoming a commodity, with some services that are unique with distinguishable attributes (virtual reality processing systems and edge computing simulations) that are proprietary to a single cloud provider and not found in all cloud providers. The more unique services that launch on a public cloud provider, the less likely they are to become commodities. My view is that we may see most of the cloud services become commodities, certainly the most used ones, while the many unique services are unlikely to commoditize anytime soon.

If that's a bit confusing, you can think again about our streaming service example. Although they show much of the same content from streaming service to streaming service, there is content that only they provide, such as movies and shows that are made by the production companies that own the streaming services. Examples would be movies and series content that's produced and owned by Netflix, HBO Max, Apple TV, Prime Video, Paramount Plus, Discovery+, Disney+, and many more. The content that they have in common is a commodity, whereas the content that only they own and stream is not. Their continued market ranks also depend on the quality of their unique content, which is also how we judge cloud providers, on the quality of their unique services.

Rise of the Supercloud or Metacloud

The rise of common cloud services is driving quicker commodification of cloud providers. *Super-cloud* and *metacloud* are the most common names applied to the platform for these common services. Although we've already covered what common services are in the chapter on multicloud, it's useful to look at how this trend is impacting the cloud market and how it will likely impact public cloud providers.

As you can see in Figure 9-8, cross-cloud services are services that logically exist above the public cloud providers. These services may run on specific cloud providers, but they exist logically and operate across all providers, such as those that are part of a multicloud. These services are best placed above all clouds, such as common security, operations, FinOps, and other services where it does not make good architectural sense to run redundant services; that is, each cloud should not run its own versions of services such as security and operations.

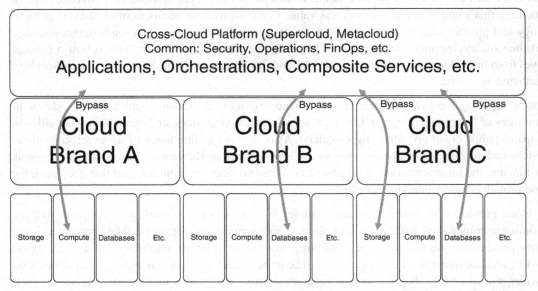

FIGURE 9-8 The rise of a common cloud known as a supercloud or metacloud means that the platform is moving to another layer of abstraction. More and more users will bypass the experiences of leveraging a specific cloud service and instead use abstract interfaces to interact with core cloud services.

As you can also see in Figure 9-8, we don't go through specific public cloud interfaces and dashboards. Instead, we can go directly to cloud services that run on the public cloud platforms and bypass the cloud-branded services altogether. It does not matter if our database runs on any public cloud; we can leverage that database equally well on each platform. The public cloud platforms now provide less value because we treat them as a common host, and not as a single destination platform.

As you may have already figured out, as the supercloud/metacloud model becomes more widely adopted, it will put the commoditization of public cloud providers into hyperdrive. We will leverage cloud providers through layers of abstraction and automation. They will look pretty much the same through common interfaces and cross-cloud services that hide the specific features of a public cloud provider from the users and systems that access specific cloud services.

Our ability to deal with clouds using these common interfaces will allow us to deal with the resulting complexity of deployments such as multicloud. A by-product of the supercloud/metacloud model will be the commoditization of the cloud providers.

Likely Cost Shifts over Time

What could widespread adoption of a supercloud/metacloud model mean to our bottom line, considering that cloud is already more costly than most executives were originally told? Figure 9-9 shows the likely shift that we'll see over time, with the current state showing most enterprises moving from single cloud deployments to multicloud. (See Chapter 6, "The Truths Behind Multicloud That Few Understand.") The supercloud/metacloud model will rise from that point with cross-cloud services that will drive more commoditization, which should drive more price reductions, with this submarket of cloud computing taking three to seven years to mature.

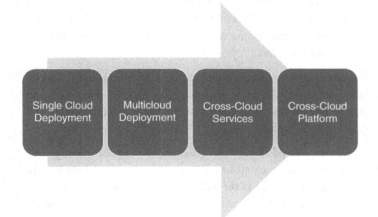

FIGURE 9-9   The most likely shift we'll see over time is the movement from single cloud to multicloud deployments. Then the focus will turn to building services that span public clouds, and then the cloud will morph into an abstract cross-cloud platform made up of many clouds and cloud services. The supercloud/metacloud model will become the new platform of choice for most enterprises. Although the final optimized state will take many years to accomplish, it's important to understand the vision and the value of undertaking this journey.

Cross-cloud platforms will become de facto technology stacks of technology that will provide repeatable sets of services that support the rise of cross-cloud services. The underlying services will be largely commoditized, with the ability to leverage whichever service is the cheapest and best supports the functionality required for your project or application. When we get to this state of the market, the underlying cloud platforms won't be as important to the users, but they will still be needed to support and provide the more primitive services such as storage and compute. You will find the differences between cross-cloud platforms and cross-cloud services in terms of how they are consumed.

The cross-cloud services emerging today are still being set up around unique business requirements, and the technology stacks are typically customized around the unique needs of a single problem domain. Cross-cloud platforms will provide many of the same services via the same technology that's configurable for each problem domain, so you end up having the same platforms that are adaptable and do not need to be completely replaced. Cross-cloud platforms are science fiction at the time I'm writing this book, but they are bound to evolve at some point. We cover this topic in much greater detail in the next chapter.

The Emergence of System Repatriation

Another shift we're likely to see, at least in the short term, is the repatriation of applications and data back to traditional on-premises systems. This, in response to rising cloud costs relative to traditional computing consumption models (for example, the data center). You will repatriate or repurchase hardware and software that you own and maintain, and resume responsibility for all the cost and risk involved in that model versus using public cloud providers.

Keep in mind the repatriation usually means returning to traditional systems after migrating them to a public cloud provider. But this shift also includes those who are considering migration to cloud and have not done so yet. Or those considering where net-new systems and databases will be built and deployed. You need to consider all use cases of traditional versus cloud-based platform selection.

Cost issues will drive most repatriation. As we covered in previous chapters, the cost of owning your own hardware fell substantially at the same time public cloud usage rose. This decrease went largely unnoticed as cloud computing innovations took center stage in the technology press. However, it makes a lot of economic sense to run certain data storage and application processing on traditionally owned hardware platforms. Right now, this option is often overlooked.

As you can see in Figure 9-10, enterprise cloud costs remain fairly static although many clouds' ongoing costs are well above what enterprises expected, which in turn drives interest in repatriation. At the same time, hardware costs such as hard disk storage and compute that you purchase and host yourself have fallen significantly. The interest in repatriation will become significant as enterprise IT looks for more bang for the buck.

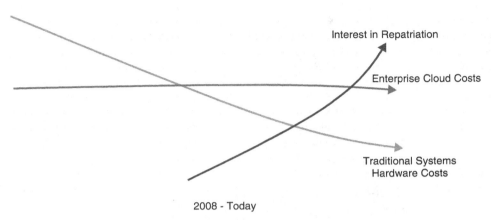

Interest in Repatriation

Enterprise Cloud Costs

Traditional Systems
Hardware Costs

2008 - Today

FIGURE 9-10 What drives interest in system repatriation from public cloud platforms? The cost of hardware and hardware maintenance experienced a significant drop, as we covered in Chapter 2, "The Realities and Opportunities of Cloud-Based Storage Services…." As the prices dropped, the cost of cloud computing remained pretty much the same per system. The shift to owned or managed platforms will likely occur for cost reasons.

Why Organizations Move to a Hybrid Model

Although most enterprises are not giving up on cloud computing, some are making economic decisions to run applications and store data in the most cost-effective spaces that might not be in the cloud. Again, cloud costs are typically much higher than many enterprises expected, and the huge potential cost savings of cloud computing have not yet materialized for most organizations. Many executives now understand that the lion's share of net-new and innovative development is done for cloud platforms these days, and yet they still decide to take a hybrid approach. They decide to put some data and applications on public cloud providers, and other data and applications in enterprises data centers.

These days it's almost impossible to run your entire application portfolio and store data on traditional systems without suffering from an inability to participate in cloud-focused technology such as business analytics, AI, and serverless computing. But all applications and all data stores may not need or even use that technology, and thus it makes more sense to take advantage of rock-bottom hardware prices and keep some applications and data stores on more traditional platforms. There is not an either/or model here; we're not giving up cloud computing to go to enterprise data centers. We do both to find the most cost-optimized platforms.

Why You Need to Justify the Move to Cloud as a Business Value

Too often the hype leads the decision-making process. Cloud architects and IT architects in general need to keep an open mind when it comes to what platforms to pick. You need to justify any platform by the business value it can provide, cloud or not. The drive to move everything to cloud-based platforms could mean you don't leverage the most cost-optimized platforms. I've seen too many projects shift to cloud computing platforms to do uncomplicated tasks such as data storage and simple application processing that resulted in the enterprise spending six to seven figures more per year on cloud-based resources versus the cost of resources leveraged from an existing enterprise data center, with all factors considered.

The core message here? No matter how the cloud market progresses, you must consider all options, old and new. Remember, innovations now take place on the public cloud platforms, so there's a certain need to take advantage of those upgrades and modernization. However, for a substantial amount of time, more traditional solutions could prove much more cost-effective. It doesn't matter if you've moved to a public cloud and need to move back to save money, or if you're looking to migrate to a public cloud provider or build net-new systems and databases, all solutions should be considered in terms of their ability to return value back to the business.

The Rise of Federated Cloud Applications and Data

Another shift in the market is the anticipated rise of the federated cloud. A federated cloud contains a logical application(s) and logical database(s) that span public cloud providers, and sometimes legacy and edge-based systems as well. An example of federated cloud applications and data is depicted in Figure 9-11. However, they are typically more complex than that in real life, where we have common services that support cross-cloud functions such as operations, security, and FinOps that run on some physical cloud, or even within a traditional data center, but they logically exist cross-cloud. What's more unique is a set of federated applications and coupled data that runs across various cloud providers as well.

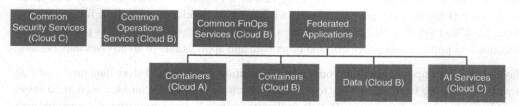

FIGURE 9-11   Federated applications and data mean that we can deploy applications and data using any number of mechanisms, such as containers, on an intra- or inter-cloud platform. This allows us to mix and match the right parts of the cloud-based application to the right cloud platform, such as one cloud platform having a superior AI system and another a better database. Of course, there will be common services as well, such as operations, security, and FinOps.

For example, let's say we're dealing with customer data that physically exists on three different cloud providers' databases. We have customer sales data running on one public cloud provider, customer shipping data that runs on a sales order entry system that exists on another public cloud provider, and finally a set of inventory shipping data that resides on yet another public cloud provider. We need to access all that data in such a way that a single application does not have to deal with three different cloud native database interfaces. Thus, we leverage some technical tricks such as database virtualization. This trick provides a layer of software between the three different cloud native databases and the applications or humans that need to access that data. Of course, we could relocate the data to a single database so that all the data would physically reside on a single cloud provider. However, that is not cost efficient in this example, especially because the data serves other purposes on each cloud provider, which is common in most cases. Therefore, we employ database federation within a federated cloud to deal with the data where it exists and use mechanisms to remove the complexity of dealing with many different data stores using the terms of that data store. We end up making our own terms, and the databases accommodate us.

We're just dealing with data in the preceding example. Other things that can be federated include AI systems, container orchestration, business analytics, and any other technology that may work best on one cloud provider over another. Of course, we need common services as well as those depicted in Figure 9-11. These services provide things like security, operations, and FinOps across all cloud providers, and thus across all federated applications and data. We federate these services so we don't need to deploy redundant systems (like security) on each and every cloud provider. This approach makes the federated architecture less complex and more cost-effective to operate.

We typically partition the application around functions, or where specific types of services (such as containers) run on one cloud. This may be done for many logical reasons, but the specific cloud may provide the best platform for containers, while another is better for data, and a third is better for high-speed transactions. We would also run the data on a cloud provider that provides the best platform to maintain data. Basically, we would mix and match cloud providers to host parts of the application each hosts best, with those parts of the application distributed among the cloud providers.

The market will likely move in the federated direction for a few core reasons:

- The ability to leverage specific cloud providers for specific application attributes that will provide the most cost-effective approach to run each part of the application.

- The use of abstraction and automation to remove the developers and operators from the underlying complexity of leveraging many different cloud providers as hosts for those services.

- The use of cross-cloud services to provide common operational and security services that span a federated architecture. Thus, it's functionally treated as a single architecture and platform.

- The ability to support resilience using redundancy that's built into these federated systems, which means a single failure is unlikely to take down the entire federated application.

Figure 9-12 depicts another view of how we deal with federated applications that span more than a single cloud. In this example, we're dealing with two layers of services: The application services or APIs, and the native cloud services that are specific to the public cloud platforms. Each provides its own set of functions with the application services and/or APIs that interact with the application and are part of the application. An example would be an application service that's written to request that a credit check be done. This becomes a common application service that can be called many times, but from different components of the application.

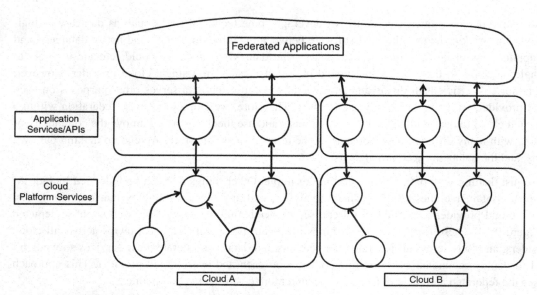

FIGURE 9-12 Federated applications deal with two layers of services: services such as database and AI that are leveraged by the applications, and services that are leveraged by core services such as storage and compute.

Federated applications can also access the cloud platform services, or services that are native to specific cloud platforms such as databases, storage, and compute services. Taking our credit check example, we would need to leverage data access that typically occurs on a database that's native to a specific cloud provider to gather the data required to provide the credit check, which is the application-specific service. These services work together to carry out the needs of an application with the application services and/or API that span across cloud providers, and those services leverage the native services of whatever cloud provider is needed to carry out a platform service such as data storage and retrieval.

The downside of federation is the main reason we don't see it much today, as depicted in Figure 9-13. This figure shows an actual design of a federated system built on a multicloud that was designed to run across cloud providers, legacy systems, and a private cloud. Note the applications at the top of this stack, the number and layers of services that are needed to support the federation, and the use of core resources such as storage and compute that exist at the lower-level platforms (legacy, cloud, and private cloud). Also, the services on the right side provide governance, security, operations, and so on, that must span all layers, including abstractions, data integration, and orchestration.

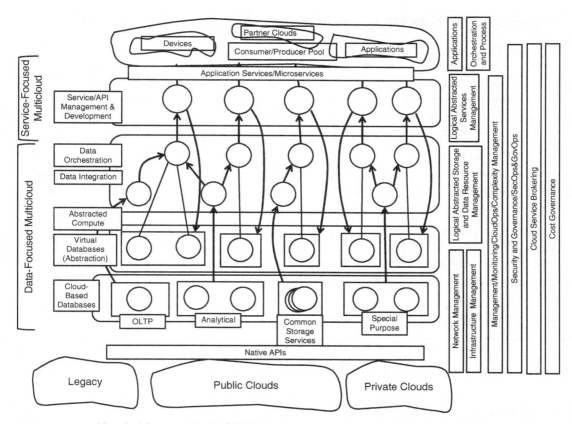

FIGURE 9-13 Headed for complexity? This is what systems are evolving into right now, with some of them already in existence. With the progression of distributed development, the number and types of services that applications need will only expand. Moreover, we're moving to ubiquitous platforms where the types, locations, and ownership of the platforms make little difference in terms of how enterprises will leverage systems and common core services.

Now we have to face the reality that this federation will lead to complexity. As we discussed in Chapter 6 on multicloud, complexity must be managed and mediated. We'll need to reduce the number of boxes and items shown in Figure 9-13 to create common services that can span services up and down this stack as well as side to side. Creating such services will be the mission of the cloud computing industry as it matures and finds new ways to make itself more useful and cost effective.

Clearly, the need to run systems across cloud providers will be the ultimate solution that most enterprises seek, with the ability to mix and match what's needed from each provider. The problem is that most enterprises don't have the know-how and/or the tools to deal with today's complexity, much less tomorrow's complexity issues. This evolution will be long, but, when done right, the end results will provide more business value and better and more optimized use of technology.

Traditional Systems Remain...Why?

Each month I'm asked when legacy or traditional systems will go away. The short answer is, "They won't." Although we'll see a diminished interest in older legacy systems and even more modern legacy systems such as Intel-based development using LAMP (Linux, Apache, MySQL, Python), all types of legacy systems will hang around for a specific reason: They will prove too costly to migrate to cloud-based systems. Better put, a business case cannot be made to remove them from a physical data center and put them on some cloud provider.

There will come a point when we've migrated as many systems to the cloud as we can that made economic sense to migrate. Although we won't hit this milestone anytime soon, what will remain are legacy systems that don't have good pathways to get them to cloud...although enough time and money can accomplish anything.

The core hindrance to moving most of these systems will be the numbers. Let's say it costs $2,000 per month to maintain certain applications in the data center space using all-in costs that include power, humans, and networking. However, it costs $.5 million to migrate those systems to a public cloud provider, and another $3,000 per month on cloud service fees to operate them. What would you do?

Figure 9-14 depicts how this scenario will likely play out. We'll hit a saturation point at what I suspect will land between the 70–80 percent mark for applications and data that are migrating to the cloud, which means that 20–30 percent of applications and data won't move to the cloud. The reason is not that we can't migrate them, but that it does not pay to migrate them.

Many will argue that enterprises need to get rid of their owned data centers, and I agree with that viewpoint...to a certain extent. There are more cost-effective alternatives available, including managed services vendors that provide platform analytics for most traditional systems as well as cloud access. Also, co-location (co-lo) providers that offer data center space for rent. I suspect we'll see an inflection point in this market as well, as many enterprises see the writing on the wall when it comes to some of their older and more traditional applications.

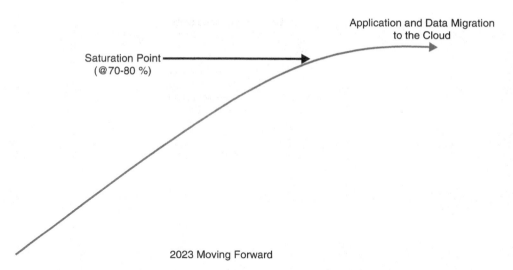

FIGURE 9-14   Most enterprises will find that about 20–30 percent of their systems are not economically viable to move to "the cloud." This means they will hit a saturation point, and these legacy systems will likely remain where they are or move to other viable options such as co-location providers or managed services vendors. Given the issues we've discussed around holding onto legacy systems and the applications that reside on them, enterprises will have some trade-offs to think about.

I do not mean that these legacy applications will never move. We're putting stuff on public clouds that I did not think possible just a few years ago, and it will make sense that cloud providers will accommodate this part of the market at some point. However, they will do the same math when it comes to what enterprises would like to move versus what it pays to move. It all comes down to finding the best business value, and for that, we'll leave 20–30 percent of those traditional applications behind for good reasons.

Battle for Human Talent

Finally, let's get into a non-cloud topic that's rapidly becoming the most limiting aspect of cloud computing for most enterprises. I'm talking about your ability to hire the right people to deal with cloud computing, including those with skill sets in migration, operations, FinOps, security, and other things that need to be done right the first time.

Figure 9-15 shows what we see today and what we saw in the past, in terms of available cloud skills. The demand for cloud skills grew at a steady pace for the past 15 years but accelerated over the last 3–5 years. What drove this skills shortage? The rise of cloud use in general, existing systems aging out, and worldwide events such as the COVID-19 pandemic that accelerated the move to the relative safety of public clouds, and the subsequent need to support a distributed remote workforce. The demand for skills outpaced the supply, with not enough skilled cloud professionals entering the workforce to meet the demand.

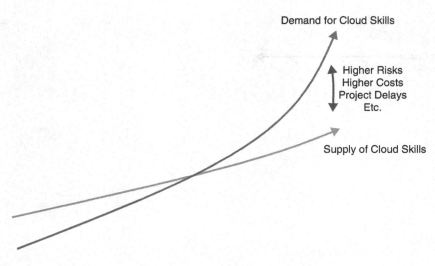

FIGURE 9-15   It's no secret that demand for cloud skills outpaced supply by a wide margin. This margin is what holds up cloud development and migration progress. Many enterprises feel forced to hire less qualified talent who make mistakes large and small as they acquire their cloud skills on-the-job. These mistakes and missteps can and often do cost a substantial amount of time and money to fix, and they incur a great deal of risk.

The cloud skills shortage resulted in higher risk, higher costs, and project delays for both enterprises and consulting firms as they tried to make do with whatever talent they could find. Working with less skilled talent often delays or cancels cloud computing migration projects or reduces expectations as to what enterprises can operate on the cloud, and the types of technology they can employ. In more general terms, it's slowing things down. In many instances, enterprises are hiring below qualifications, and major mistakes are being made with ill-conceived cloud solutions that must be fixed at some point. Yes, this is a bad. What can you do about it?

What to Exploit Right Now

It's hard to buy the right talent in a seller's market. There are no foolproof ways to eliminate this problem, but there are ways to better manage it. Compounding the problem, colleges and universities are not producing the number of qualified candidates needed to fill even the entry-level job openings. Although you should have a relationship with and pipelines to traditional learning institutes, a better option would be to hire in less traditional and more innovative ways. I'm often taken aback by the number of enterprises that still rely on college degrees to determine who should be considered for cloud jobs or not.

The dirty little secret about cloud computing skills is that you don't need a computer science degree from an Ivy League university to gain access to some hot public cloud computing skills. Those skills can be acquired in many other places with almost no limitations on access. For myself, I don't require a college degree for someone to work my cloud jobs. However, new hires must have the desired skills to quickly provide productive value and, more importantly, the willingness to be a continuous learner. You're not much good to me if you don't want to update your own skills as you go versus me requiring that you attend mandatory training to keep your skills up to date.

So, I work with learning services and even community colleges that focus on providing core cloud skills but lack requirements for nonrelated courses. Thus, you get somebody who other hiring organizations may avoid because they don't have a college degree, but they turn out to be a superior hire because you want them to play a single role, such as cloud security, cloud development, or cloud databases, and you encourage them to build their own career from there.

Other people to consider include those who are reentering the workforce after a long span of raising families or other life events. They may have had some computer experience in the past, but they don't have current skills such as cloud computing. I've worked within programs that have provided training free of charge for those who are looking to reenter the workforce with more modern skills (such as cloud computing). These individuals are often successful because they already understand the basics of computing and often make an easy transition to cloud computing. Moreover, they tend to be more motivated with a stronger drive to learn. Women are most of the job candidates here—again, a group often overlooked by the traditional hiring organizations.

My success in hiring the right cloud skills is largely due to looking where others do not and being more pragmatic about assessing a potential employee's near-term usefulness as well as their long-term ability to grow as a teammate and not just an employee. Yes, I'm often criticized for this approach to hiring. Some point out that I won't get employees with more rounded skill sets. So far, that hasn't been my experience. Good people are good people, no matter where you find them.

The Secrets of Keeping Cloud Talent

Let's say you manage to hire the cloud staff you need. With all the competition and opportunities out there for cloud talent, how do you keep them? Incentives sometimes work, but the best approach is to foster a culture that keeps and attracts the right talent.

The first thing you need to understand is what motivates people. Why do they stay or leave jobs? Surveys are often done to determine the reasons, but often they miss what employees don't tell surveys or tell their former employers, or what they may not understand themselves. Complaints might focus on their pay, or the lack of parking, or even the need to adhere to a strict expense account. Even with those issues fixed, they still leave. What are we missing?

Figure 9-16 shows a good framework to understand what talent may expect; again, in many instances they may not have externalized any of these expectations. Early in my career, I was "encouraged" to address the results of employee surveys, to fix issues that showed up in the surveys, and the enterprise still experienced huge turnover. After watching the same scenario play out in many peer organizations, I went with my gut to address what I felt needed to be fixed to create a positive work environment. Turnover dropped significantly, while hiring through word of mouth increased. Figure 9-16 depicts a simplistic representation of basic employee expectations, but it's a good example to start with.

Working from the top down, we can look at trends in "give-a-damn" about certain aspects of work, starting with income. Almost everyone thinks that they're underpaid, so they want more money. That's a no-brainer. However, money is not always as important as you might think, with considerations for income trending slightly up over the last five years. Yes, they still want more money, but other aspects of their jobs have equal or more importance, even if they don't say so out loud.

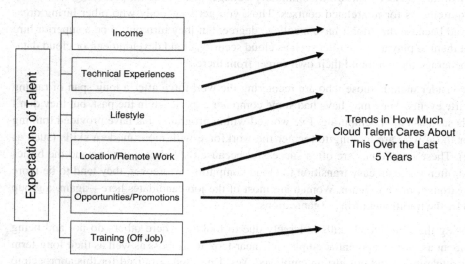

FIGURE 9-16 The secret to hiring and keeping talented people with solid cloud computing skills is to understand their underlying motivations. Surprisingly, it's not like the old days when companies that could pay the most or offer the most perks retained the best talent. Today, most skilled staff want fair compensation with new challenges and experiences that make the job interesting. Many want a flexible work environment where they can live and work anywhere in the world. Are you ready to meet those expectations?

Working down from there, the opportunity to gain more or better technical experiences is what many IT- and cloud-focused employees seek. They are in the technology sector because they find it interesting. Their ability to gain on-the-job experience with more current and exciting technology is often a motivator for people to remain in a cloud job. The lack of new technical experiences is a reason many people cite when they leave cloud jobs.

Lifestyle is rarely considered a significant employee expectation. This does not mean that the cool cloud team leader has a gaming console in the office, but it's important to understand that everyone has different expectations of what they want to do and the life that they want to live. Which naturally leads to location/remote work.

The best lifestyle and location assets are not assets at all, but flexibility around working hours, work location, and the resources to support these nontraditional types of work lifestyles. I often say to employees, "You can work anywhere in the world and keep any hours you like, as long as you meet the agreed-upon expectations. Find your best path." On the other hand, some people like structure and the ability to work in an office environment. They should be accommodated as well, even if it's a nontraditional setting such as coworking office spaces.

Few cloud people resign due to the lack of promotional opportunities. More than once I've promoted someone and they soon quit anyway, so the promotion was not the motivator. Most enterprises have a flat organizational structure these days. Those who need to look at an org chart to determine their value are perhaps the people you don't want on your team. While people do want to get recognized for their work, they don't care as much about where they sit in the hierarchy as they did a few years ago.

Finally, access to training. While you should provide access to training, it's not productive to have mandatory training. You need to let everyone know that training is available, and you'll be paid while you take the approved training courses. For those who want to get better at their jobs, it's desirable to further their education. Keep in mind that people learn in different ways. Some are good at classroom learning; others need to learn by doing. Don't put too much emphasis on certificates and other traditional ways to prove that they completed a certain set of steps that makes them an "expert" on a job description.

There are many (including myself) who learn best through doing, and they don't provide certificates for that kind of knowledge. "Hands-on" knowledge is the type of experience most enterprises want or need, although almost all insist that qualified candidates possess a coursework degree of some sort and/ or a certain amount of on-the-job experience. But few people have substantial amounts of on-the-job cloud experience. See the Catch-22 here?

Someone once said, "You go to college to get the piece of paper that gets you the job. Then you learn how to do the job." There are fields that still require degrees or certifications or internships of various sorts to prove you're capable of doing the job. You don't want a surgeon, lawyer, or electrician to purchase the tools of their trade one day and open for business the next.

Many IT jobs are the same, with degrees and certificates that prove someone knows enough about the job to not fall flat on their face on day one. However, at this point in the cloud skills shortage life cycle, an equally important skill is that of a hiring executive who's good at identifying potential cloud talent. Many of today's hires with the potential to be good or even great future cloud employees are found outside the degree/certificate/internship mills. Be open to the possibilities.

Call to Action

Out of all these chapters, this one was the most difficult to write. Not because the topic of the cloud market is that complex; it's that it requires me to speculate about where it's moving. Yes, this is an educated prediction in some instances, but so far my predictions track record is pretty good. Other trends are obvious to anyone who watches the cloud computing market.

If you're reading this chapter, chances are good that you'll be called on at some point to make predictions and plan where to invest your enterprise's time and money. This important chapter gives you the inside story as to how this all plays out. The calls I make are based on what I've seen play out in the past, and on what I see happening today. I've tried to be as open and as honest as possible. My prediction is that my predictions will be about 95 percent correct, but you tell me.

Chapter | **10**

Here's the Future of Cloud Computing from an Insider's Perspective... Be Prepared

If you don't think about the future, you cannot have one.

— *John Galsworthy*

In the preceding chapter, we looked at where cloud computing is today and what your next moves should be. This chapter is a continuation of that conversation that will look much deeper into the future. I don't have a crystal ball, but I have made a pretty good living by placing bets on certain technology patterns that may emerge, and then they did emerge. That doesn't mean I'm clairvoyant or have a uniquely special talent, or that I'm always right. Accurate predictions require good guesswork backed by data, research, and past experiences.

The upside is that I'm right so much of the time that I've been hailed as a genius by some in the industry. Even if I'm right about most of cloud's future, I doubt many people will notice or care. The technology world tends to have ADHD. We move so fast that we never really notice who was right and who got things wrong...unless they were spectacularly wrong. The best way to play this game around all the evolutions of technology is to pay attention and listen to your gut. We usually have a sense of emerging patterns and can feel and understand how these evolutions of technology are likely to play out over time. When you have a sense of the patterns, it's relatively easy to figure out what technology innovations will be needed, and thus what we're likely to be talking about in the tech press in 5, 10, or even 20 years in the future. All without validation from the $20,000 per month analyst firms that aren't always on track.

You'll find that some of the predictions in this book are more obvious than others, such as in the next section where I talk about the growth of complex data architectures and deployments. Although those are easy to predict, it's not so easy to predict what they mean to enterprises and technology providers.

That's another level of predictions, but they address the information you'll find most useful to yourself, your business, and/or the technology you're building or planning to build.

As an insider, I do my best in this chapter to provide you with what will likely happen in the future, as well as why it will happen, and what that means for technology users and builders. The "why" and "what that means" are often the most valuable part of the conversation, but they usually get left out of the end-of-the-year predictions from technology articles. Instead, they let you know things like, "Cloud security will continue to be important," which is a cop-out unto itself. Those types of generalized statements rarely get backed up with any assertions as to what specific changes we'll see around that prediction. In this forward-looking chapter of the book, I do my best to fill in those blanks.

Continued Rise of Complex Cloud Deployments

Okay, I hear you barking, "Dave really went out on a limb for this obvious prediction that cloud computing will become more complex." Stay with me. We've already covered multicloud in its current and evolving state in this book. The likelihood that its evolution will continue is close to 100 percent. However, I'm going to take things a bit further and talk about what will most likely come next after complexity settles into our everyday reality. After that, I'll take us forward from now until about 20 years from now.

There are three main things that make hybrid and multicloud deployments harder to secure:

■ The first is visibility. Specifically, when you mix public and private cloud with on-premises infrastructure, you need not only visibility but also deep visibility to manage the complexity and make sure that gaps don't develop. If you can't see it, you can't secure it.

■ The second thing to think about in these types of environments is insecure data transmission. Data that flows between public and private clouds or from on-premises or in a co-location, or co-lo, can be vulnerable to attack. We're seeing organizations turn to tools that encrypt data both in flight and at rest.

■ The third thing that keeps some customers up at night, particularly if their data is globally dispersed, is the idea of falling out of compliance. The stakes for that are high from both a reputation and financial perspective. We're seeing teams look at compliance at the start of their hybrid deployment and plan through a lens of compliance.

Figure 10-1 depicts our move from "Single-Cloud Deployments" into "Cross-Cloud Services" (also known as Supercloud/Metacloud Services). We covered this move earlier in the book. The only thing I would add here is that we're just beginning our journey to cross-cloud services. Most of you will be operating single-cloud and multicloud deployments until well after this book hits the streets. Cross-cloud services will continue to evolve in the meantime, and I'm sure they will be the focus of my day-to-day activities for at least the next five years. The future "Cross-Cloud Services" journey is depicted in Figure 10-1. "Cross-Cloud Platform" and "Ubiquitous Deployment" are what I believe will be the next evolutions of cloud technology. Let me tell you why.

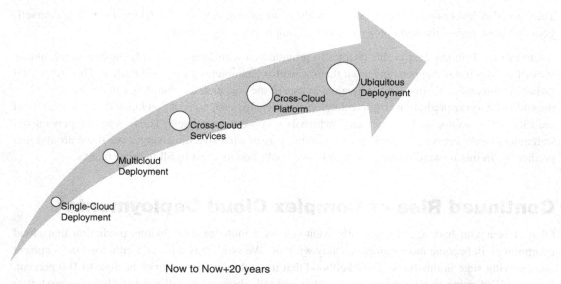

Now to Now+20 years

FIGURE 10-1   The progression of cloud computing clearly moves from single-cloud deployments to multicloud, where we are now, and then to more common cross-cloud services (supercloud/metacloud,), and then to ubiquitous cloud deployments and services. This is when cloud services and application services may exist anywhere, and auto migrate to the platform that provides the best cost efficiency.

Keep in mind that a cross-cloud architecture is a combination of software and services that will be delivered to give organizations freedom and control of private and public clouds. We do this by designing above the physical public cloud providers, thus removing the limitations of those physical cloud deployments from the cross-cloud architecture.

Let's define what a cross-cloud platform is and how it will likely evolve from cross-cloud services. First, no two enterprises are the same. Each will have different requirements for security, governance, FinOps, compliance, and application and data, and different technology to fulfill those requirements. Most cross-cloud services that reside in a supercloud/metacloud are not predefined platforms, but layers of technology that need to be custom fit for each enterprise. There are no turnkey solutions, and each cross-cloud layer will be a bespoke layer of technologies that will vary from enterprise to enterprise.

Any custom fit technology gets us back to the two words enterprises hate to hear, "It depends." In the case of every supercloud/metacloud, it *does* depend, and that's why you'll need very skilled architects to define the technology stacks that make up cross-cloud services.

As cross-cloud platforms begin to emerge, the technology industry will adapt to new market demands. Ubiquitous sets of cross-cloud services can be configured in many ways to deal with many different types of requirements. Rather than look at each set of clouds as a new problem that needs a customized solution, we'll leverage a single platform (supercloud/metacloud) that can provide everything the enterprise needs for security, operations, AI, data, data integration, and so forth. It will be one-stop shopping for all the services you need to exist above and between cloud providers.

If cross-cloud platforms work as planned, which they should, most enterprises will move in this direction even if they already have some custom cross-cloud solutions in place. They'll make this move for the same reasons we began the move to the cloud: We want to make the technology stack somebody else's problem. By moving to a cross-cloud platform, we do just that.

Of course, the development of supercloud/metacloud architectures and the services that work on them will take a staggering amount of provider-supplied capital, much like cloud computing providers had to invest and spend millions of dollars at the onset of cloud computing. The larger cloud computing providers will likely offer the first commercial-grade cross-cloud platforms and end up owning that market as well. Only major players will have the resources required to build a new technology and develop its market from the ground up, and then be capable of funding the years of investments that need to be made. Here we go again.

The next phase following cross-cloud supercloud/metacloud platforms comes along further into the future. Ubiquitous deployments will install autonomous services onto a distributed array of technologies that we're authorized to use. We won't deploy them to a specific platform, but to a technology pool in general. This pool will include public clouds, edge computing, and on-site systems. Anything you own that is connected to a network, can store data, and has a processor can be a candidate to run these ubiquitous and fully autonomous services.

The kicker here is that these services, once developed and/or deployed, can exist by finding the best platform to run on, or even divide themselves so they can run on many platforms at the same time. The objective will be for these services to operate with the most efficiency, and thus use the least number of resources and money. They will be intelligent and have awareness of every other service around them, including hosting platforms, and will bring along security, governance, operations, and other services needed to provide the best operational efficiency.

The reason a ubiquitous service deployment is so attractive is around its underlying simplicity. We'll no longer build centralized systems for security, operations, FinOps, and so on, as we did with the previous two evolutions. Instead, all those services will be contained within the ubiquitous deployment and thus exist wherever the service exists, all aware of each other, all working together in a distributed configuration. Everything will be self-contained and thus require very little human intervention (if any) and be intelligent, self-aware, and completely automated.

We're working toward this end during today's growth of multicloud technology and in what we'll see developed for the next 10 years. During this time, we'll also master the successful use of containers. In many respects, today's containers are the prototypes for ubiquitous deployments. We'll see containers evolve in this direction and eventually subsume traditional infrastructure tooling to provide something more flexible and scalable. Ubiquitous deployments will combine containerized applications and data, which will add much improved functionality to those containers to build a full operational stack. Ubiquitous deployments are on the horizon, but commonplace use is still many years into the future. I can't wait to see if I live that long!

Refocus on Cross-Cloud Systems

This is my predicted progression of cloud computing: The focus will be on multicloud in the short term and will turn next toward cross-cloud platforms (supercloud/metacloud). As cross-cloud platforms become a more repeatable pattern, the longer-term focus will progress toward ubiquitous systems (as seen in Figure 10-1).

In this section we look at the specifics of this future, including its effects on security, operations, the rise of observability, governance, FinOps, and data federation. Because we covered these topics in other chapters in other contexts, here we focus more on the forward-looking topics, both near and long term. As cloud computing users, you'll get a sense of where things are going to ensure that you make the right investments in time, resources, and technology. IT success requires good insights and vision to support both long- and short-term planning. Cloud computing is no different.

You'll notice that we leave the *cloud* word alone for this section, opting instead for *platform*. Of course, a platform can be a cloud, but here we also include platforms that comprise the future core of cloud computing (that is, edge computing and traditional/legacy systems). The future will see the continued rise of technology stacks that are born and live on cloud-based platforms, but also include non-cloud platforms in that mix as well. We can't just evolve security solutions and supporting technology that only solve problems for public cloud providers. We must also provide a valuable holistic technology solution for the enterprise. The goal will be to extend these ideas and solutions to other platforms using the same cross-platform services to secure, govern, and operate those systems, thus increasing the value of what we discuss in this section of the chapter. In other words, the future of cloud computing is not all about cloud computing, and that's for a good reason.

Cross-Platform Security

The future focus on cross-cloud security means that we need to examine the current state as well as what's next. We begin by discussing the basic changes that are happening now and finish up with a more far-reaching outlook. Given the importance of security, it needs to shift and evolve to protect us moving forward. Let's get started.

Right now, security is becoming more complex to make it easier to leverage. How can that be? Security is moving from single monoethnic systems designed for use on a specific platform (such as a single public cloud provider) to systems that work with a mixture of systems and databases. These new systems comprise many pieces that must be encompassed by a larger security net. Moreover, most of these larger security nets will be custom configured for the specific business and its current technology solutions to deal with the problems and requirements at hand. Security will become this "whole of its parts" security net rather than a single security brand or a single set of tools.

This cross-platform security net encompasses several tiers of security. The native security features on platforms below the cross-platform security layer could include hundreds of things that focus on security for just that public cloud platform. This is where most of the heavy lifting occurs such as encryption, authentication, role-based security, or whatever else you need to deal with on those specific platforms. Those of you who worked with security systems throughout the years will understand the differences between security on legacy systems (that is, mainframes), security on edge-based platforms, and even those on more modern on-premises systems (that is, traditional Intel-based servers that still crowd data centers). Each has its own way to deal with security that is specific to that platform or native security layer.

Figure 10-2 depicts the concept of a cross-platform security manager, which is the key to all cross-cloud operations. This high-level platform can coordinate between all the native security layers on their own terms. The cross-platform security manager provides an orchestrated and automated system with holistic security, meaning security across all platforms.

As you can see in Figure 10-2, the cross-platform security manager covers each brand's native security system. These individual security systems are very different and highly heterogeneous because they support different models, approaches, and mechanisms. We don't want to deal with branded security on a case-by-case basis, so it's best to leverage abstraction and automation that use simplistic approaches and mechanisms to deal with this very complex security tier.

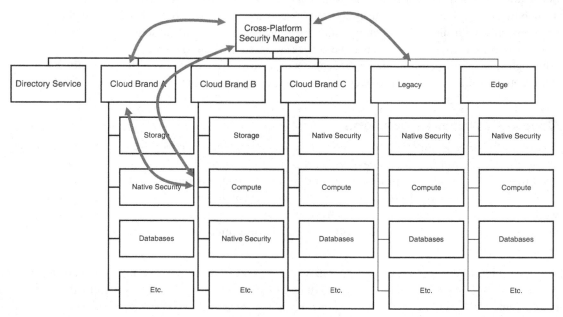

FIGURE 10-2 Cross-platform security is the next generation of cloud security. It focuses on a cross-platform security layer (cloud and not) that can address each component by identity, and then track each identity in a directory service. From here, the cross-platform security manager can use the features of its own system, or leverage cloud-native and legacy-native features without forcing the security administrator to learn about native features and operations. This approach provides more simplicity and less complexity.

Cross-platform security is not a new concept. We've been aiming for this ability because security needed to exist across more than a single computing system. It's why a single security technology brand typically provides our security systems, but we don't have systems that work together in tightly coupled ways. There is centralized command and control, but it works by using loosely coupled distributed security mechanisms that deal with their platforms using best-of-breed approaches and technology.

The fundamental difference is that we will not deal with security on each platform using each platform's terms, which would require the use of different tools, technologies, skills, and approaches. Instead, we will deal with security holistically and the same. A cross-platform security manager abstracts each native security system into sets of common services that can be orchestrated and automated, but we don't deal with the trade-off of having to leverage least common denominator approaches, where we would force all system security to fit a single set of mechanisms that ultimately downgrade the solution from the native best-of-breed mechanisms that each platform provides.

Today, most breaches are caused by human mistakes, such as unauthorized access or simple misconfigurations. Security is better with a cross-platform security approach because we will remove humans from the process and instead focus on repeatable higher-level processes that are consistently carried out within each native security mechanism. Although we're a few years away from the widespread availability of cross-platform security systems that work, we're slowly moving toward these types of approaches with the rise of identity and access management (IAM) systems that authorize identities such as humans, machines, data, and processes based on their known identities and credentials. Although some cross-platform identity management security systems do exist, this is mostly deployed intra-platform, and each cloud provider has its own identity management approach and technology.

Cross-Platform Operations

The outlook for cross-platform operations is much the same as security. Rather than focus on a single platform's operations processes, approaches, and technology, we will instead focus at a level higher on several operations managers that can abstract and automate platform-native operations systems. Typically, if you do it right, this layer exists logically above all cloud providers as well as above legacy, edge, and so on. Physically, cross-platform operations may exist anywhere, and typically run on a public cloud provider or even on-premises. It really does not matter to the value we want to obtain.

The idea with cloud operations, and operations in general, is to remove as much redundancy and complexity as possible. That means doing things in the middle of the platforms, cloud and non-cloud, rather than within each platform. Some of this is possible using emerging tools such as artificial intelligence operations (AIOps), which can monitor and manage many services on many platforms at the same time, cloud and non-cloud. However, they can't do it all. Right now, you'll end up with a collection of tools and technology that can logically exist over the platforms. They deal with operational functions such as performance management and operations, applications management and operations, data management and operations, FinOps, and other things that need to be monitored and managed ongoing.

The future of cross-platform operations is clear:

- Core operational services will be combined in a logical layer that exists above all the cloud and non-cloud platforms. (Getting the trends here?) Again, this cross-cloud platform will have physical components that run on any type and number of platforms, cloud and non-cloud, but logically speaking they sit above the platforms to provide core operational services to all platforms.

- Ubiquitous services will run in any number of host platforms. They will provide automated deployment and redeployment based on the needs of the applications, and they will have the ability to provide more value to the business by running on one platform over another, or many platforms at the same time (that is, federated applications, as covered in earlier chapters).

- Automated services will proactively deal with operational issues, primarily by using the concept of observability (covered next). This means that things get fixed before they become issues.

Cross-Platform Observability

Observability is a concept being kicked around today that will evolve around the use of cross-platform services. It's about the future of cloud computing, and computing in general. A large portion of this chapter talks about observability because it is key to taking your cloud computing game to the next level. My goal is to provide you with insights and information you simply don't have access to right now.

At its core, observability allows us to monitor internal states of systems. Observability uses externally exhibited characteristics that can predict the future behavior of monitored systems using data analysis and other technologies. Core to the observability concept is the ability to find insights that are unapparent by just looking at the monitored data.

Observability is often associated with operations, certainly with AIOps tools. However, observability is a concept with much wider applications. Observability can enhance security, governance, and any aspect of computing where there is an advantage to seeing beyond the more obvious states of systems, data, applications, and so forth. This is about taking the understanding game to the next level. Later in this chapter, we cover some of the more interesting applications for observability that will probably affect the decisions you make about systems in the short and long term.

Back to general trends, future cross-cloud observability will move the enterprise to a state where core business systems in and out of the cloud are operated in a way that solves issues before they become issues. Proactive maintenance and operations will lead to much higher uptime that approaches zero outages and lowers operational costs. The inflection point of complexity and heterogeneity no longer impacts the business. Thus, no complexity wall and no tipping point, as we discussed in earlier chapters.

Proactive observability helps predict issues before they become issues. A proactive enterprise can deploy very complex systems without impacting the ROI value of those systems. If used correctly, observability allows enterprises to leverage best-of-breed technology and its resulting complexity with little or no impact on the business.

Figure 10-3 represents the major components of observability as related to IT operations, cloud and non-cloud.

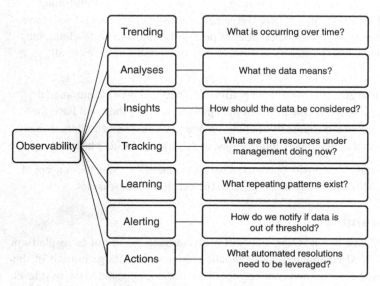

FIGURE 10-3 Observability for general operations, security, and other aspects of cloud operations can gain insights from an enormous amount of gathered data. This is different from monitoring, which just reveals the current state of things. Observability tells you what is happening and what will happen, and it can even trigger automated mechanisms that fix problems before they cause outages or other negative events.

Let's explore each component of observability and why it's important to the future of cloud computing:

- **Trending:** What patterns occur over time, and what do they mean for future behavior? For example, if performance trends downward, that indicates likely I/O problems that arise from organic database growth. This is based on historical and current data, and then the observability system uses this information as training data for an AI system such as AIOps.

- **Analyses:** What does the data mean, and what insights can we draw from it? Observability provides the ability to analyze data, using AI, to interpret that data and determine insights. This core feature of observability sets it apart from just monitoring the data. Observability analysis can be very deep and complex, such as determining AI system training requirements based on an analysis of system outages. Or it can be rudimentary, such as determining that a drop in network traffic means there is a 67 percent probability that an I/O error exists in a core storage system.

- **Insights:** What can we understand from the data, or what do we need to understand from the data? Observability finds meaning in data that's not readily understood or apparent. For example, observability can find correlations between a rise in sales revenue and a drop in overall system performance. This doesn't make sense on the surface. A decrease in system performance usually has a negative impact on customer access and sales order entry. However, in this case, excessive users on the sales order system (including the e-commerce website) pushed down system performance. Thus, the operations team can take action to ensure that capacity will elastically increase to support more sales activities. Many won't suspect that these data points are connected, but observability allows you to get such insights into past, current, and even forecasted data.

- **Tracking:** Monitoring system activity data in real time or near-real time allows observability to leverage this data to find, diagnose, and fix issues ongoing. Traditional tracking monitors the activity of multiple systems in the cloud and in the data center. Under the concept of observability, the system can find dynamic insights around real-time data and look at it in the context of related operations data. The system may determine and diagnose issues that can be self-healed through automation. For example, tracking CPU performance of a single virtual server that exists on a major IaaS provider. Tracking can provide real-time insights as to what this performance data means in relation to future performance, processor failure, memory failure, and other insights that may be derived from this relatively innocuous data that was once displayed on an operator's dashboard for a few seconds and then gone forever.

- **Learning:** Learning systems look at massive amounts of data to find trends and insights, and then leverage that data to learn about emerging patterns and what they mean. Any system that embraces the concept of observability leverages AI systems to train knowledge engines around patterns of data. This can be simple patterns such as an increase in the internal temperature of a server that will accurately indicate an impending failure, which is something that most humans with IT operations experience already understand. Looking at the correlation of systems' data from hundreds of sources involves much more complex uses of learning to look at patterns over time and what they typically indicate. This can include performance data from specific applications, networks, databases, I/O, and so forth. The knowledge engine can identify and use these patterns to predict and avoid negative issues that impact operations. Complex patterns will emerge that may encompass a detailed review of thousands of current and historical data sets to pinpoint most network, storage, and application failures before they happen. Humans can never physically replicate the same processes to achieve this level of understanding.

- **Alerting:** What issues need to be dealt with in a timely manner? For example, a low-level priority alert for a network performance issue that will eventually lead to the replacement of a network hub. Or an immediate alert that requires immediate attention, such as capacity that needs to be automatically expanded because an application processing load is nearing the limits of a virtual server cluster in the cloud. Again, these can be simple alerts that just let a system or human know about some issue or warning, whereas complex alerts could go out based on different humans and/or systems that need to be involved.

- **Actions:** What happens because of an alert? It could result in a manual action such as a text to IT to reboot a cloud-based server, or some automated action such as kicking off very sophisticated processing to automatically recover from a ransomware attack before there is an impact on core business systems. Complex actions may involve dozens of actions taken by humans and thousands of automated actions to carry out immediate self-healing operations.

Observability provides the ability to manage and monitor modern systems that include applications built to run at faster velocities with more agile features. It will no longer work to deploy applications and then bolt on monitoring and management tools. The new tools must do much more than simply monitor operations data. Again, what's core to the value of observability are the insights that observability systems can provide by leveraging data that they gather from all platforms under management—for instance, cloud, legacy, and edge-based systems. Keep in mind that "legacy" refers to systems typically over 10 years old but is really anything existing that needs to work and play well with the cloud-based systems.

Figure 10-4 depicts what these insights are now or will likely be. Note that it's a matter of understanding the present, the past, and what will happen in the future. This is a tall order for most observability systems now, even if the data exists to generate these insights. The trick is to get things right, and that can only be done by the repeated use of data as training data, and the ability to derive outcome patterns of that data. In other words, the answers are somewhere in the data, but we don't have the approaches and processes to find and interpret the answers. The value of observability is not in its ability to gather and monitor random data. Its value lies in its ability to find answers in overwhelming quantities of seemingly random data.

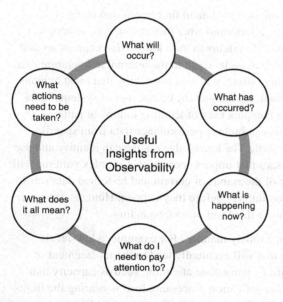

FIGURE 10-4   Useful insights from observability include an understanding of the current state of systems, such as active cloud services. More useful insights include what happened in the past, what the current state of things really means, and, most importantly, what will happen in the future and how to correct impending problems before they become true problems.

Figure 10-5 is an observability maturity model for IT operations, including cloud and legacy operations. It's a good guide for the progression of a company that wants to optimize observability for IT operations.

> **Note**
>
> We define the degrees of maturity as CloudOps (cloud operations) 1.0, 2.0, 3.0, and 4.0. The lower number, 1.0, is the least amount of observability maturity, and the highest amount of maturity is 4.0. The higher numbers come with more advanced capabilities and technologies deployed and thus generate the most business value. Obviously, it's desirable to move from the lowest to the highest maturity levels, and this will hold true for most enterprises well into the future.

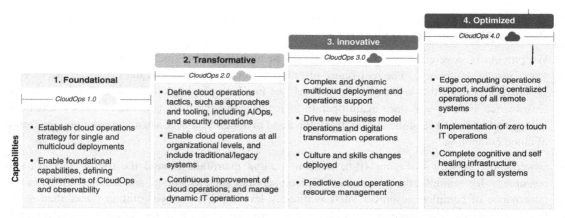

FIGURE 10-5 Operations-oriented observability can define several steps of maturity that enterprises will progress through to achieve "zero touch" IT operations that include all cloud and non-cloud resources.

To begin the journey, our company would first start with capabilities that are considered "Foundational," or, CloudOps 1.0. They could build on existing IT operational approaches and tooling to find a starting point for next-generation IT operations in the cloud. The most important capability here would be to establish a cloud operations strategy that would cover a single and multicloud deployment, as well as extend operations to legacy systems. If our company progressed to CloudOps 2.0, "Transformative," the most important step for that level of maturity would be to define the cloud operations tactics to support observability. This would include the addition of AIOps and other tooling, which is just an implementation of the cloud operations strategy that we created at the previous level of maturity.

Moving into the future, CloudOps 3.0 and 4.0, "Innovative" and "Optimized," respectively, many of these capabilities take our company to levels that produce ROI values back to the business for the investment made in observability approaches and tooling. Some of the most important capabilities include the ability to support complex cloud deployments, such as complex and distributed multi-clouds that would also include legacy systems under the observability umbrella. Moving up, a fully optimized maturity state includes the ultimate destination of zero touch IT operations with fully optimized and automated legacy and cloud operations. Humans have been removed from the operations processes, including fully automated self-healing systems that proactively correct operational issues using cognitive tools such as AIOps and other force multipliers to fully automate all IT operations.

Note that this is an example of an application of observability that uses observability to add value to cloud operations. Observability can as easily apply to security, application operations, and other areas that can reap benefits from these insights to better deal with their cross-platform jobs. Thus, you need to consider how to use observability generally, meaning just for operations, and observability for specific purposes and its benefit to cloud computing (which is where the future of this concept lies), as well as its benefit to other platforms. Keep cross-cloud observability on your radar.

Cross-Platform Governance

We previously covered governance as it relates to multicloud and single-cloud deployments, so I won't restate things here. The real future of cross-platform governance is the expanded use of core governance systems that work across platforms, not just for a single platform as it's leveraged today. Governance systems will once again operate logically above the platforms, which is how this technology and concept will shine. Again, that's the trend to understand best when you peek into the future of cloud computing.

Governance, as seen in Figure 10-6, is about putting guardrails around the use of services and resources—for example, the governance of cloud services such as storage and database APIs, or the governance of complete resources such as directly leveraging a storage solution rather than going through a service. The future of cross-platform governance begins with the initial use of governance in single and multicloud deployments by those who operate cloud and non-cloud systems. This trend includes or will include

- The rise of security and governance systems that work together. For example, ensuring that someone is not granted access to a specific resource or service by using set policies that deny access.

- The rise in the use of compliance governance. For example, having cross-platform governance systems and underlying policies that enforce legal and corporate compliance. An example would be to disallow data transfers out of the country, if laws exist that prohibit such transfers.

- The rise of governance systems linked with operations. Right now, there is little or no integration between operational tools such as the ones discussed earlier in this chapter and earlier in this book. Moving forward, this lack of integration can't stand. Governance systems need to work across platforms to work and play well with systems that operate infrastructure, applications, data, and so on, and to control who has access to all the various pieces and parts. This is not about denying access to something just to ensure that everyone and everything is following the rules, it's about protecting core systems from mistakes that are likely to cause core problems.

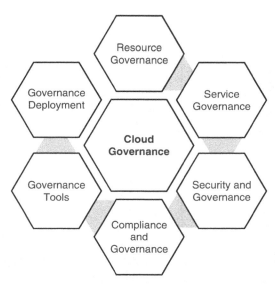

FIGURE 10-6 Governance is core to cloud computing success now and into the future. Governance puts limits or guardrails around resources and services to protect them from misuse, and over- or underuse. Today, most enterprises don't leverage formal governance and will soon find that it's unavoidable.

Cross-Platform Financial Operations (FinOps)

FinOps has just emerged as the primary means to deal with cloud costs, and the management and optimization of cloud costs. Moving forward, FinOps will cross all platforms to provide true cost optimization.

Cloud-based systems can't work on an island. They need visibility into the other systems as well, including legacy and edge computing systems. Just because we own the hardware, the idea that we don't need to manage costs on those systems is just not true. The focus moving forward needs to be on cloud-based resources, as well as how they interact with existing and net-new systems, cloud or not, and how that impacts the ROI value for the business.

Figure 10-7 depicts the benefits of FinOps programs now and into the future. FinOps programs can obtain the maximum amount of value from system resources, which means FinOps will monitor all cloud and non-cloud resources, which allows us to look at how everything works together to provide optimized business value. This approach is a bit different than the FinOps of today that focuses more on cloud resources, or even the resources of a single-cloud provider. That information does not tell us much, other than how a few systems are optimized.

Tomorrow's FinOps will help developers, operations, finance, and other business teams understand and control all system costs. As we mentioned earlier in this book, there will come a time when non-cloud options offer the most cost-effective solutions. Thus, non-cloud options need to be included in a FinOps program and include observability around how non-cloud and cloud-based resources utilize non-cloud options, and how much business value they generate. If your FinOps program is limited to cloud-only operations, you won't get the entire picture and you will have limited visibility into cloud-only parts of the cost optimization story.

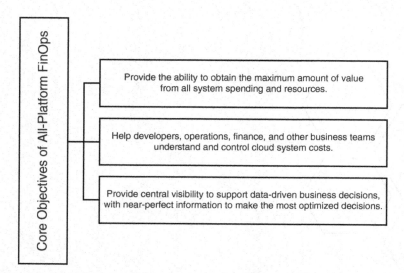

FIGURE 10-7   The core objective of any FinOps program is to monitor cloud costs ongoing and provide information that allows organizations to obtain the maximum amount of value from all computing resources, cloud and non-cloud. FinOps will extend to all systems in the future.

FinOps also needs central visibility to support data-driven business decisions using near-perfect information to make the most optimized decisions. Again, this goes to observability as the primary objective of future FinOps: Understand what the current state means in the context of many other things that happened and are happening now. Based on that information, make forecasts as to what's most likely to happen in the future.

The way we view value will change as well. Right now, the focus is on hard cloud values, such as operational cost savings or how much of our own computing equipment we can shut down in favor of cloud computing. As shown in Figure 10-8, this only tells part of the story. Existing and future net-new cloud deployments must work with other technology consumption solutions such as co-location (co-lo) providers, managed services providers (MSPs), and even some of our own hardware.

Moving forward, soft values will be much more important. However, they are much more difficult to determine. Most enterprises don't trust "dart board" soft value estimates, or they don't know how to estimate soft values such as business agility, speed-to-market, and other factors that are much more complicated to put a number on. Most systems' spending doesn't make much sense without trusted soft value numbers, including cloud computing.

The dirty little secret of cloud computing is that the hard values are just not there, and it's not so secret anymore. It's time to look at soft values to justify cloud and non-cloud systems for modernization and expansion. Hype drove yesterday's decisions, business value drives today's systems decisions. Hard values may or may not exist. Soft values need to be included in your FinOps program as well.

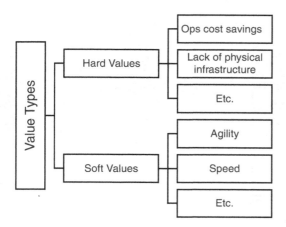

FIGURE 10-8 The two major types of cloud values are hard and soft values. Hard values are easy to determine, such as the decreased cost of using cloud resources versus more traditional approaches. Soft values are more difficult to determine but end up being of much higher value. Examples include the enhanced values of business agility and speed-to-market delivered by cloud computing.

Cross-Platform Data Federation

Data is the most difficult problem to solve for those looking to modernize their systems. For the last 20 years, I've listened to enterprise after enterprise complain about the state of their data, and how they vow to redo and consolidate everything. It's never done. Instead, the data situation gets worse as more net-new databases are added and complexity is compounded by new database models—for example, the addition of purpose-built databases to deal with a specific application that's added to pre-existing relational and object databases.

Every enterprise has scads of legacy data that may exist in dated database technology, or even in direct I/O to storage that needs to be part of the database story as well. If we ignore that data and just refocus on cloud-based databases, that approach won't provide the value needed to make a business case for moving to the cloud. All data needs to be included and leveraged using managed and secured mechanisms that can span all data, cloud and non-cloud. So, how do we solve this values problem moving forward?

Data federation is the most-likely candidate to fix most of the value issues. The data physically will stay where it exists in cloud-based systems or traditional platforms, and data federation will leverage the data using a common control panel. This is depicted in Figure 10-9. Although aspects of this approach are possible today, complete data federation across all platforms, cloud and non-cloud, is difficult to pull off. Data control panels must provide full database virtualization, or the ability to view all data using any schema and metadata model that works best for the application or human that consumes the data. It won't matter where the data physically exists. You may not even know its location for security reasons, but you will access any data you are authorized to access, at any time, for any reason, in the way you need to access it. The consumption and production of the data will be handled using a common layer that spans all platforms.

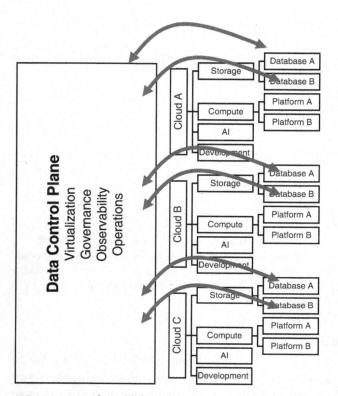

FIGURE 10-9   A multicloud leverages data across many public clouds, and it needs a common data control panel. This control panel includes data virtualization or data abstraction, data governance, and data operations, including data observability.

The data control panel should include controls that manage fundamental data issues, such as compliance, and data governance, which allows us to put limitations on data consumption. Observability also needs to be on the control panel for reasons presented earlier in this chapter. The final control panel options should include data operations, security operations, backup and recovery, cross-database management, performance management, and all the blocking and tackling that goes into managing a database. Again, aspects of this data control panel exist today, but only in bits and pieces. The final solution will require more innovation and acceptance in enterprise IT. I suspect that enterprises will have little choice but to adopt a data control panel approach—especially after they come to the hard realization that data complexity will reduce or eliminate the value that data could bring to the business.

Changing Skills Demands

Addressing skills again, let's focus on what the future will bring. Although the need and demand for cloud skills will most likely increase (if past patterns are any indication), the profile of the in-demand skills will change as well, as it always does. It's in your best interest to keep skills in mind as you define the next generation of systems to build. This skills list should include cloud and non-cloud skills.

A limited supply of skills will limit your ability to modernize and evolve your systems. Thus, the availability of the required on-staff and on-demand IT skills will determine the enterprise's degree of success. As I write this book, I'm hearing about all kinds of cancellations and limitation issues with cloud migrations and net-new cloud deployments due to the unavailability of qualified cloud technologists. Although many enterprises believe they can just toss money at a hiring problem, that's typically not the case with cloud computing. It's a constant game of "Where's Waldo?" with a single qualified candidate hiding within a sea of unqualified candidates, or Waldo already works for your competition. Paying more helps, but it does not solve the longer-term problem. So, it's advantageous to look at how the demand for skills will evolve to make sure you have as many Waldos on staff when they're needed.

Cloud Generalists vs. Cloud Specialist

One of the issues that keeps arising is the demand for a specific skill set. Just a few years ago, a cloud certification focusing on a single popular cloud provider was enough to get you a "cloud job." These days, the focus is on specialization such as [name a public cloud brand] security engineer, or [brand] developer, or [brand] architect. The focus is on very specific skills in the narrow versus general skills in the wide.

Figure 10-10 depicts what this demand looks like moving forward. Specialized [cloud brand] technology skill sets become more desirable than cloud computing generalists in architectures, security engineers, operations architects, and so on. Looking from the wide to the narrow will hurt us at some point, and many enterprises have already hit that hiring wall.

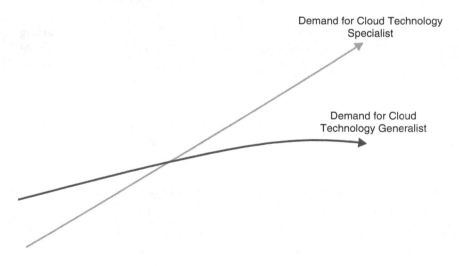

FIGURE 10-10 In-demand cloud skills seem to be shifting from generalists to those with specialized skills. It's no longer a qualifier to be a cloud data expert; it's best to specialize in a specific cloud provider and cloud-native database. Generalists, including good cloud architects, are in demand as well, but not as much. This could lead to problems if only a few hires are looking at more holistic issues within the cloud architecture.

I'm telling you this for a few reasons. If you focus your career on general cloud computing skills, you will still find a cloud job. It just won't be as readily available or pay as well as the job that requires specific cloud skills. Cloud providers offer certifications for these narrow skill sets and then convince enterprises that they need these specific skill sets to survive. It will take time for enterprises to realize they also need cloud generalist skill sets.

There are valid reasons why providers take this strategic path—namely, to expand their role in a specific enterprise to expand their business. The unintended consequence of branded certification requirements is that IT often misses the bigger picture issues that will only be caught by those with a broader knowledge of all solutions, cloud and non-cloud; thus, IT staffs will often lack the ability to take a more strategic look at the big picture of cloud technology.

I suspect that this inability to see the big picture will have a few negative effects, including the fact that many viable solutions won't be considered because no one in the organization understands how they work, or why they should be leveraged as an alternative to the current path. As we discussed earlier in this book, on-premises systems should still be considered a potentially viable solution, as well as other cloud providers and other deployment architectures such as edge computing. Without knowing what the other options are or how they could provide potentially better fits, enterprises often leverage suboptimized architecture (which we cover later in this chapter).

Less Code, More Design

As I write this book, there's a lot of buzz about low-code and no-code development. Simply put, this type of development can create applications using visual interfaces that sometimes have the ability to add code. The idea is that it democratizes development by allowing those without much training to build and deploy their own applications. Although this capability sounds compelling, it's not right for all development work. In many other instances, this approach leads to more robust software development projects where the low-code and no-code development is moved to more common application development and deployment approaches.

The point here is that the likely path moving forward will be on systems built using less code, with the focus on the design rather than the underlying mechanisms that make up the application. This approach will provide several core benefits:

- The ability to create systems and applications faster and deploy them closer to the speed requirements of most businesses.

- The ability to change these applications and systems faster, including core databases and application functionality. Again, we can create and change these applications at the "speed of need."

- The inclusion of the end users in the design of these systems and applications. Right now, requirements are fed into developers who turn out their interpretation of the application solutions. In this low- or no-code scenario, end users actively participate in the design of the applications and even create portions of the applications themselves. This approach should deliver a better final product that better meets the specific needs of the business.

Architectural Optimization Is the Focus

Future optimization will include all systems, cloud and non-cloud, and thus we must move to more strategically focused system deployments. Most initial cloud deployments are much less optimized than they should be, with survey after survey reporting substandard ROIs relative to the promised values of cloud computing. We've covered aspects of this type of optimization already, so I don't redefine it in as much detail here.

It's time to stop deploying the most popular technology that might "work" but typically results in underoptimized solutions. Figure 10-11 depicts the next shift that will align the end-state solutions with both the business requirements and the optimized use of technology that returns the maximum ROI. This will be a nice change.

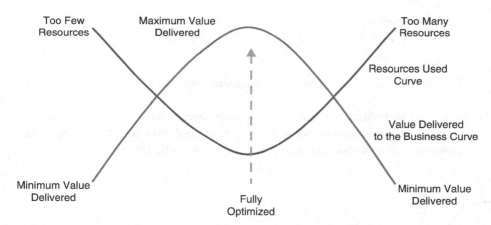

FIGURE 10-11 Architecture shifts to become an optimization exercise where we look for a solution pattern that provides the most value for the business. This is a change from cloud architectures that are grossly underoptimized and thus much less efficient than they should be, although they may appear to "work."

Cloud Security Shifts Focus

Cloud security focused on specific siloed deployments to solve cloud security problems in the past. As mentioned earlier, security will most likely become more centralized and exist logically above all public clouds, and even traditional systems in operations. Let's look at what security systems themselves are now and what they will likely become in the future.

Figure 10-12 depicts the as-is state of cloud security and security in general. There is nothing surprising about how we deal with security today. We typically focus on identity-based security for each cloud deployment as well as some encryption services. Although biometrics are there for multifactor authentication (MFA) (that is, fingerprint recognition on your iPhone), it's not leveraged at scale. Neither is observability, where we could look for insights into states that may be an indication of a breach and then take defensive actions as an automatic response.

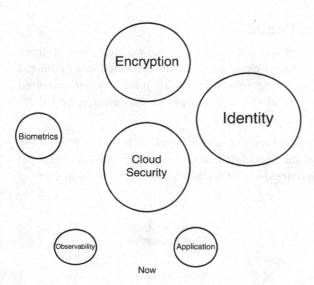

FIGURE 10-12 Today's security focuses on core security services such as identity and encryption.

Figure 10-13 depicts the most likely future that features centrally deployed security at the higher layers of the architecture (for example, supercloud/metacloud), which is systemic to all these forward-looking evolutions. New security evolutions will make cloud and non-cloud security more effective than it is today.

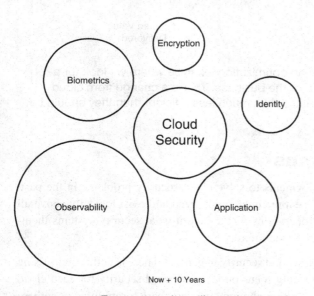

FIGURE 10-13 Future security will watch many things and determine insights into those things, that is, security observability. We will spot issues using any number of data points and determine the underlying meaning that relates to security issues, and then automate protection from those issues. This will become the preferred security approach because it considers many things at the same time and thus becomes much more effective.

Figure 10-13 also depicts the most obvious change, the rise of observability. The focus is on proactive security with insights into system states, and what that means to the active security posture. For example, CPU saturation on several cloud-based servers could be an indication of a breach attempt. Observability gathers future insights to determine whether that's true or not. Today, we wait for things to happen and then respond. A good analogy would be if you have an outdated home security system and burglars break in through an unmonitored window. You must wait until (and hope) they set off an indoor alarm to notify you and authorities. This wait results in more damages and losses, and potentially puts responders in more danger. Instead, today's security cameras and motion detectors can determine suspicious activity near your home and respond defensively with sirens and notifications to you and/or authorities, which could help avoid the break-in altogether along with its costs or risks.

Biometrics will rise in use for a few core reasons. First, devices that interface with fingerprints and retina scans are getting much less expensive and more accessible. Sometimes people use the same passwords for everything, and that gives the bad guys access to everything after they crack the first password. An astonishing number of passwords are still on Post-It notes stuck to monitors around the world. You know who you are. In your defense, technology users have also hit a complexity wall. Most people can't possibly memorize all the passwords now involved in our daily lives. It's much easier to invest in a retina, face, or palm scanner than it is to memorize and/or constantly update passwords, and/or hope no one hacks into your online password manager. Passwords do work, but biometrics are much better.

Cloud Computing Becomes Local

The heading of this section really says it all. Figure 10-14 reflects how future points-of-presence (the physical location of cloud data centers) will multiply and disseminate. Right now, cloud data centers are concentrated in a few physical regions, including one a few miles from where this book is being written. As we move into the future and the workforce continues to geographically disperse itself, the number of cloud computing data centers located just down the street from you will increase no matter how remote you choose to live.

Why? The cost of deploying data centers continues to fall, and remote locations will provide more economically viable alternatives. Higher-performing applications that require less latency will drive this demand as well. Public cloud providers should respond to this shift with more flexible billing terms, and not focus as much on regions as they do today. Data centers should be deployed anywhere and run anywhere at some point in the future.

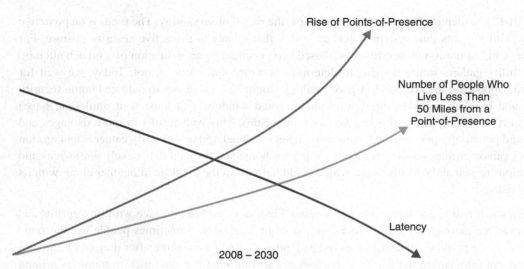

FIGURE 10-14   Today most providers cluster data centers at or near the same locations. More modern clouds will place cloud data centers everywhere so that they will be closer to their ultimate users. This placement should provide better performance and reliability.

Industry Clouds Become Important

Industry clouds with purpose-built industry-specific services will increase in popularity, as depicted in Figure 10-15. These types of clouds will support faster solutions development, because many of the services required for a specific vertical (that is, retail, finance, health care) are easier to leverage as prebuilt services rather them building them from scratch each time.

Industry-specific services will include database schemas and specialized security for certain industries (such as banking and health care). Again, the market motivation is to move faster by leveraging services you don't have to build yourself. Currently, public cloud providers are teaming up with industry-specific consulting firms and developers to build and deploy these services. It will take years for these new services to significantly impact affected businesses, but you should have them on your radar.

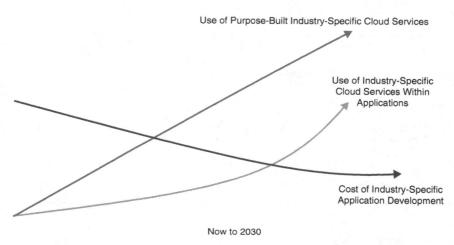

Use of Purpose-Built Industry-Specific Cloud Services

Use of Industry-Specific
Cloud Services Within
Applications

Cost of Industry-Specific
Application Development

Now to 2030

FIGURE 10-15   Cloud providers are beginning to offer deep industry-specific services, such as the services that finance, government, and retail find most valuable. The more work that's already done for you, the lower the cost. The industry-specific services will also be more reliable because they are better tested through sharing.

Where Is Edge Computing?

It's not going out on a limb to say that edge computing will continue to rise, with many of the systems and services that are now a part of public clouds moving to the edge. However, edge computing must be at the edge of something. That "something" will be public cloud providers. After all, the two are related.

If you look at today's most popular edge computing technology providers, they include all the big public cloud providers. So, edge computing will become just another architectural option that you can leverage if it makes good business and technical sense for your application and/or system. Therefore, it should continue to be on your radar for future evolutions of cloud, and of technology in general.

Figure 10-16 is an example of a modern edge computing system; in this case, it provides a set of services for a motorcycle. Note how the core subsystems are divided into systems that are on the device—in this case, on the bike—and systems that exist on the back-end system on a public cloud provider. The reason for edge computing here is obvious. The system needs to make immediate decisions on the bike, such as turning off the fuel pump if the bike is tipped over. Other systems are more effective off the bike and on the public cloud provider, such as gathering mechanical metrics over time to determine if you have an impeding breakdown event that's preventable if caught before it happens, such as a part that's known to break at a certain wear level. The potential system value and ROI are huge if we keep this architectural option in our back pocket.

Connected Motorcycle

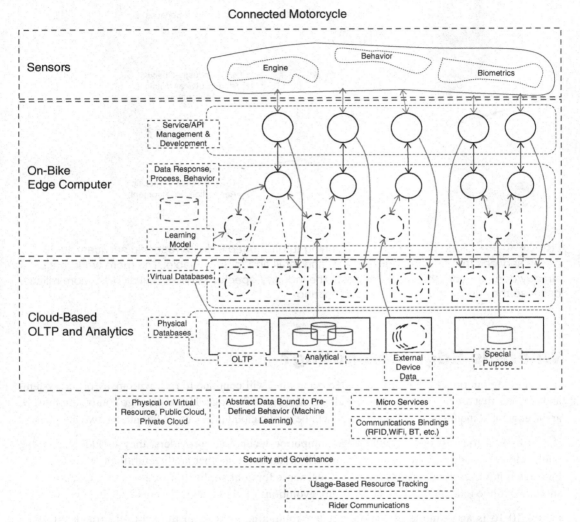

FIGURE 10-16 This example of edge computing depicts a connected vehicle (motorcycle), which hosts an edge device. That device has three different architectural layers. The sensors are physically attached to the bike to gather data. The on-bike edge computer contains the edge computing system that locally gathers and stores data with some processing (even lightweight analytics), and AI (knowledge at the edge). The cloud-based back-end system does some of the heavier processing and provides deeper capabilities around the use of AI and data analytics.

Call to Action

The primary reason we'll continue to leverage cloud computing is due to its ability to promote innovation, as well as to build products and services that are innovative unto themselves. In Figure 10-17, you'll notice we flipped the pyramid. Innovation was a smaller result of leveraging most technologies, with the focus being on business efficiency using automations that provided a better product and customer experience. The need to provide a good customer experience remains important, and it's now more achievable with better technology. Now and moving forward, the focus turns to innovation.

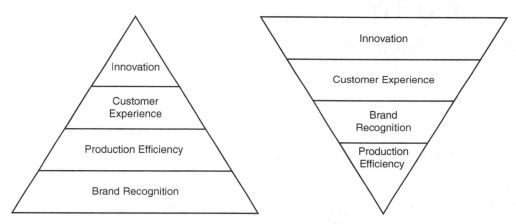

FIGURE 10-17 Innovation was once a random by-product of any technology, valued far less than the customer experience or production efficiency. Today, innovation is the primary value driver for cloud computing and the reason most enterprises go through a data transformation to get the business to a better state.

Value comes from innovation in our modern economy. It's the reason innovation will remain the focus of cloud computing. If you think about it, we live in a time when we have major transportation companies such as Uber and Lyft that don't own most of the vehicles that provide their services; they just provide the innovation around how you find and leverage those vehicles. The economy will evolve as innovation becomes the ultimate value. Cloud computing enables faster innovation, which is a major motivator to continue using these technologies.

The future value of cloud computing will be defined as the fastest path to a more innovative business, which is the fastest path to value for the business. Innovation is the reason cloud exists and thrives today and will into the future. Apply the points made in this chapter to make some good bets on where the market is moving and how you and/or your company can take advantage of the evolutions.

11

Wrapping Things Up: Miscellaneous Insider Insights

Success consists of going from failure to failure without loss of enthusiasm.

— *Winston Churchill*

In this last chapter of the book, I wrap up what's been said from an insider's point of view and put a bow on how we need to think about the evolution of cloud computing…and computing in general. This book approaches the topics from the standpoint of what's not being said in other books, articles, and podcasts to provide you with a unique perspective. There are no biases or conflicts of interest to color the truth, so you can make more informed decisions moving forward with cloud computing. If you've read each chapter in sequence or moved directly to this one, both types of readers will find good perspectives here.

I also understand that you, the reader, have many unique perspectives. Some of you work within the cloud computing industry as technology builders and providers, or as consultants and trusted advisers like me. Others are just starting their cloud computing journey and are hungry for the knowledge that will give you a leg up in your field, or to confirm someone else's take on the current and future states of cloud computing. A few others are in traditional IT right now and want to shift their career to cloud computing. One book can't be all things to all people, but I did write this chapter and this book with all these perspectives in mind.

Now let's look at some overall benefits of cloud computing.

Cloud Can Make Life Better

The fundamental role of any technology, including cloud computing, is to make our lives better in some way. While our primary cloud focus is to return value to the business, the end game should always be to do specific human things such as serve the customer better, allow employees to be more productive, return equity to the investors, and return more to the humans than the amount of time and resources invested. If you keep those goals in mind, success will track directly to your technology project's ability to meet those objectives.

"How will this proposal make most of the people involved happier than they are today?" That's a question I often ask in meetings to discuss and decide any sort of technological shift or transformation: If the question meets with blank stares, chances are the work should not take place and the investment should not be made. Those who promote cloud computing, including myself at times, need to ensure there is a link back to the happiness of people. A project's "before" and "after" happiness quotient often relates directly to business success.

Let's break down this idea using an insider's perspective. In other words, this perspective probably won't match much of the hype and glad-handing out in the cultural zeitgeist of cloud computing. The goal here is to look at the true realities behind each benefit or issue described in this chapter. Let's get going.

Cloud Supports Remote Work

A good result of the recent pandemic is the acceptance that work can occur anywhere, and employees should have the freedom to work where they want, even when they want, with some practical exceptions. For instance, airline pilots can't fly via a Zoom call, and most manual labor doesn't support remote work. However, most of the information processing workforce can now work from home, at the local Starbucks, or even at a remote cabin to change up the scenery. Anywhere that has access to a reliable high-speed Internet connection is a potential workforce location

As someone whose job can be done via the Internet from anywhere, I've been a remote workforce disciple for most of my career. Its advantages include employee retention, productivity, flexibility, and the often-underrated advantage of not having to spend hours in traffic each day. My round-trip commute took two to four hours daily throughout my 20s, 30s, and 40s. In that same amount of time, I could have written two books each year, spent more time with my family, and perhaps started a hobby. Instead, I was required to commute to an office where I would have very short interactions with other humans while there. If you add the time on planes and trains, that would have been well into 1,000 unproductive hours each year spent burning time and fuel.

Yes, we do need to meet with our coworkers outside of a Zoom call on occasion, and companies should promote a culture where there are structured human-to-human employee interactions. However, it's an outdated concept to require all staff to report to an office each day, regardless of what they are working on or any true need to interact with others in person. Many businesses take an extreme view on the remote work issue and don't allow it at all, including a surprising number of otherwise progressive enterprises.

Other businesses embrace remote work in its entirety and even allow creative options to foster business relationships that were once nurtured in an office environment. Examples include allowing travel to client sites to meet customers in person or coordinating employee attendance at a trade conference and then renting nearby meeting space so more diverse groups of employees could meet in person, such as an IT team and the stakeholder sales reps and sales managers who will use the team's product. Even meeting quarterly with your team in a conference room could be more about the social aspect than it is about getting specific things accomplished.

Remember, companies that are still successful today had sales representatives located nationwide to call on customers within a geographical location rather than work from a centralized corporate office. Employee morale and human connections were of as much concern then as now. Good sales managers came up with solutions to those concerns, even in the days before Zoom and cell phones. Today 29 Google pages are returned on a search that addresses "How to successfully manage a remote workforce," with links to dozens of books, blogs, and articles on the subject. The ground to break here is not as new as you think.

As a manager, you need a pragmatic understanding of what should be done to maximize productivity, retention, and thus profitability. So, the "it depends" answer comes back again. The ability to work remotely depends on what the job is and/or what the project requires. Take each remote work opportunity on a case-by-case basis. Almost every job involves hybrid work, which is a mix of remote with in-office work or vice versa, but the location should relate directly to the needs of the business and the employee, and not to some hard-and-fast rule that negatively affects employee productivity and retention.

Cloud computing also received praise during the recent pandemic for supporting a quick shift to a remote workforce. Cloud-based resources were already set up for access over the open Internet, including the ability to scale and the ability to support a reasonable level of security. You could consume those cloud resources anywhere over the open Internet. Enterprises that kept more traditional systems with limited remote access capabilities quickly installed more virtual private networks (VPNs), augmented security for remote workers, and even retrained staff that was mostly unprepared to work outside the corporate office building.

Enterprises that leveraged cloud computing prepandemic were often more technologically aggressive with more adaptable cultures and an existing remote workforce. They did much better at adapting to the "new normal" of work during and even after the pandemic (see Figure 11-1). Cultural adaptation is just as important as the adoption of cloud computing technology. Enterprises that were caught by their inability to adapt…well, many are now paying the price to dig out from their mistakes. "Adapt or die" has never been a truer idiom in this business climate.

Many enterprises that did cloud "wrong" lost productivity and thus market share, and still struggle to adapt as I'm writing this book. It's a mistake they now regret. Big, strong companies won't survive this latest technological revolution unless they maintain an adaptable and agile culture and technology stack. The insider advice? You're either a disruptor, or you'll be disrupted.

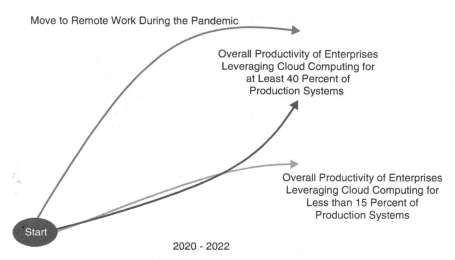

Move to Remote Work During the Pandemic

Overall Productivity of Enterprises
Leveraging Cloud Computing for
at Least 40 Percent of
Production Systems

Overall Productivity of Enterprises
Leveraging Cloud Computing for
Less than 15 Percent of
Production Systems

Start

2020 - 2022

FIGURE 11-1   We saw huge differences in productivity recovery between 2020 and 2022 among those who used cloud computing extensively during the pandemic and those who did not. Although many factors need to be considered, cloud computing made enterprises more agile overall with the ability to make quick shifts as needed, which proved especially important at the onset of workplace shutdowns in 2020. This time it was a pandemic, but the next work location disaster could as easily be manmade or another natural disaster.

Support for Remote and Virtual Enterprises

The rise of the born-in-the-cloud enterprise is a result of cloud computing being around long enough that younger companies could take full advantage of cloud computing from the start. This typically includes organizations founded less than 20 years ago, with most between 5 and 15 years old. These organizations have almost all of their IT delivered as cloud services. You've likely heard about a few of these, including Netflix and Uber. Although not all have 100 percent cloud-based infrastructure, they lean more into public cloud computing than many traditional enterprises or more modern companies that act more traditionally than they should.

We found out during the pandemic that these born-in-the-cloud companies had a greater advantage for the reasons we covered earlier. Lockdown in place or not, it was easier to support a remote workforce if an enterprise did not have a traditional data center and thus did not need access to one. Companies often found that access to some data centers was either not allowed for the time being, or, in many instances, they could not find employees who were willing to venture out to fix stuff in their data center. I've heard story after story of CIOs struggling to find the ways and means to fix simple problems, such as the power supply for a router or a storage server that was failing, things that would take less than a few hours to fix and usually cost almost nothing to repair. They ended up stopping all IT processing for hours until the CIOs could find creative ways to remotely fix these issues. A huge number of enterprises learned painful lessons during that time. Thus, today's more aggressive moves to cloud-based platforms hardly come as a surprise.

This climate gave rise to complex virtual companies that don't own or rent real estate or offices, at least not permanent ones. Most importantly, they own few if any servers, and they typically lease data center space. Company-issued laptops, smartphones, and/or tablets are the only potentially owned hardware, although it's often leased, or remote workstations are employee-owned. Most of what a virtual company "is" exists as a concept versus a brick-and-mortar company that's measured by its physical assets. Virtual companies feature a loosely coupled group of people who work together using technology to achieve whatever goals the company needs to achieve, such as building a cloud service, building a physical product (outsourcing manufacturing), selling products, or selling services. For the most part, unless you specifically investigate a virtual company, you would never guess it's completely virtual.

The insider perspective here is that cloud computing makes virtual companies possible. Cloud proves that all IT services including sales, order management, accounting, inventory control, collaboration, DevOps, and most other core business and technology services can be delivered as services to any person or system in the company that needs access. While completely virtual companies are still few and far between, the lessons learned from the pandemic are leading many new companies to sell their office real estate and/or cancel office leases, and only rent data center space.

Existing and more traditional companies now see a hardware path to a virtual state, but it's difficult if not impossible for these types of companies to give up all physical buildings and physical data centers that depend on what they sell. The core issue here is culture. For a company that maintained an office for the last 100 years, and for employees who joined the company to work in an office, it's much tougher to reduce or eliminate the traditional office. The same can be said for owned computer hardware and even owned data center space. As we said earlier, legacy systems are hard to dispatch. However, there are creative alternatives to maintaining your own data centers such as co-location providers that rent out data center space much like real estate, or managed services providers that own and maintain the hardware for you and may even manage your public cloud services, if needed.

This area becomes another one where companies need cloud computing if they want to be completely virtual and enable all employees to work remotely. What limits this movement for many companies is culture and a lack of willingness to make drastic changes. News flash, the market may make those changes for you.

Support for World Changes and Evolutions

The feature I point to as the core value driver of cloud computing is agility. Traditional IT approaches and components cannot expand or change as quickly around new and emerging opportunities. Cloud-based systems can deal with most agility issues. Success with agility comes down to understanding those capabilities and how to leverage the right solution to solve the right problems. We've covered agility already systemically throughout this book, at least conceptually, but it's helpful to point out specific areas where the benefits are better realized.

Support for Sustainability

We have an entire chapter on sustainability (Chapter 8), so I won't restate those concepts here. However, it's important to support sustainability, and that means you must understand how to support it. Many companies with good cloud sustainability intentions make things worse when they leverage cloud computing. Some get confused because *private cloud* has the word *cloud* in it. For instance, many don't realize a private cloud's carbon impact is much greater because you still own and run your hardware in an existing data center.

The real sustainability value we get from cloud computing is more difficult to define than most enterprises understand. Just using "a cloud" does not guarantee a return on sustainable value, and it's easy to make things worse if you're not careful. Figure 11-2 depicts what this process should look like to evaluate the use of sustainable technologies such as the cloud. The goal is to save carbon *and* return value to the business. A positive sustainability audit could mean access to more business and/or compliance with regulations. It could even save energy, which saves the company money. Of course, being a good citizen of the world is the overall motivation for reducing carbon output.

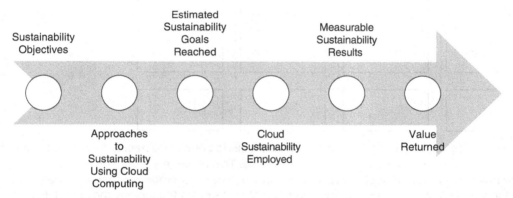

FIGURE 11-2 Sustainable cloud computing is not as easy to achieve as most people believe. You must create a process to clearly define the objectives, approaches, and goals, and then determine how you will approach sustainability using cloud computing. Then you need to measure the results and figure out how much value is returned.

Democratization of Computing

The democratization of computing is nothing new. COBOL, a programing language developed in the 1970s, theoretically allowed executives to write programs themselves. Spoiler alert, few executives in the 1970s had mastered the use of automatic teller machines, so even fewer volunteered to write software programs. However, the idea stuck and evolved. Today we no longer need to translate requirements from the end users to build our vision of *their* vision of business-critical systems. Now that most users are familiar with the use of apps on laptops, pads, and phones, they have greater potential than the execs of 50 years ago to use an app or dashboard to build what they need themselves. The advantage is speed, cost of development, and empowerment to get the end users to take ownership of their solutions (see Figure 11-3). Win-win.

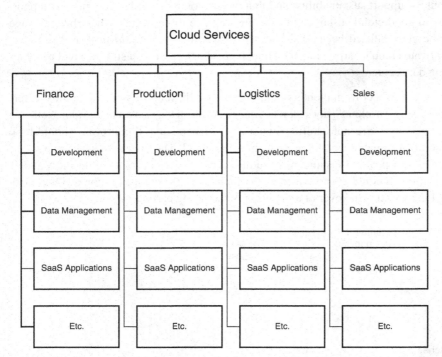

FIGURE 11-3 Democratization of computing by using cloud computing means that IT functions can be spread among the departments in an enterprise. This allows each department or team the power to build and deploy applications, manage data, leverage purpose-built SaaS applications, and so on. They are empowered to employ the exact technology they need. Be aware that there are many trade-offs with this approach.

Of course, democratization does not work all the time for all people. It's people rather than technology problems that usually eliminate a democratization approach. It's understandable. Most people are hired to do a non-IT job; then we push a programming tool in their faces and ask them to become software engineers, as well as do their core job. Remember, most people still think "the cloud" is where they store their pictures, music, and files from their phone and/or laptop. Think about the likely response if you ask those same people to write a custom business app or program. In my view, the technical aptitude of users will continue to evolve, but democratization for current non-IT workers will have limited success until they become sufficiently incentivized to become part of the process, or after they see a few peer successes with projects.

In that same vein of aptitude evolution, several new cloud-based innovations provide an easier entry into development for laypeople. A recent rise in the popularity of low-code and no-code development resulted in application development tools that are purpose-built to allow anyone with a bit of training to build, deploy, and operate applications. These tools use mostly visual interfaces that allow most semi-technical people to "drag and drop" their way to application development. Some of these tools also allow code to be added behind the application components to define custom behavior. Other low-no-code tools either don't require coding, or they provide visual methods to create code-like mechanisms. They also provide database access, and some tools provide access to any number of APIs that exist outside of the tool.

The downsides are what you would think. Because most of these low-no-code tools are cloud-based, they are limited in what they can do. Although they can build applications that are 100 percent defined by a trained end user, they are not optimized applications. They leverage only one technology stack that is typically unoptimized for that application's performance and thus can be costly to run on public cloud systems that charge for the extra CPU cycles used and extra data stores. That's why I have reservations about the widespread use of low-no-code technology, especially on the heels of preaching the need to optimize cloud solutions for technical and cost efficiency.

But don't let that dissuade you from leveraging the democratization of cloud computing systems for business purposes. It's fine to do things like create a prototype or build quick systems that will be improved later. However, for fully optimized applications, you still need to leverage more robust tools (we can call these "high-code" tools). So, I'm not buying that low-no-code development will replace more traditional approaches to cloud-based development. However, like any solution, there are some problems that low-no-code tools will solve best.

Punching Above Your Weight

A great thing about cloud computing is that it allows once insignificant and undercapitalized businesses to punch above their weight, which also relates to democratization—this time as computing power. Almost any business can leverage advanced computing systems that were once too costly for the "little guys" to leverage. They could not afford hardware and software that cost millions, so they had to make do with suboptimal solutions. That gave most big competitors a huge advantage over new and/or smaller competitors in their markets, and the big guys often pushed the little guys out of the race altogether.

Those race days ended with the evolution of cloud computing over the last 20 years, especially with the rise of SaaS in the early 2000s that allowed ERP and CRM systems to be leveraged as-a-service. This evolved into the rise of IaaS clouds which allowed businesses to leverage expensive storage and compute systems without a single investment needed in data centers or the hardware that lives in data centers. I saw this play out firsthand in my tenure as CTO and CEO of various startups over the years.

I had to raise at least $1 million of funding just to get the bare minimum infrastructure in place needed to develop and market the resulting technology products. Of course, that was just for entry-level startup activities. There were also upgrade and expansion cycles that drained most of my startup cash. At the time, there was no working around that startup scenario.

Today, the five powers of cloud computing make a true difference in how we do business now versus how we did business just a short time ago (see Figure 11-4). These powers break down as follows:

- **Growth** is the ability to scale cloud computing technology up and down as needed, now and into the future. There are few or no restrictions as to how fast you can grow, albeit you'll pay for all that you leverage.

- **Usage** is usage-based cost, in that you'll pay only for what you leverage. As you scale the business and your revenue grows, you'll use more compute and storage resources, and pay more for using a greater amount of those services. This lines up with how we want to run our businesses, where costs track with usage, which tracks with revenue.

- **Agility** is the ability to change when you need to change and do so at the speed of need. It doesn't matter if you're moving from a relational database to an object-based database for better analytics support or moving applications to serverless computing. With cloud computing, you can adjust as needed to respond faster to market changes or move fast when you need to quickly push a new product into the market based on a rising opportunity. Look at companies that pivoted during the pandemic from manufacturing dresses or safety helmets to making masks and face shields as demand for those products far outpaced supply during the pandemic. Or the designer clothing manufacturers that sped new designer masks to market to meet exploding demand.

- **Disembodied** means we can use cloud-based resources at any time, for any reason, from anywhere. There is no physical requirement that people or systems be at a specific location, as we covered earlier in this chapter. Entire companies that use cloud computing can be 100 percent virtual, which means they can adjust quickly and burn less cash because they don't have to rent office or data center space. Talent should also be easier to find since the virtual business can employ anyone from anywhere.

- **Democratization** empowers employees, departments, and other areas of the business to directly participate in system development, deployment, and operations.

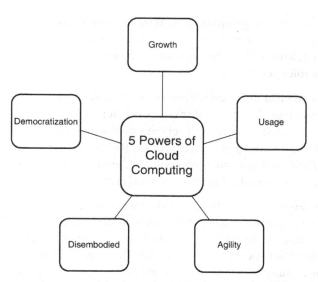

FIGURE 11-4 Cloud computing allows small- and medium-sized businesses to punch above their weight. They can leverage cloud computing as a force multiplier to build a business faster and disrupt more traditional businesses. These powers make cloud computing the great equalizer.

Changes in the Skills Mix

Back to people. Cloud and IT job descriptions and qualifications are undergoing major changes as we identify the mix of skills required to drive cloud computing within enterprises. Some of these changes won't come as a surprise, some of you will disagree with me, and others will be a tad confused. Let's walk through it.

The trouble with any substantial change in the skills mix needed to drive any new technology is the latency between demand for the skills and the labor market's ability to respond and adjust. This happens so often in the evolution of technology that I find it surprising when the supply and demand for new skills seem to take so many people by surprise. Indeed, during the pandemic, most believed there would be a huge downturn and all technologies, including cloud computing, would be negatively impacted. The opposite occurred. Enterprises and consulting firms scrambled for talent to build cloud systems to support the new remote workforce demands. What more of us realize now is that technology and spending do not limit progress; it's limited by the number of skills you can quickly recruit into your organization to implement that technology.

It's a huge value if you can see how those virtual skills will change moving forward because you can proactively train and recruit to make sure those skills are at your fingertips when you need them. Ironically, hiring and/or training ahead of demand is something most enterprises don't like to do, seeing the risk if the demand never materializes and the new hires or newly trained staff won't provide their anticipated value to the company, at least not right away.

However, if you create a true vision of your company or government organization, you'll understand what technologies you'll be using now, two years from now, five years from now, and so forth. It's just a matter of doing skills planning that will determine if it's best to recruit new hires, train existing personnel, or use outside contractors to fill the roles you'll need.

If you must respond at the last minute, any value that cloud computing or other technologies could bring goes right out the window as you compete with dozens of other companies for each somewhat qualified candidate. While you wait for the right people to show up, your enterprise will die the death of a thousand cuts. It's more likely that you'll hire the wrong people, or projects will be delayed while you wait for skills to show up that get more difficult to find as time progresses. So, understanding when and where the skills will likely change is not only a good idea but also a survival skill.

Figure 11-5 depicts where we were at the time this book was published. This is an amalgamation of all cloud skills that exist within enterprises, covering the major technology patterns that enterprises use in their current deployments. There are a few things to note. Cloud operations are important because most enterprises are not focused on obtaining cloud operations-specific skills. Instead, they assign operational duties to people in other technology categories such as data and AI. In many instances, cloud operations skills are not being formally addressed as a specific skill set and discipline. You need a separate team that focuses exclusively on holistic cloud operations.

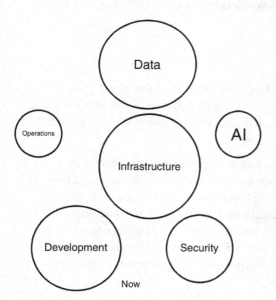

FIGURE 11-5   The cloud computing skills mix today is even between data storage, infrastructure (computing, networking, and so on), security, and development while AI and operations skills lag. Figures 11-5 and 11-6 show how needed skills will shrink or grow, relative to the larger cloud computing space. They're designed to depict what changes will be made in the number of people you'll need for each category of cloud technology, relative to the entire skills market space. Although this is just an educated guess, it encourages a discussion about what skills will be needed in the future and the necessary planning.

Figure 11-6 shows my insider estimate about how skill needs will break out in the years to come, say, in the next 5 to 10 years. There will be a huge increase in demand for cloud operations skills that will include AIOps, observability, FinOps, and so on. We spent a lot of time and money building and migrating systems over the last 10 years. We'll put in a similar effort to keep these things running smoothly. This effort will partly focus on employing cloud operations across enterprises because it makes more sense to consolidate operations skills within a cloud operations team. A CloudOps team can do this job more efficiently because we combine many similar or related operations tasks within the same team and the same technology stacks. We also need to understand that the CloudOps team must deal with increasing overlap in operations such as performance, backup, recovery, and reliability, all being types of services that need to span all aspects of cloud computing, including all circles (see Figures 11-5 and 11-6).

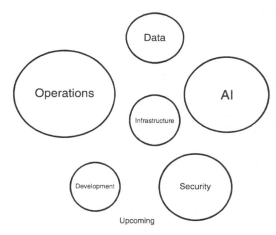

FIGURE 11-6 Moving forward, we'll need many more people with operations skills. AI engineers will be in even higher demand. Security will grow a bit, but not as much as many would predict. Development automation will reduce the need for development and deployment skills, as infrastructure automation will reduce the need for infrastructure skills.

Other changes in skills mixes are easier to predict, such as the rise of AI, considering how important it will be to businesses moving forward. The rise in security is now growing as fast as most predicted. We'll soon deliver much better security with fewer people as advanced security tooling automates manual tasks and provides better coverage to AI systems, observability, and automation; thus, the demand for people with cloud security skills will remain relatively flat.

The need for cloud data skills will shrink for the same reasons. Automation, abstraction, and federated data will require fewer people relative to the growth of the cloud computing space. Their data skills will likely shift to focus more on data usage and data value than traditional database admin tasks such as changing structures, adding features to databases, and overseeing the use of data within applications. Again, development work shrinks relative to the growth of the space. It's not that we'll build fewer cloud applications, but the tools will become more efficient and optimized so that it will take fewer people to crank out the same number of applications. Also, the adoption of low-code and no-code solutions will democratize some of the development. However, as I've previously asserted, not as much as the market now believes.

The idea here is simple, but the execution is tough. We're making some educated calls about what skills we'll need in the short and long term for the business. It takes as much as a year to hire a good cloud operations engineer or a good cloud AI specialist. Creation of a plan for the skills to hire and what and how to train new hires can affect your ability to succeed with cloud computing more than any other factor. Who would have thought that cloud success would revolve around people issues rather than technology issues? (Well, I did predict this too.) People are becoming the most important resource for cloud computing. Funny how people are such important assets these days when many once believed that all human value could be completely automated. That's not the case now, and I doubt it will ever be the case.

The Objectives Change

Cloud computing value as defined in the past has been a bit of a moving target. You may recall from the earlier chapters that cloud value was once based on operational savings created by avoiding capital expenditures. Now it's more about business agility and the ability to scale. This shouldn't be news to anyone who's read along this far into this book, but it's thinking that most enterprises still don't share. So, the next lead story should be: Enterprises finally accept that cloud computing is not just a movement to cheaper servers; it's a fundamental foundation to improve and modernize the business.

My question to new clients is often, "What do you consider the core value of cloud computing?" If the answer is "cost savings," there needs to be another discussion before we get started because they are missing the true value of cloud computing. Based on each company's unique situation and criteria, I sometimes advise them not to move to public cloud servers because staying put will likely be the cheaper path, at least for the time being. It's always interesting to see the looks on their faces when I give that answer.

There are a few hard realities about moving to the cloud that we all need to understand. For most, you have little choice. Consider the cloud innovation dollars that enterprises have spent for the last five to seven years. They can't stay off public clouds because they're already on them, and they won't gain an advantage from the technology providers' investments in innovations. Another confusing spin on this fact is that not all applications and data should reside on public cloud providers. Moving forward, you need to wisely pick the applications and data sets that move to the cloud. Look at the true value of cloud computing as it relates to these applications, meaning business advantages such as agility and scalability, with the pragmatic review of an application and data in terms of where they should be hosted to bring the most value back to the business.

Confused yet? Long story short, we now have options for where applications and data should exist to bring the most value back to the business. All things and all places need to be considered. How we view cloud and non-cloud resources is changing and will always change. While we have cost/benefit data points to consider, at the end of the day we must take the criteria and metrics and then determine the right location for applications and data. The criteria should include values to the business, such as operational cost savings, agility, speed, and scalability. The analysis should point to and cost justify one of three possibilities: Leave it be, lift-and-shift, or refactor.

As you can see in Figure 11-7, what I assert here is that business agility and growth become stronger drivers because, right now, most enterprises don't even consider them as value factors. At the same time, the "migrate, build, and deploy" approach to move to the cloud as fast as possible will fade as the primary driver to migrate to the cloud. Although many understood this years ago (including yours truly), agility and growth (agility) are just now catching on as the primary drivers and objectives for moving to public cloud providers. It's about time.

FIGURE 11-7   The current drivers to quickly migrate to the cloud and create net-new cloud applications will be slowly replaced by business agility and growth drivers. The focus will turn to optimization and how people find cloud technology useful. In other words, it will become more of a business-oriented objective versus a technology-oriented objective.

The Market Absorbs the Weak, and the Weak Emerge Again

The public cloud market was very crowded around 2009 when every enterprise technology company, managed services provider, co-location provider, and a bunch of telecom companies and underfunded startups had a public cloud of some sort. The functionality of their versions of a public cloud was all over the place, with some even setting up physical servers when their cloud computing customers requested them. So, you would request a resource, such as a storage and/or compute server as you do today from a "public cloud dashboard." It would take several hours for the resource to come online while a physical server was installed in a rack on your behalf, meaning that it would be removed from the box by a human, configured, tested, and physically put online. Although that's a funny story I sometimes tell when keynoting cloud computing conferences, it's a scheme that worked well, all things considered.

We know now that cloud providers quickly normalized as the market understood the huge amounts of investments required for a cloud provider to exist. This happened from about 2010 to 2016, as depicted on the left side of Figure 11-8. This is a pattern we've seen repeat itself in the technology space when the market absorbs weaker players that don't have enough cash to compete in a resource-intensive technology space such as public cloud computing. The smaller players are purchased by the bigger players and the market consolidates. In the case of public clouds, the market consolidated around three primary players with a few secondary players.

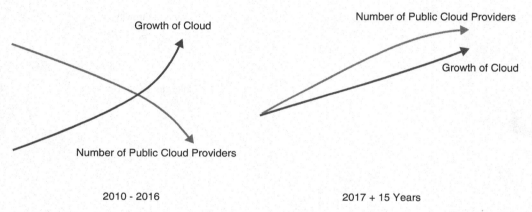

2010 - 2016   2017 + 15 Years

FIGURE 11-8 At the start of cloud computing, the number of public cloud providers numbered in the dozens, with most telecom companies promoting a public cloud. Then the market normalized when providers realized the large investment required to succeed. There will be more public cloud providers again that focus on industry cloud services and other niches moving forward. Because most enterprises already leverage multicloud, adding smaller cloud providers will become easier as we continue to solve multicloud complexity problems.

As the cloud computing market matures, we'll again see a familiar pattern emerge. Smaller players are beginning to enter the public cloud marketplace with a specialty focus on niches that the larger providers do not yet address. As the number of public clouds grows, the cloud market will again mature (see Figure 11-8).

Secondary niche IaaS public cloud providers are nothing new, by the way, with offerings such as file sharing, backup, and recovery services. These secondary public clouds provide a niche service designed to compete directly with the larger public cloud providers. What's most interesting is that they are becoming public clouds unto themselves, purpose-built to compete with more traditional cloud providers. Thus, this is an existing pattern of evolution that's been underway for the last 10+ years; I'm just calling out the growth that is about to occur.

The niche market is a bit different from cloud computing ecosystem technology (a technology designed to add value to a cloud computing provider's product). For example, if you go to the "marketplaces" for any larger public cloud provider, you'll see hundreds or thousands of providers that offer everything from security to automated spelling correction that works with a specific public cloud provider. The difference between an ecosystem and a niche product? When leveraging an ecosystem product, you'll typically do so by working through a public cloud provider such as accessing a particular enterprise's database. The new IaaS niche public clouds provide direct access to their cloud without going through another cloud provider. They are legit public clouds that I call "baby clouds."

A rising number of smaller public clouds may replace specific niche and standard cloud services markets that the public cloud providers now dominate. These public clouds may have services that compete directly with public cloud providers, but they have specialized public cloud services that are not offered by traditional public cloud providers. Most of these will be industry-specific services, such as databases that are purpose-built for retail, health care, or finance, or even specific supercomputing and quantum computing services that the larger public clouds may also provide.

Typically, the reason an enterprise would go with one of these emerging "baby clouds" is that they offer a full package of cloud products and services that existing public cloud providers don't offer, such as data and APIs that are purpose-built for trauma centers. Eventually, larger public cloud providers will also enter industry-specific cloud markets. For now, baby clouds will continue to pop up like mushrooms, and one or more may someday evolve into a behemoth capable of head-to-head competition with today's Big Three public cloud providers. However, history indicates that an emerging contender will be purchased and absorbed into one of its larger competitors.

This coming evolution makes the public cloud computing space more interesting for a few good reasons:

- First, the widespread use of multicloud makes it much easier to include other nonstandard public cloud providers and place them under the same operational and security frameworks as we do other public cloud providers, as you may recall from the multicloud chapter. This opens the number of options that cloud solutions architects now have by not limiting their choices to the "walled garden" of a single public cloud provider. This also assumes that enterprises will first optimize their cloud systems to bring multicloud complexity under control.

- Second, and most interesting, baby clouds provide a third choice when it comes to public cloud providers and traditional data center systems. They are still a public cloud and should come with the convenience and scalability of "traditional" public cloud services. Baby clouds may also provide analog resources at greatly reduced prices. For instance, you may pay .002 cents a gigabyte for object storage on a larger public cloud provider while a smaller public cloud upstart offers the same service at .0001 cents a gigabyte. If all things are equal (and they never are), then that would be a good fiscal choice if no other integrated features are needed that are only offered by a larger public cloud provider. In most cases, I suspect a cheaper analog service will not attract the largest share of baby cloud clients. The lure will be a niche service that the larger public cloud providers may not provide such as risk analytics to support financial trading, or the ability to calculate the best investment path for a portfolio. Those are deep specialty niche services that can't be easily replicated.

- Third, the additional competition will promote more entrants into the public cloud space but also provide pressure on public cloud providers' prices. The larger public cloud providers with their many billions of dollars in resources have built clouds that are pretty much the same. The prices and terms are a bit different, but they have more in common than not in common. That situation levels the cost of using a large public cloud from provider to provider. They have R&D and production expenses that are built into their pricing models, and those costs are higher than the smaller more efficient players. The existence of more baby cloud providers that can be easily incorporated into a multicloud will put pressure on existing cloud pricing. At the very least, it removes worries about cloud lock-in.

Of course, there are and will be downsides to leveraging baby clouds. They typically don't have the same number of points of presence as larger cloud providers. However, some of the smaller public cloud providers may leverage the larger cloud providers to support their infrastructure, including points of presence. This is done today. A baby cloud may use a public cloud provider to manage access and storage on the back end for services such as personal file storage. You never even know that they are leveraging an IaaS public cloud provider, even though that is where your data exists.

We'll see cases where baby cloud providers don't own physical servers but instead leverage a larger public cloud provider to host their specific cloud services. This may fall out of favor if baby clouds become true threats to the public cloud provider's business and the provider abruptly kicks the baby cloud off their cloud. Also, baby clouds could not offer a profitable discount to another public cloud provider's analog resources. So, I see many baby clouds moving to physical systems they own, much like we saw over the last five years when some gaming services moved from public clouds to owned systems to have more control and save money.

The insider takeaway? Watch for the growth of choice. Enterprises are much more likely to add all the larger cloud providers to their multicloud cloud services portfolio, but many of the baby clouds will present a more difficult decision as enterprises struggle to tame the complexity monster. Eventually, I suspect the market will instigate the evolution and integration of baby clouds into more multicloud portfolios. It will be a step in the right direction.

Cloud Technology Continues to Be a Value Multiplier

As depicted in Figure 11-9, the cloud remains the single most effective technology that enterprises can leverage to take their value to the next level. Cloud computing allows enterprises to punch far above their weight in the marketplace. In terms of cash spent relative to value delivered and acceleration to value, the ability to find and capitalize on innovation remains the single most compelling reason to leverage cloud computing today and into the future.

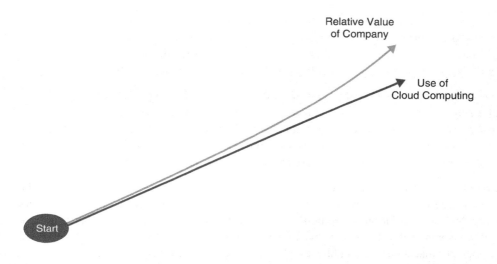

FIGURE 11-9 The cloud will continue to be a not-so-secret weapon to increase corporate value, either through innovation or better productivity. While many businesses missed the first wave of cloud computing, I predict we'll see a surge in digital transformation and IT modernization using cloud computing as a force multiplier to expand value.

Not all enterprises will leverage cloud effectively. Most won't. Missing will be the skills and vision required to configure the use of cloud computing as a net benefit to the business. There are lots of ways to succeed with cloud computing and lots of ways to fail. Many who promoted cloud computing in their enterprises assumed that success was a foregone conclusion just by using cloud computing. Most cloud providers also promoted that point of view to accelerate adoption when cloud computing was new.

Now we know that cloud computing is another enabling technology that enterprises can use and misuse. The inside advice I hope you take away from this book is that cloud computing is not magic, and its adoption does not ensure success. Enterprises need to make a series of strategically sound decisions for cloud computing to deliver its promised value. For many enterprises, cloud computing will be another path of trial and error, certainly for most of those who did not read this book.

Call to Action

In writing this insider-focused book, I tried to provide information that you won't find in other places. These days I'm a bit concerned that many information resources are not as candid and pragmatic as they once were. This is an evolution of the media in general to address the fact that most of today's readers have short attention spans. Many technical articles now feature short sound bites of advice rather than in-depth and concise information about the topic of the article. A problem or evidence that a problem exists is often the topic of an article, with no guidance or advice about how to solve the problem. Even books are written in such a manner these days, which is bothersome. For example, your car has a flat tire. Here are the bad things that will happen if you drive on that flat tire. Change the words *flat tire* to *cloud complexity*, and you will see the theme emerge in many technical publications.

The key here is to question everything as you move forward with cloud computing or any other technology. Don't assume a security approach and technology are right for you just because an analyst or another company's CTO used them successfully for a different project. Every project is unique. Also, be aware that analysts often have as many technology providers as paying clients. I would consider their advice with a grain of salt, despite any statements of unbiased advice.

The tech press suffers from the same issue. However, it's just the maturation of the market. (1) The press and analysts need to find sources of revenue. (2) Technology providers have marketing dollars to spend. (3) Problem, meet solution. To be honest, some of the publications I've contributed to have these kinds of sponsorship issues, meaning we're asked to opine on specific technologies that are provided by companies that support the publication through advertising or Webinar hosting. Or, look at the vast number of surveys about technology subjects. You'll rarely or never see a survey sponsored by a technology provider that returns information that's not in the sponsor's favor.

Some technical publishers and their publications are hyper-ethical, and they will even turn down lucrative advertising that could imply a conflict of interest. Other publishers and publications act as mouthpieces of technology companies. Learn to recognize the difference.

You may still gain valuable information about the reasons for the existence of a problem from a mouthpiece article, but the solution will be focused on the product that sponsors the article. Search for articles sponsored by competitors of that product to get a more well-rounded point of view about potential solutions.

Different points of view lead to more correct solution choices, which lead to greater success. That's why it's important to continue supporting the tech press and tech analysts. Gather data points wherever they exist, from normal channels that include the tech press, analysts, and product providers themselves, and from those who have an insider track on this technology, people like myself and a handful of others.

Whenever I undertake a technology project, I consider potential conflicts of interest with data points that may prove helpful. Two things can be true. Information can be useful and correct but also purposely slanted toward a particular conclusion. Be savvy about where you get your information and the motivations of the people providing it.

Today, many IT decision-makers have only a fraction of the information they need to make informed decisions about cloud computing. These decisions will eventually prove pivotal to an enterprise's success or failure. This book's purpose is to even the playing field and spread cloud knowledge that can lead to cloud success. Perhaps you learned more about a few new cloud computing concepts and facts. At the very least, I hope the information in this book will encourage you to ask more informed questions about how all this cloud stuff works together.

Remember, you can't get answers if you don't know the questions.

Index

A

abstraction, 79, 90, 131, 146
additive technology, 98
add-ons, storage, 39–40
adoption, multicloud, 113–114
Agile, 78
agility, 7, 8–9, 14, 24, 106, 227, 232, 237
AI (artificial intelligence), 10, 12–13, 42. *See also* **analytics**

  business optimization, 70–71
  business solutions, 67–68
  cost of, 66, 68–69
  data analytics, 80, 81–82
  deep learning, 67
  fraud detection, 42
  IoT (Internet of Things), 86
  leveraging, 70
  ML (machine learning), 66–67
  overuse, 67
  pattern searching, 149
  proactive security, 149
  security, 139, 146
  training data, 69
  use cases, 69–70
  Watson, 66
alerts, 207
all-cloud DevOps, 77
analytics, 78–79

  AI (artificial intelligence), 81–82
  business optimization, 82–83
  connecting the data, 79–80
  insights, 80
  overutilization, 81
  underutilization, 81
APIs, 27, 102–103, 104
application/s. *See also* **cloud native; container/s; DevOps (development and operations)**

  AI (artificial intelligence), optimizing, 70–71
  bloatware, 166–167
  cloud native, 101–102
    architecture, 102–104
    CNCF, 102
    portability, 104–105
  container-based development, 91–92
  decoupling, 28
  federated, 188–191
  green development, 166–167
  legacy, 192–193
  performance, 52–54
  profiler, 53
architecture

  CNCF cloud native, 102–104
  cross-cloud, 200–201
  optimization, 217
ASPs (application service providers), 4–5
asset scatter, 79

assumptions, market, 8–9, 11–12
attack/s
    cross-channel, 49–51
    detection, 135–136
    response, 136
authentication, peer-to-peer, 145
automation, 3, 116
    container, 89
    data analytics, 82
    multicloud, 131
    security, 138, 146, 149–151
    serverless technology, 72
    storage, 41–42
    sustainability and, 170–171

B

baby clouds, 239–240
back-end database, 28
backup and recovery, 142
BC/DR (business continuity and disaster recovery), 142
"being elastic", 5
best practices, 25
best-of-breed technology, 16–17
    flexibility, 116
    leveraging, 114–116
biometrics, 219
bloatware, 166–167
block storage, 40
blockchain, 145
"bolt-on" model, 45
born-in-the-cloud companies, 227–228
breaches, 140, 204. *See also* security
    detection, 135–136
    learning from, 150
    protecting against, 135
business
    agility, 7, 8–9

AI (artificial intelligence)
    optimizing, 70–71
    solutions, 67–68
    use cases, 69–70
CapEx versus OpEx, 5–6, 15
ESG (environmental, social, and corporate governance) score, 153
optimization
    AI (artificial intelligence), 70–71
    cloud native, 105–106
    data analytics, 82–83
    DevOps (development and operations), 78
    edge computing and IoT, 86–87
    ML (machine learning), 70–71
    serverless technology, 75
startups, 14–15
sustainability goals, 153
systems operations, 4
value. *See also* value
    hard, 6, 107
    moving to the cloud as, 187–188
    soft, 6–8, 9, 11–12, 13, 107

C

CapEx, 5–6, 15
capital, 3
cloud computing. *See also* multicloud
    AI (artificial intelligence). *See also* AI (artificial intelligence)
        optimizing, 70–71
        use cases, 69–70
    analytics, 78–79
        connecting the data, 79–80
        overutilization, 81
        underutilization, 81
    benefits, 224–225
        democratization of computing, 229–231
        punching above your weight, 231–233, 240–241

support for remote and virtual enterprises, 227–228

support for remote work, 225–227

support for sustainability, 229

support for world changes and evolutions, 228

breaches

detection, 135–136

protecting against, 135

compute, 44

container/s, 91–92

abstraction, 90

-based development, 96–98

benefits, 89

costs, 92–93

host operating system, 90

isolation, 90

J2EE, 89

operational complexity, 98–99

orchestration, 88, 93–96

portability, 92–93

structure, 90

use cases, 91

cost savings, 4–5, 12–13

data center/s, 4

power consumption, 154, 156–157

private, 159

resource sharing, 159–160

security, 17

system utilization, 157–158

development trends, 18–19

DevOps (development and operations), 75. *See also* DevOps (development and operations)

all-cloud, 77

some-cloud, 77–78

edge computing, 84–85

feature parity, 112

federation, 188–191

five powers, 232

hybrid, 110–113

IaaS (Infrastructure as a Service), 5, 22–23

lift-fix-and-shift approach, 25–27

market, 178–180, 237–240

MSP (managed service provider), 61

multitenancy, 45–46

"bolt-on" model, 45

resource utilization, 158

"share nothing" approach, 45

sustainability and, 160–161

trade-offs, 45–46

PaaS (Platform as a Service), 5

performance

application, 52–53

network, 51–52

power consumption, 154, 160–164

pricing, 177–178

providers. See provider/s

resource sharing, 46, 47

cross-channel attack, 49–51

dedicated host, 47

dedicated instance, 47

Shared model, 46–47

SaaS (Software as a Service), 4–5

second-tier providers, 62

security, 17–18, 112, 132–134, 137

abstraction and automation, 146

AI/ML integration, 139

automation, 138

BC/DR (business continuity and disaster recovery), 142

blockchain, 145

cross-cloud, 144

cross-platform, 202–204

detect, 135–136

encryption, 137–138

failure to manage complexity, 141–142

future of, 217–219

IAM (identity and access management), 138

non-native, 144

observability, 146, 147–148

proactive, 147

protect, 134–135

removing focus from non-cloud systems, 139–141

response, 136

talent shortage, 142–143

track, 136

versus traditional security, 137

services, 12–13. *See also* service/s

"share nothing" approach, 45

shared responsibility, 25

skills, 214–215

changes in the mix, 233–236

cost of, 13

finding the right people, 194–195

generalist versus specialist, 214–215

shortage, 193–194

SLA (service-level agreement), 176

storage, 23

add-ons, 39–40

automation, 41–42

efficiency, 24, 25

future of, 43

leveraging growth, 38–39

migration, 23–24, 25

versus on-premises, 33–37

raw, 22–23

support for change, 24

sustainability, 160, 165

measuring, 162–163

resource optimization, 165–166

time-share model, 3, 155–156

trends, 172–173

utility model, 3–4

value, 2–3, 14, 19–20, 236–237

agility, 8–9

curve, 7–8, 11

disruptors, 16

hard, 6

innovation, 9–12

soft, 6–8, 11–12, 13

speed, 9

transformative business, 6

cloud native, 88, 91, 101–104

architecture, 102–104

cost argument, 106–108

definition, 102

optimization argument, 105–106

portability, 104–105

CloudOps, 209–210, 234–235

clustering, 88, 93, 94–95. *See also* container/s

master node, 94

slave node, 94

CNCF cloud native, 101, 102–104, 107

architecture, 102–104

cost argument, 106–108

optimization argument, 105–106

portability, 104–105

collaboration, provider, 180–181

commoditization, 182–183, 185

complexity

container orchestration, 98–99

failure to manage, 141–142

federation, 191

multicloud, 114, 119–121, 124–125, 126

security, 204

compliance, hybrid cloud, 199

compute, 44, 63

costs, 48–49

cross-channel attack, 49–51

overbuying, reasons for, 57–58

packages, 56–57

performance

    application, 52–54

    network, 51–52

picking the most optimized configuration,
54–57

reserved instance, 59–61

resource sharing, 46, 47

    dedicated host, 47

    dedicated instance, 47

    Shared model, 46–47

consultants, 58

container/s, 88, 89, 90–92

abstraction, 90

-based development, 96–98

benefits, 89

cluster, 95

cost considerations, 92–93

host operating system, 90

isolation, 90

J2EE, 89

leveraging, 93

multicloud, 119

orchestration, 88, 93–96

    cost considerations, 99–100

    declarative programming, 96

    imperative programming, 96

    master node, 94

    operational complexity, 98–99

    scalability, 95

    slave node, 94

portability, 92–93

structure, 90

use cases, 91

cost/s. See also value

AI (artificial intelligence), 66, 68–69

cloud computing, 14

cloud egress, 43

cloud native, 106–108

compute, 48–49, 57–58

container and container orchestration, 92–93,
99–100

hard, 6

multicloud, 116–117

    complexity, 124–125

    heterogeneity, 125–126

overallocation, 72

savings, 4–5

serverless technology, 73–74, 75

of skills, 13

storage

    leveraging, 38–39

    on-premises versus cloud, 35–37

CPU (central processing unit), 44, 51–52, 55

cross-channel attack, 49–51

cross-cloud

platforms, 199–201, 202

security, 144

services, 32–33, 130, 184, 185–186

cross-platform

data federation, 213–214

FinOps, 211–212

governance, 210–211

observability, 205–210

operations, 204–205

security, 202–204

CSBs (cloud service brokers), 116

D

data, 27–28

AI and, 68

analytics, 78–80

    AI (artificial intelligence), 81–82

    overutilization, 81

underutilization, 81
compliance, 199
encryption, 50, 137–138
fabric, 79
federated, 188–191, 213–214
governance, 27
insecure transmission, 199
layer, unified, 27
meta, 27
migrating to the cloud, 23–24
patterns, 67–68
PII (personally identifiable information), 33
security, 27, 31
silos, 31
structured versus unstructured, 30–33
support for change, 24
training, 69
underutilized, 80
virtualization, 29–30, 32, 79
data center/s, 4
enterprise, 192
locations, 219
power consumption, 154, 156–157
private, 159
resource sharing, 159–160
security, 17
system utilization, 157–158
time-share model, 155–156
database/s, 28
application performance and, 53
back-end, 28
decoupling, 28
federation, 188–189
purpose-built, 40
virtualization, 188–189
declarative programming, 96
decoupling, 28
dedicated host, 47
dedicated instance, 47

deep learning, 66, 67, 149
democratization of computing, 229–231
detection, 135–136
development
cloud-based, 18–19
container-based, 97–98
green, 166–167
low-code/no-code approach, 216, 231
DevOps (development and operations), 19, 75
all-cloud, 77
cloud native, 103
disruptive approach, 76
finding business optimization, 78
innovative solutions, 76
iteration, 76
no-cloud, 77
some-cloud, 77–78
tool pipeline, 75
DevSecOps (development, security, and operations), 19
disruptors, 65, 172. *See also* **innovation**
DevOps (development and operations), 76
value of cloud computing, 16
Docker, 88, 89, 90
DR (disaster recovery), 19
dumb terminals, 155

E

edge computing, 83–84, 221–222
finding business optimization, 86–87
IoT and, 85–86
public cloud and, 84
EDP (Enterprise Discount Program), 61
efficiency, 24, 25. *See also* **sustainability**
elasticity, 5
encryption, 50, 137–138
ESG (environmental, social, and corporate governance) score, 153

F

feature parity, 112
federation, 188–191, 213–214
FinOps (Financial Operations) system, 57–58, 116, 211–212
five powers of cloud computing, 232
flexibility, best-of-breed, 116
fraud detection, AI (artificial intelligence), 42

G

GB (gigabyte), 59
governance, 27, 33
    cross-platform, 210–211
    multicloud, 123, 127
green application development, 166–167

H

hard value, 6, 107
HDD (hard disk drive), versus cloud storage, 33–37
heterogeneity, multicloud, 125–126
hiring and keeping talented people, 195–197. See also skills
HPC (high-performance computing), 10
hybrid cloud, 110–112
    compliance, 199
    feature parity, 112
    reasons for adoption, 187
    services, 112
    visibility, 199

I

IaaS (Infrastructure as a Service), 5, 22–23, 231–232. See also storage
IAM (identity and access management), 138, 217
imperative programming, 96

industry-specific services, 220
infrastructure, 65
innovation, 7, 14, 87, 114, 115, 119, 120, 178
    cloud security, 17–18
    DevOps (development and operations), 76
    disruptors, 13, 16, 117, 172
    service, 65–66
    value, 9–12, 223
insights, 80, 146, 206–207, 208
investment
    R&D, 174–175
    technology, 175
IoT (Internet of Things), 10, 83
    AI (artificial intelligence), 86
    edge computing, 85–86
    finding business optimization, 86–87
    scaling, 85–86
    updates, 85
IPCs (inter-process communications), 51
isolation, 90
IT, 4. See also skills
    carbon emissions, 153–154
    hiring and keeping talented people, 195–197
    power consumption, 154–155
    zero-touch, 209
iteration, 76

J-K

J2EE, 89
Kubernetes, 88, 90, 93–96

L

LAMP (Linux, Apache, MySQL, and Python) stacks, 125–126
learning systems, 207
legacy systems, 192–193, 208
leveraging

AI (artificial intelligence), 70

best-of-breed technology, 114–116

cloud storage, 40

container/s, 93

MSPs (managed service provider), 62–63

reserved instances, 60–61

resources, 54–55

second-tier providers, 62

serverless, 72

storage growth, 38–39

technology, 87, 100–101

lift-and shift, 25

lift-fix-and-shift, 25–27

Linthicum, D., Enterprise Application Integration, 29

lock-in, 92–93, 102, 104–105, 118–119, 126

M

MagLev (magnetic levitation), 10

maintenance, automation, 41–42

market, 7

assumptions, 8–9, 11–12

capture, 180

cloud computing, 178–180, 237–240

commoditization, 183

innovation, 10

micro-cloud, 180

shift toward federated applications and data, 189

speed-to-, 9

technology, 176, 178

master node, 94

maturity model, 208–209

MDM (master data management), 27

measuring, sustainability, 162–163

memory

cache, 59

picking the right configuration, 59

size, 59

speed, 59

metacloud, 129–130, 184–186, 201

metadata, 27

metered service, 3

micro-cloud, market, 180

migration to the cloud, 23–24, 25

lift-and shift, 25

lift-fix-and-shift approach, 25–27

shared responsibility, 25

ML (machine learning), 66–67

business optimization, 70–71

leveraging, 70

security, 139

use cases, 69–70

model

"bolt-on", 45

maturity, 208–209

supercloud/metacloud, 185–186

time-share, 3, 4, 155–156

utility, 3–4

monitoring, security threats, 136

MSP (managed service provider), 61, 62–63, 179

multicloud, 43, 62, 63, 110, 239

adoption, 113–114

benefits, 118

abundance of choices, 119–122

owning your own destiny, 122

risk reduction, 122

best-of-breed technology, leveraging, 114–116

business realities, 116–118

complexity, 124–125

containerization, 119

cost argument, 116

deployment approaches, 127–128, 130–131

consolidation, 128
isolation, 128
leverage technologies, 128
metacloud, 129–130
replication, 128
governance, 123, 127
heterogeneity, 125–126
lock-in, 118–119, 126
operations, 123, 127
providers, 113, 181
security, 123, 126–127
sustainability, 167–168
ubiquitous deployments, 201
visibility, 199
multitenancy, 45–46
"bolt-on" model, 45
cross-channel attack, 49–51
resource sharing, 46, 47
dedicated host, 47
dedicated instance, 47
Shared model, 46–47
resource utilization, 158
"share nothing" approach, 45
sustainability and, 160–161
trade-offs, 45–46

N

NDA (nondisclosure agreement), 39
network/s
performance, 51–52, 53
virtual private, 138
zero-trust access, 138
NIST (National Institute of Standards and Technology), 5
no-cloud DevOps, 77
non-native cloud security, 144

O

object storage, 40
observability, 219
actions, 207
alerts, 207
analysis, 206
cross-platform, 205–210
insights, 206–207
learning, 207
maturity model, 208–209
security, 146, 147–148
obsolete technology, 175
operating system, 56
host, 90
picking the right one, 58–59
operational complexity, container orchestration, 98–99
operations
artificial intelligence, 204
cloud, 209–210, 234
cross-platform, 204–205
multicloud, 123, 127
security observability, 146
storage, automation, 41–42
OpEx, 5–6, 12–13, 15
overallocation, 72
overbuying
compute, 57–58
reserved instances, 60–61

P

PaaS (Platform as a Service), 5
packages, 56–57
passive response, 136
pattern/s, 67–68, 81, 198, 206
encryption, 2–3

searching, 149
peer-to-peer authentication, 145
performance, 24
application, 52–54
data virtualization, 30
network, 51–52
PII (personally identifiable information), 33
pipeline, DevOps, 75
platform, 44
compute, picking the most optimized
configuration, 54–57
cross-
data federation, 213–214
FinOps, 211–212
governance, 210–211
operations, 204–205
security, 202–204
cross-cloud, 199–201, 202
security, 140
politics of sustainability, 158–159
portability
cloud native applications, 104–105
container, 92–93
power. *See also* **sustainability**
consumption
cloud computing, 160–164
data centers, 156–157
IT-related, 154–155
utilization, 164–165
prebuilt configurations, 56–57
predictions, 198–199
architectural optimization, 217
changing skills demands, 214–216
cloud computing becomes local, 219
cloud security shifts focus, 217–219
continue rise of complex cloud deployments,
199–201
continued rise of edge computing, 221–222

cross-platform data federation, 213–214
cross-platform FinOps, 211–212
cross-platform governance, 210–211
cross-platform observability, 205–210
cross-platform operations, 204–205
cross-platform security, 202–204
industry clouds become important, 220
less code, more design, 216
refocus on cross-cloud systems, 202
on-premises storage, versus cloud storage, 33–37
pricing. *See also* **cost/s**
cloud services, 177–178
storage
discounts, 39
on-premises versus cloud, 35–37
private cloud, 111
proactive
response, 136
security, 147
AI, 149
pattern searching, 149
"Production Ready", 175
programming
declarative, 96
imperative, 96
protection, 134–138
provider/s
application service, 4–5
baby cloud, 239–240
cloud computing, 14, 178–180
collaboration, 180–181
co-location, 192
commoditization, 183
edge computing, 221
managed service, 61, 179
market, 179–180

market capture, 180

multicloud, 113

overlapping technology, 182–183

power consumption, 161–162

pricing, 177–178

second-tier, 62

SLA (service-level agreement), 176

public cloud, 4, 16. *See also* **cloud computing**

edge computing, 84

security, 112

publications, technical, 241–242

purpose-built databases, 40

R

R&D (research and development), 4, 17–18, 174–175

ransomware, 151

raw storage, 22–23

recommendation engines, 68

remote work, cloud support for, 225–227

renewable power, 163–164

repatriation, 186–187

replication, 128

reserved instance, 59–61

resource/s

allocation, 54–55, 73–74

optimization, 165–166

provisioning, serverless technology, 72

sharing, 46, 47. *See also* multitenancy

costs, 48–49

cross-channel attack, 49–51

dedicated host, 47

dedicated instance, 47

multitenancy, 160–161

security, 49

Shared model, 46–47

utilization, 158

response, 136

passive, 136

proactive, 136

revenue, usage and, 15

risk. *See also* **cost/s**

of maintaining traditional systems, 174–177

multicloud, 122

ROI (return on investment), 3

S

SaaS (Software as a Service), 4–5

Salesforce.com, 4–5

scaling and scalability, 5

automated, 18

containers, 93, 95

IoT (Internet of Things), 85–86

second-tier providers, leveraging, 62

security, 27, 33

abstraction, 146

AI (artificial intelligence), 146, 149

automation, 146, 149–151

biometric, 219

cloud, 17–18, 132–134, 137

AI/ML integration, 139

automation, 138

breaches, 135

cross-, 144

detect, 135–136

encryption, 137–138

future of, 217–219

non-native, 144

observability, 146

proactive, 147

protect, 134–135

response, 136

track, 136

versus traditional security, 137

cross-platform, 202–204

data, 31

identity-based, 138

mistakes

    failure to manage complexity, 141–142

    lack of talent, 142–143

    little focus on BC/DR, 142

    removing focus from non-cloud systems, 139–141

multicloud, 123, 126–127

native, 140

observability, 147–148

pattern searching, 149

peer-to-peer authentication, 145

public cloud, 112

resource sharing, 49–51

skill, 134

storage, automation, 41–42

SEO (search engine optimization), 101

serverless technology, 71–72

cost versus value, 73–74

finding business optimization, 75

leveraging, 72

resource provisioning, 72

use cases, 74–75

service/s, 27. *See also* **compute**

AI (artificial intelligence), 68

cloud, 12–13

commoditization, 183, 185

cross-cloud, 32–33, 130, 184, 185–186

federated, 189

hybrid cloud, 112

industry-specific, 220

infrastructure, 64–65

innovative, 65–66

management, 32

metered, 3

value, 121–122

video streaming, 181–183

"share nothing" approach, 45

Shared model, 46–47, 159–160. *See also* **multitenancy**

shared responsibility, 25

single tenancy, dedicated instance, 47

skills

cloud, 214–215

    changes in the mix, 233–236

    cost of, 13

    finding the right people, 194–195

    generalist versus specialist, 215–216

    shortage, 193–194

container-based development, 99

security, 134, 142–143

training, 197

SLA (service-level agreement), 176

slave node, 94

"smart" devices, 83, 85

SOA (service-oriented architecture), 119

soft value, 6–8, 9, 13, 107

agility, 7, 8–9, 14, 24

of cloud computing, 11–12

innovation, 9–12, 13, 14

speed, 9, 14

some-cloud DevOps, 77–78

speed, 9, 14, 59. *See also* **agility**

spending, R&D, 174–175

SSD (solid-state device), 34

startups, 14–15

storage, 22

add-ons, 39–40

automation, 41–42

block, 40

databases, decoupling, 28

efficiency, 24, 25

growth of, 43

leveraging, 38–39, 40

lift-and shift, 25

lift-fix-and-shift approach, 25–27
object, 40
on-premises versus cloud, 33–37
raw, 22–23
shared responsibility, 25
support for change, 24
unified data access, 32, 33
value, 33
structured data, 30–33
"sunset", 173, 175
supercloud, 184–186, 201
support for change, 24
sustainability, 153, 165, 169
automation and, 170–171
cloud, 160, 229
measuring, 162–163
multicloud, 167–168
multitenancy and, 160–161
negative impacts, 169–170
politics of, 158–159
renewable power, 163–164
resource optimization, 165–166
system utilization, data center, 157–158
systems operations, 4

T

technical publications, 241–242
technology, 4. *See also* **AI (artificial
intelligence); container/s**
additive, 98
best-of-breed, 16–17
blockchain, 145
chasing the hype, 100
data virtualization, 29–30
J2EE, 89
leveraging, 87, 100–101
limited, 175

market, 176, 178
obsolete, 175
OpEx, 5–6
picking the right solution, 108–109
pool, 201
"Production Ready", 175
provider, 182–183
repatriation, 186–187
serverless, 71–72
cost versus value, 73–74
finding business optimization, 75
resource provisioning, 72
use cases, 74–75
"sunset", 173, 175
value curve, 7–8
time-share model, 3, 4, 155–156
tracking. *See also* **observability, security
threats, 136**
trade-offs
multicloud, 118
multitenancy, 45–46
training, cloud skill, 197
transaction, blockchain, 145
transformative business value, 6
trends, cloud computing, 172–173

U

Uber, 9–10, 15
ubiquitous deployments, 201
underallocation, 72
unified data access, 27, 28, 32, 33. *See also*
data
unstructured data, 30–33
use cases
AI (artificial intelligence), 69–70
containers, 91
utility model, 3–4

V

value, 15

 AI (artificial intelligence), optimizing, 70–71

 of ASPs (application service providers), 4–5

 business

  hard, 6

  moving to the cloud as, 187–188

  soft, 6–8, 9

 capital, 3

 cloud computing, 14, 19–20, 236–237

  agility, 8–9

  CapEx versus OpEx, 5–6

  innovation, 9–12

  speed, 9

  storage, 33

  time-share model, 3

  utility model, 3–4

 of containers, 96–98

 curve, 7–8, 54, 105–106

 differentiator calculation, 11

 hard, 107

 innovation, 223

 optimizing, 54–55

 serverless technology, 73–74

 service, 121–122

 soft, 13, 107

  agility, 7, 8–9, 14, 24

  of cloud computing, 11–12

  innovation, 9–12, 13, 14

  speed, 9, 14

 transformative business, 6

video streaming, 181–183

virtual companies, 228

virtualization, 4, 29–30, 32, 79

 database, 188–189

 structured versus unstructured data, 30–33

VPNs (virtual private networks), 138

W-X-Y-Z

Watson, 66

zero-touch IT, 209

ZTNA (zero-trust network access), 138

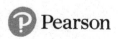